EXCITING AND DELICIOUS NEW WAYS TO PREPARE PASTA EVERY DAY OF THE YEAR

366 Delicious Ways to Cook Pasta with Vegetables offers more than a year's worth of creative and flavorful recipes that will liven up your pasta and satisfy your palate.

Arranged alphabetically by vegetable, from artichoke to zucchini, this book offers an array of tempting recipes, from salads to soups to casseroles, that you can enjoy as either a first course or entrée. You will delight in such inviting dishes as Stir-Fried Broccoli with Shiitake Mushrooms and Vermicelli, Cauliflower with Peanut Sauce and Asian Noodles, Fennel, Apple, and Walnut Pasta Salad, and even New England Corn Chowder with Shells.

This unique, practical cookbook also contains invaluable information on how to cook pasta, a glossary of its many shapes, advice on sauces, and tips on how to select and store vegetables. *366 Delicious Ways to Cook Pasta with Vegetables* is essential for any cook who wants to prepare simple, tasty, and healthy meals for every day of the year.

DOLORES RICCIO is the author of *Superfoods* and *Superfoods for Women*. She makes her home in Warwick, Rhode Island.

D1406590

Also by Dolores Riccio

Superfoods
Superfoods for Women

366

DELICIOUS WAYS TO COOK
Pasta with Vegetables

DOLORES RICCIO

A PLUME BOOK

Ed Blonz, Ph.D., is a nationally syndicated columnist and author of Your Personal Nutritionist series (Signet, 1996). He is president of Nutrition Resource. Nutrition analysis was supplied using Nutritionist IV™ software.

PLUME
Published by the Penguin Group
Penguin Putnam Inc., 375 Hudson Street,
New York, New York 10014, U.S.A.
Penguin Books Ltd, 27 Wrights Lane,
London W8 5TZ, England
Penguin Books Australia Ltd, Ringwood,
Victoria, Australia
Penguin Books Canada Ltd, 10 Alcorn Avenue,
Toronto, Ontario, Canada M4V 3B2
Penguin Books (N.Z.) Ltd, 182–190 Wairau Road,
Auckland 10, New Zealand

Penguin Books Ltd, Registered Offices:
Harmondsworth, Middlesex, England

First published by Plume, an imprint of Dutton Signet,
a member of Penguin Putnam Inc.

First Printing, October, 1997
10 9 8 7 6 5 4 3 2 1

Copyright © Dolores Riccio, 1997
All rights reserved

 REGISTERED TRADEMARK—MARCA REGISTRADA

LIBRARY OF CONGRESS CATALOGING-IN-PUBLICATION DATA:
Riccio, Dolores, 1931–
366 healthful ways to cook pasta with vegetables / Dolores Riccio.
    p.   cm.
Includes index.
ISBN 0-452-27727-2
1. Cookery (Pasta)   2. Cookery (Vegetables)   I. Title.
TX809.M17R52   1997
641.8'22—dc21   97-17697
                                                                                  CIP

Printed in the United States of America
Set in Garamond Light
Designed by Leonard Telesca

BOOKS ARE AVAILABLE AT QUANTITY DISCOUNTS WHEN USED TO PROMOTE PRODUCTS OR SERVICES. FOR INFORMATION PLEASE WRITE TO PREMIUM MARKETING DIVISION, PENGUIN PUTNAM INC., 375 HUDSON STREET, NEW YORK, NEW YORK 10014.

This book is dedicated to my wonderful husband, Rick,
a true pasta lover.

ACKNOWLEDGMENTS

Special thanks to my super agent,
Blanche Schlessinger,
and my thoughtful editor,
Jennifer Moore,
for all they have done
to make this book a reality.

Contents

CONTENTS

Introduction: Combining Two Fabulous Foods in Fresh, Fast Ways

---

Vegetables and pasta—they're two of the world's most versatile and nutritious foods. A cornucopia of fresh vegetables, changing with every season, brightens every supermarket. An infinite variety of pasta shapes await saucing. And they've suddenly come into their own as stars of an all-around healthy diet.

Check out the United States Department of Agriculture's new Food Guide Pyramid, and you'll find vegetables and pasta featured among foods that should be the mainstay of our daily fare. Three to five servings of vegetables and six to eleven from the grains group (which includes pasta) are the recommended amounts. (If that seems like a lot of servings, consider that a half cup counts as one serving of pasta.)

In this cookbook, I've combined vegetables and pasta into dishes that are the essence of simplicity to prepare, beautiful to behold, and perfectly scrumptious—ideal choices for casual entertaining as well as for family meals. Speaking of the latter, it's amazing to see how much more warmly vegetables are welcomed at the family dinner table when they're tossed with an inviting pasta.

There's an existing treasury of time-honored family recipes, the gift of America's immigrant populations, that inspired many of these medleys. Good home cooks from other countries often blended vegetables and pasta into one glorious dish. This is especially true of the Mediterranean region, whose natural, wholesome cuisine has been widely recognized for its role in promoting a long, robust life. Asian cultures, too, have contributed to the treasury of simple, satisfying vegetable-and-noodle stir-fries and soups. It's reassuring to know (when you're tucking into something

1

as tasty as broccoli de rabe with sweet red peppers, spicy black olives, and ziti) that vegetables lavishly confer the benefits of life-extending anti-oxidants, phytochemicals (plant chemicals), and abundant vitamins and minerals. Not only are these classic dishes delicious, fast, easy, inexpensive, and crowd pleasing, they also generously provide substances that help to prevent many diseases, including heart disease and cancer. According to the latest research, vegetables are looking more and more like the preventive medicine of the future.

And pasta is the quintessential good-mood food, revving up the brain's production of the neurotransmitter serotonin to keep you focused and cheery. Today's athletes are especially well aware of the sustaining value of complex carbohydrates. The day before strenuous events like the Boston Marathon, runners fortify themselves with plentiful bowls of macaroni for the long haul.

Vegetables and pasta—shall it be an appetizer, an entrée, or a side dish? This depends entirely on your dining style. Vegetarians and the cholesterol-shy will enjoy serving vegetables and pasta as a stylish, satisfying center-of-the-table entrée. Mediterraneans often serve pasta as a *primo*, or first course. (But in Italy, pasta portions are smaller and more lightly sauced than in America.) Traditionalists for whom a meal is not complete without that serving of meat or fish will find the vegetable-pasta combination a perfect side dish. It needs no other accompaniment to produce a perfectly balanced meal.

For the weight conscious (and who isn't?), vegetables and pasta can be an exemplary diet food. If you forgo the meat course and are a miser with the oil (within reason—because olive oil carries the flavor and is good for your heart, too), you'll probably halve the calories for that meal. Enjoy a good honest plateful of food at dinner, and chances are you won't be looking in the refrigerator later that evening for sandwich makings.

Vegetables and pasta are also the ultimate in fast food as well as light cuisine. Vegetable "sauces" are generally prepared in less time than it takes to cook the pasta. None of the recipes in this cookbook requires you to make homemade fresh pasta. It's great stuff, of course, but making fresh pasta has to be a kind of hobby for those with leisurely afternoons to devote to its art. For those whose hobbies are otherwise, excellent fresh and dried pastas are readily available. Asian noodles are often sold in the produce section of supermarkets. A selection of fresh vegetables is plentiful at every time of year, and occasionally frozen ones can be called on to fill in during off-seasons. You can buy the ingredients for these recipes quickly, perhaps on your way home from work, and cook a fabulous dish in a half hour or so.

The recipes in this book are arranged alphabetically by vegetable, from artichokes to zucchini, for the convenience of the seasonal shopper. If you've just brought home a wonderful head of cauliflower or bunch of asparagus, it will be easy to find some tempting possibilities to make the most of your selection. The great majority of these recipes are meatless, but a few include meat or fish.

Vegetables and pasta have been shown to be a miracle combination for good health, as well as a marvelous-tasting and enjoyable mainstay of the nineties menu. And with 366 recipes from which to choose, you can revel in seasonal vegetables and enjoy pasta every day of the year!

A GUIDE TO THE MANY FORMS OF PASTA

With pasta, you always have a myriad of options! You'll find that many pasta shapes are available fresh as well as dried. Although fresh pasta cooks more quickly, it's not necessarily superior; much depends on the dish you're preparing. Fresh pastas are particularly good with light, creamy sauces.

Filled pastas, such as tortellini and ravioli, are available frozen. There's a wide difference in quality, so when you find a good brand, stick with it.

The same may be said of domestic versus imported pastas. There's a difference in quality among brands of both domestic and imported pastas. It's worthwhile to do some serious taste-testing and find the brand that pleases you best. Look for a chewy not mushy texture, good retention of shape, and a mild yet detectable wheat flavor and aroma.

Names ending in *-ini* or *-ette* denote the smaller sizes. Names ending in *-oni* signify the larger sizes.

Asian pastas are also available both fresh and dried. Many packages don't have English (or any) cooking directions, in which case, cook them as you would any pasta, testing for doneness by taste. As a general rule, Asian pastas cook in a very few minutes, perhaps three to five.

Fresh pastas usually display a "sell by" date; if you want to keep a package for a longer time, you can store it in the freezer. Frozen fresh pasta can be cooked without thawing and will take only a minute or two longer.

Unopened dry pasta can be stored in a cool, dry place for a year or more, and egg noodles for six to eight months, so you can stock up on as many shapes as will fit on your pasta shelf. It's a comforting feeling to know that lots of quick, easy, nutritious, and delicious dishes can be prepared from the contents of one's pantry and freezer. Enjoy the infinite "pastabilities"!

A Vast Variety of Shapes

Acini di Pepe: peppercorn size
Alphabets: a kid-pleasing soup pasta
Anelli or Anellini: "rings," small circles
Cavatelli: shell-shaped with ruffled edge
Conchiglie and Conchigliette, Shells and Seashells: shell shapes that range from tiny to jumbo
Ditali and Ditalini: "little thimbles," short tubes
Elbows: small or medium ("casserole" size)
Farfalle and Farfallini: "butterflies," bow shapes
Fusilli: screw-shaped, similar to rotelle
Gemelli and Gemellini: "twins," two short spaghetti pieces, twisted together
Gnocchi: potato-pasta dumplings; homemade or frozen
Mezzani: smooth, 1- to 2-inch tubes
Mezzani Rigati: same as mezzani, with ridges
Mostaccioli: "mustaches," ridged macaroni cut diagonally
Orecchiette: "little ears"
Orzo: shaped like rice
Pastina: "little pasta," tiny grains
Penne: "pens," smooth macaroni cut diagonally
Quadrettini: small flat squares
Rigatoni: "grooved, large," large, grooved, curved macaroni
Rotelle or Rotini: "spirals," screw-shaped, similar to fusilli
Ruote: "wagon wheels"
Stellini: "little stars"
Tubetti and Tubettini: "tubes"
Ziti: "bridegrooms," medium tubes, slightly curved

Strands for Twirling

Bucatini: thin, long tube
Capelli d'Angelo or Capellini: "angel hair," delicate thin threads
Fettuccine: "ribbons," wider than linguine
Fusilli Lungi: long twists
Linguine: long flat strands
Thin Linguine: thin flat strands
Perciatelli: long tubes

Spaghetti and Spaghettini: "strings," long smooth strands
Tagliatelle: wide ribbons
Vermicelli: "little worms," very round, thin

Shapes for Filling

Cannelloni: "big pipes," large tubes for stuffing
Curly Lasagna: curly-edged lasagna
Lasagna: large flat pasta for filled dishes
Manicotti: "small muffs," large long tubes for stuffing
Ravioli: filled squares or rounds, available fresh and frozen
Shells (Jumbo): very large, for filling
Tortellini: small "filled hats"; available fresh and frozen

Egg Noodles

American, Pennsylvania Dutch, and Jewish brands are widely available.

Broad Egg Noodles: may be long or short, curly or flat
Medium Egg Noodles: may be long or short, curly or flat
Fine Egg Noodles: thin strands
Egg bows: see Farfalle

Greek Pasta

Hilopites: egg noodle squares
Makaronia: basic short cuts of macaroni
Orzo and wide egg noodles are also popular in Greek cuisine.

North African Pasta

Couscous: tiny grains, the size of pastina; prepared by soaking or
    steaming rather than by boiling

Asian Noodles

Vermicelli, spaghetti, whole wheat spaghetti, and thin fettuccine (dried or
    fresh) can be substituted for Asian noodles.

Japanese Noodles: thin (somen) or wide (udon), and buckwheat (soba)
Chinese Rice Sticks, rice noodles, rice vermicelli
Korean Glass Noodles: made from sweet potato starch
Asian Vermicelli and Thin Fettuccine: made from mung bean starch

Preparing Perfect Pasta

Pasta is an easy dish to prepare, providing you follow a few simple, but important, guidelines. Because the timing is critical, it's always best to have the sauce ready or almost ready before cooking the pasta. As a matter of fact, have the table set and the diners handy, also. Pasta, unless baked in a casserole, should not be kept waiting.

Four to five quarts of water are needed for 1 pound of pasta. Use 3 quarts for a half pound, 2 quarts for 6 ounces or less. Bring the water to a full rolling boil, add the salt (2 teaspoons per pound, but don't worry, most of it will go down the drain), then the pasta. If salt is not added at this point, the pasta will taste flat no matter how much salt you add to the dish later. Stir several times to separate. Use a cooking fork to bend long strands as they soften to get them under the boiling water as quickly as possible.

Don't add oil to the cooking water. Oil does reduce the tendency of the water to foam up, but it makes the pasta too slick for some sauces. Instead, if the pot threatens to boil over, reduce the heat a little.

The cooking time given on the package should be taken as a guide, not a commandment. Usually a range is given. The lesser time is meant to produce a pasta that is cooked *al dente* (literally, "to the tooth," meaning firm and chewy). The greater time should yield a more tender pasta. Tastes vary, so you must make the final determination on your own, by tasting a piece or strand. When you've cooked a particular shape of pasta several times, you'll know just how to set your timer—but give it the taste test anyway!

If the pasta will be subjected to additional heat, as in a casserole or a soup, it should be undercooked slightly. The same is true if the recipe directs you to heat the pasta a minute or two with the sauce in a skillet.

Salad pasta should be cooked al dente to allow for the softening effect of the dressing. As soon as salad pasta is drained, rinse it in cold water to stop the cooking and mix it with the dressing.

There is no need to rinse pasta that will be served hot. Simply drain, allowing the cooking water to flow out, but don't shake it bone dry. A little moisture helps to distribute the sauce evenly, especially in a vegetable sauce with a minimum of oil, such as those found in this book.

As soon as the pasta is drained, mix it with the sauce to keep it from sticking together. Ideally, it should be served within three minutes of saucing. If cooked pasta must be held for any amount of time, however, toss it with a tablespoon of oil (per pound) and keep it separate from the sauce.

Cooked pasta, if tossed with oil, can be kept refrigerated for three to four days (separately from the sauce).

Lasagna or large shells can be cooked and stuffed or layered with filling in advance and frozen; then the dish can be baked when needed. Allow as much as thirty minutes extra cooking time for a frozen dish, fifteen minutes for a refrigerated casserole.

How much pasta to cook is subject to many variables, starting with how chunky the sauce is—and many of the vegetable sauces in this book are quite substantial and filling. You must also consider what else will be served. Is the pasta to be a first course, as it would be in Italy, or an American-style dish served with meat, or a vegetarian entrée with a light salad to accompany it? In most of the recipes that follow, I have indicated the servings one may expect as a side dish (or first course). As an entrée, the number of servings would be half as many. In other words, a recipe that serves four as a side dish would serve two as the main dish.

However you dish up pasta with vegetables, you can be sure of serving the world's favorite food with a wonderful bonus of good nutrition. *Bon appétit!*

ABOUT THE INGREDIENTS

Broth—Vegetable, Chicken, or Beef

Recipes for soups and other "saucy" dishes in this book often call for broth. If you customarily make soup stock and freeze it, you'll have the best of all broth ingredients. (See Index for recipes.) But if making stock doesn't fit into your schedule, canned low-sodium broths can be substituted and will work well. In a pinch, you can even used prepared bouillon. Vegetable bouillon is harder to find. Knorr makes vegetable bouillon as well as other flavors; this brand is favored by many cooks.

Flour, Superfine

I often used this shortcut ingredient to thicken sauces and soups because it blends easily and cooks quickly without the need to combine with butter in a classic roux. You can always substitute all-purpose flour; simply cook a few minutes longer to eliminate any raw flour taste.

Fresh Bread Crumbs

To make fresh bread crumbs, tear day-old bread into rough pieces and drop one piece after another down the feed tube of a food processor with the motor running until coarse, even crumbs have been formed.

Herbs, Dried

Measurements in the recipes that follow are based on dried herbs less than six months old. If you keep herbs longer, they will lose much of their pungency and aroma.

Milk, Nonfat Dry

You'll find this ingredient in many recipes for "creamy" dishes. It's a low-fat way of making a milk-based sauce taste more like the high-fat cream sauces of yesteryear. If you don't have this ingredient on hand, you can make the recipe anyway; however, the sauce or soup will not taste as rich.

Parsley

Most of the following recipes call for fresh flat-leaf parsley, which is chock-full of vitamin C and other nutrients. To keep fresh parsley longer, rinse and spin it quite dry. Spread it out on a towel-covered tray for a half hour or so, then wrap it in a towel and place the towel in a plastic bag in the refrigerator. It should keep a week to ten days. Dried parsley is not a good substitute for fresh.

BASIC RECIPES

Here are a few basic recipes that have been used as ingredients throughout this book. Some of them can be replaced by prepared products from a jar or package—but homemade always tastes best!

Basil Pesto

———————————◼———————————

MAKES ABOUT 1 CUP (8 2-TABLESPOON SERVINGS)

Leftover pesto can be frozen for later use. Spoon heaping tablespoons of pesto onto a foil-covered pan and freeze them solid. Remove the pesto and store in a plastic bag in the freezer. Mighty nice to have on hand!

2 cloves garlic, peeled
2 cups basil leaves, rinsed,
   thoroughly dried, and well
   packed
¹/₂ cup lightly toasted pine nuts

¹/₂ teaspoon salt
¹/₄ teaspoon freshly ground
   black pepper
About ¹/₂ cup olive oil
¹/₄ cup grated Parmesan cheese

In a food processor fitted with the steel blade, turn on the motor and drop the garlic cloves down the feed tube to mince them. Add the basil, nuts, salt, and pepper, and process until very finely chopped. With the motor running, gradually add enough oil to make a smooth paste.

Remove the pesto from the work bowl and stir in the cheese.

Kilocalories 186 Kc • Protein 4 Gm • Fat 19 Gm • Percent of calories from fat 87% • Cholesterol 2 mg • Dietary Fiber 0 Gm • Sodium 193 mg • Calcium 55 mg

Parsley-Walnut Pesto

Put ¹/₂ cup walnuts in a small saucepan, cover with water, and bring to a boil. Drain and rinse the walnuts. Substitute them for the pine nuts in the Basil Pesto recipe. Substitute fresh flat-leaf parsley for the basil.

Kilocalories 185 Kc • Protein 3 Gm • Fat 19 Gm • Percent of calories from fat 88% • Cholesterol 2 mg • Dietary Fiber 1 Gm • Sodium 201 mg • Calcium 61 mg

Herb Medley Pesto

Follow the recipe for Basil Pesto, substituting fresh flat-leaf parsley (about 1 bunch, stemmed) for the basil. Add 2 teaspoons dried basil, 1 teaspoon dried oregano, $^1/_2$ teaspoon dried thyme, and $^1/_2$ teaspoon dried rosemary. This aromatic mixture is especially nice with bean dishes, or try stirring a teaspoon of it into a plate of hot soup just before serving, as a flavorful garnish.

Kilocalories 191 Kc • Protein 4 Gm • Fat 20 Gm • Percent of calories from fat 86% • Cholesterol 2 mg • Dietary Fiber 1 Gm • Sodium 201 mg • Calcium 73 mg

Herb Vinaigrette

MAKES 1 CUP (8 2-TABLESPOON SERVINGS)

Because it contains no fresh garlic, this vinaigrette will keep well at room temperature.

$^1/_3$ **cup red wine vinegar**
$^1/_2$ **teaspoon salt**
$^1/_4$ **teaspoon freshly ground black pepper**
$^1/_4$ **teaspoon dried marjoram or oregano**

$^1/_4$ **teaspoon dried basil**
$^1/_4$ **teaspoon dried cilantro**
$^1/_4$ **teaspoon dried dill**
$^2/_3$ **cup extra-virgin olive oil**

In a jar, mix together the vinegar, salt, pepper, and herbs. Add the oil and shake. When ready to use, shake well and measure quickly while the oil and vinegar are still mixed.

Some optional additions: a sprinkle of garlic powder, a pinch of sugar.

Kilocalories 160 Kc • Protein 0 Gm • Fat 18 Gm • Percent of calories from fat 100% • Cholesterol 0 mg • Dietary Fiber 0 Gm • Sodium 146 mg • Calcium 2 mg

Mustard Vinaigrette

◼

MAKES ³/₄ CUP (6 2-TABLESPOON SERVINGS)

2 tablespoons white wine
   vinegar
1 tablespoon garlic-roasted
   mustard or Dijon mustard

¹/₂ cup olive oil
¹/₄ teaspoon salt
Freshly ground black pepper
   to taste

With a hand blender or by hand with a whisk, blend the vinegar and mustard until well combined. Gradually add the oil while blending or whisking constantly until the dressing is thick and smooth. Whisk in the salt and pepper.

Kilocalories 164 Kc • Protein 0 Gm • Fat 18 Gm • Percent of calories from fat 99% • Cholesterol 0 mg • Dietary Fiber 0 Gm • Sodium 111 mg • Calcium 4 mg

Honey-Mustard Vinaigrette

Follow the preceding recipe. Whisk in 1 tablespoon warmed honey with the salt and pepper.

Kilocalories 174 Kc • Protein 0 Gm • Fat 18 Gm • Percent of calories from fat 92% • Cholesterol 0 mg • Dietary Fiber 0 Gm • Sodium 112 mg • Calcium 4 mg

Light Russian Dressing

MAKES $^1/_2$ CUP (4 2-TABLESPOON SERVINGS)

$^1/_4$ cup nonfat plain yogurt
2 tablespoons mayonnaise
2 tablespoons chili sauce

1 tablespoon sweet pickle
  relish
8 stuffed green olives, chopped

Whisk together the yogurt, mayonnaise, and chili sauce until smooth. Stir in the pickle relish and olives.

Kilocalories 83 Kc • Protein 1 Gm • Fat 7 Gm • Percent of calories from fat 70% • Cholesterol 3 mg • Dietary Fiber 0 Gm • Sodium 326 mg • Calcium 35 mg

Couscous

4 SERVINGS

Couscous, the basis of many North African dishes, is a grain-shaped pasta made of semolina wheat. It was adopted into Southern Italian cuisine when Arabs occupied Sicily.

Most American couscous is precooked and packaged; just follow the package directions. For recipes in this book calling for 1 cup raw couscous, prepare enough packaged couscous to make $2^1/_2$ cups cooked. If you buy unpackaged couscous, white or whole wheat, in a natural foods market (specializing in organic, healthful, and untreated foods), prepare as follows.

2 cups stock, canned broth, or
  water (see Note)

1 cup couscous, white or
  whole wheat

Bring the stock to a boil. Pour it over the couscous. Let stand until all the water is absorbed, 10 to 15 minutes.

Fluff the couscous and spread it on a platter. When it is cool enough to handle, rub handfuls of the couscous between your fingers to break up all the lumps.

If necessary, rewarm by steaming the couscous in a strainer (not touching the boiling water beneath) or in a microwave-safe bowl in the microwave. Fluff with 2 forks, again breaking up any lumps.

NOTE: If using water, you may wish to add ¼ teaspoon salt.

Kilocalories 191 Kc • Protein 6 Gm • Fat 0 Gm • Percent of calories from fat 2% • Cholesterol 0 mg • Dietary Fiber 3 Gm • Sodium 251 mg • Calcium 11 mg

Spanish Sauce

—————■—————

MAKES ABOUT 3 CUPS (6 ½-CUP SERVINGS)

2 tablespoons olive oil
1 large red bell pepper, seeded and thinly sliced
1 Anaheim chili, seeded and thinly sliced
1 large yellow onion, thinly sliced
2 carrots, thinly sliced
3 garlic cloves, minced
1 28-ounce can crushed tomatoes

½ cup sliced pimiento-stuffed olives
¼ cup red wine vinegar
¾ teaspoon salt
½ teaspoon hot pepper sauce, or more to your taste
¼ teaspoon pepper
¼ cup chopped fresh flat-leaf parsley

Heat the oil in a large skillet and sauté the red pepper, chili, onion, carrots, and garlic over very low heat for 10 minutes or until slightly soft.

Add all the remaining ingredients except the parsley, and simmer, uncovered, stirring often, until thickened (25 to 30 minutes).

Remove from the heat and stir in the parsley. Extra sauce can be frozen for later use.

Kilocalories 110 Kc • Protein 2 Gm • Fat 6 Gm • Percent of calories from fat 46% • Cholesterol 0 mg • Dietary Fiber 3 Gm • Sodium 644 mg • Calcium 69 mg

Boiled Shrimp

---

1 pound shrimp, raw, in shells
1 quart water
1 lemon, sliced

1 teaspoon whole peppercorns
¹/₂ bay leaf

Wash the shrimp well (rubber gloves are recommended; some people are allergic to raw shrimp).

Combine all the ingredients in a saucepan. Bring to a boil, cover, and simmer for 2 minutes. Remove from the heat and let stand 5 to 10 minutes in the hot broth, until the shrimp have all turned bright pink. Drain.

When the shrimp are cool enough to handle, remove the shell and the black vein running down the back just under the skin. (Insert the point of a paring knife right at the top, or neck, and pull off the strip of flesh and vein. Often it will come off in one piece, but if any black vein remains, clean it out with the knife point.

Kilocalories 120 Kc • Protein 23 Gm • Fat 2 Gm • Percent of calories from fat 15% • Cholesterol 172 mg • Dietary Fiber 0 Gm • Sodium 169 mg • Calcium 59 mg

Mini-Meatballs

■

Cook immediately or freeze uncooked (some or all) for later use. Frozen mini-meatballs can be steamed or cooked in soups without thawing; allow a few extra minutes cooking time.

$1/4$ cup minced shallots
2 slices Italian bread,
   moistened with water
   and crumbled
2 tablespoons grated Parmesan
   cheese
Several sprigs of fresh parsley,
   chopped

1 teaspoon Italian herbs, or
   1 pinch each dried oregano,
   basil, thyme, and rosemary
$1/4$ teaspoon salt
$1/8$ teaspoon pepper
1 egg, or $1/4$ cup prepared egg
   substitute
1 pound lean ground turkey

Mix all the ingredients well and form them into walnut-size meatballs. Drop them into hot broth or sauce, and simmer for 15 minutes.

Kilocalories 161 Kc • Protein 16 Gm • Fat 8 Gm • Percent of calories from fat 46% • Cholesterol 96 mg • Dietary Fiber 0 Gm • Sodium 268 mg • Calcium 49 mg

Vegetable Stock

■

Here's a vegetarian version of an all-purpose vegetable broth.

2 tablespoons olive oil
3 large leeks (1 bunch), well
    washed, chopped
2 onions, chopped
3 garlic cloves, finely chopped
4 celery stalks with leaves,
    chopped
2 large carrots, chopped
1 green bell pepper, seeded
    and chopped
8 cups water

2 tablespoons tomato paste
1 teaspoon chopped fresh
    thyme, or $1/4$ teaspoon dried
Several sprigs fresh dill,
    chopped
Several sprigs fresh parsley,
    chopped
1 teaspoon salt
$1/8$ to $1/4$ teaspoon freshly
    ground black pepper

Heat the oil in a large pot. Add the leeks, onions, garlic, celery, carrots, and bell pepper; "sweat" the vegetables over very low heat until they are lightly colored, not browned, 15 to 20 minutes. Add the water, tomato paste, thyme, dill, parsley, and salt. Cover and simmer for 1 hour. Stir in the pepper to your taste. Strain before using, pressing on the vegetables with the back of a spoon. Discard the solids.

Kilocalories 35 Kc • Protein 0 Gm • Fat 0 Gm • Percent of calories from fat 0% • Cholesterol 0 mg • Dietary Fiber 1 Gm • Sodium 492 mg • Calcium 0 mg

Chicken Stock

MAKES 8 CUPS STOCK (8 1-CUP SERVINGS)

This is a "bonus" chicken stock, yielding cooked chicken that can be used for many quick, tasty dishes. This flavorful stock is so nearly fat-free, it can be used immediately, or chill to skim off any traces of fat, if you wish.

**3 pounds split chicken breasts
 with bones, skinned
 (4 pieces)
1 tablespoon olive oil
1 large onion, chopped
¹/₂ cup chopped shallots or
 scallions
2 celery stalks with leaves,
 chopped
1 teaspoon chopped fresh
 thyme, or ¹/₄ teaspoon dried
1 teaspoon chopped fresh
 rosemary, or ¹/₄ teaspoon
 dried**

**8 cups water
Several sprigs of fresh parsley
 or cilantro, chopped
1 tablespoon tomato paste
1 teaspoon salt
2 large carrots, each cut into
 2 pieces
¹/₈ to ¹/₄ teaspoon freshly
 ground black pepper**

Wash the chicken in cold salted water; rinse and drain.

In a large pot, heat the oil. Add the onion, shallots, and celery, and "sweat" the vegetables over very low heat until lightly colored, not browned, 10 minutes. Add the thyme and rosemary during the last minute. Remove the vegetables and lightly brown the chicken pieces in batches over medium-high heat.

Return the vegetables to the pot. Add the water, parsley, tomato paste, and salt. Simmer the stock, covered, for 40 minutes. Add the carrots and pepper to your taste; continue cooking for 10 to 15 minutes.

Reserve the chicken and carrots for another use. Strain the stock. Discard the solids.

Kilocalories 39 Kc • Protein 5 Gm • Fat 1 Gm • Percent of calories from fat 35% • Cholesterol 0 mg • Dietary Fiber 0 Gm • Sodium 426 mg • Calcium 10 mg

INTRODUCTION

1

Artichokes, the Succulent Thistle

This culinary delicacy is more than a challenging dining experience. Artichokes are rich in folic acid, an important B vitamin, and some essential minerals—magnesium, phosphorus, and potassium. They're also a great source of fiber. All in all, artichokes can be counted among the heart-healthiest vegetables.

A member of the thistle family, fresh artichokes are treasured for the taste of their fleshy leaves and "heart" (actually, the bottom). They appear in produce departments briefly in spring and should be celebrated while they are available. Look for artichokes that are compact, heavy for their size, and still tightly closed. Once their season has passed, take advantage of the excellent quality of frozen artichoke hearts, which combine very well with pasta. In a pinch, if frozen artichokes are unavailable, you can even substitute imported canned artichokes, well rinsed.

Store fresh artichokes in a perforated plastic vegetable bag in the refrigerator crisper drawer. Use them within a day or so of purchase.

Fresh Artichokes Stuffed with Couscous

4 SERVINGS

Spiny thistles transformed into a lovely first course!

2 large fresh artichokes
1/4 cup white vinegar
4 slices lemon
1/2 cup couscous, raw
2 to 3 tablespoons freshly
  grated Romano cheese
2 tablespoons minced fresh
  flat-leaf parsley

1/4 teaspoon dried oregano
1/4 teaspoon freshly ground
  black pepper
About 1 tablespoon extra-virgin
  olive oil
Paprika

Snap off the tough outer leaves of the artichokes and cut off the stems. Use a serrated knife to cut off the top 1/2 inch and a kitchen shears to cut off the spiny tops of the remaining outer leaves. Cut the artichokes in half lengthwise and scoop out the choke (hairy inner leaves), but leave the heart intact; a serrated grapefruit spoon works well for this task.As you prepare the artichokes, immediately plunge the halves into a large pot of cold water with the white vinegar added to prevent discoloration.

When ready to cook, drain off the water. Add 2 inches of fresh water and the lemon slices. Bring to a boil, reduce the heat, and simmer the artichokes, covered, until the hearts are fork-tender, about 25 minutes. Drain.

Meanwhile, prepare the couscous, using a flavorful broth rather than water (see page 12 for basic recipe, or follow package instructions); fluff and separate the grains. Blend in the cheese, parsley, oregano, and pepper.

Using some of the oil, oil a baking dish that will hold the four artichoke halves upright. Preheat the oven to 350 degrees F.

Stuff the artichoke halves with the couscous, mounding it up well and pressing lightly so that the stuffing will hold its shape. Lay the halves in the baking dish and drizzle the remaining oil over all. Sprinkle with a few dashes of paprika. Cover the pan with foil.

Bake the artichokes, covered, for 20 to 25 minutes, until they are heated through and fragrant.

The artichokes can be prepared and stuffed beforehand and refrigerated until you are ready to bake them; if chilled, they will need a longer baking time, 30 to 35 minutes.

Kilocalories 162 Kc • Protein 6 Gm • Fat 5 Gm • Percent of calories from fat 24% • Cholesterol 3 mg • Dietary Fiber 1 Gm • Sodium 340 mg • Calcium 64 mg

Fresh Artichoke Hearts

Put the fresh artichokes in a pan with water to cover. Add a lemon slice for each artichoke. Bring the water to a boil and simmer, covered, until the artichoke bottoms are tender, about 25 minutes. Drain and cool.

Peel away the artichoke leaves and remove the chokes (tiny hairy leaves at the center). What remains is the heart. If the hearts are large, you may want to halve or quarter them.

Although you could enjoy some of the leftover leaves as a snack, obviously there is a great deal of waste in preparing fresh artichoke hearts. You may wish to use prepared frozen artichoke hearts instead; their quality is very good.

Fresh Artichokes with Pesto and Fettuccine

This dish makes a beautiful presentation and is delightfully messy to eat. Enjoy!

2 large fresh artichokes
$^1/_4$ cup white vinegar
4 slices lemon
8 ounces ($^1/_2$ pound) fettuccine

About $^1/_2$ cup Herb Medley Pesto (see page 10 for basic recipe)

Snap off the tough outer leaves of the artichokes and cut off the stems. Use a serrated knife to cut off the top $^1/_2$ inch of the artichokes. Use a kitchen shears to cut off the spiny tops of the remaining outer leaves. Cut the artichokes in half lengthwise and scoop out the choke (hairy inner leaves), but leave the heart intact. A serrated grapefruit spoon works well for this task. After removing the choke, cut the artichokes lengthwise again to make 8 quarters. As you work, immediately plunge the prepared quarters into a large pot of cold water with the white vinegar added.

Drain off the water. Add 2 inches of fresh water and the lemon slices. Bring to a boil, reduce the heat, and simmer the artichokes, covered, until the hearts are fork-tender, 15 to 20 minutes. Drain and keep warm.

Meanwhile, cook the fettuccine according to package directions and drain. In a large serving dish, toss the pasta with $^1/_3$ cup of the pesto. Arrange the artichokes on top like the spokes of a wheel, stems in the center, and fill each choke with about $^1/_2$ teaspoon pesto.

Kilocalories 465 Kc • Protein 18 Gm • Fat 21 Gm • Percent of calories from fat 38% • Cholesterol 2 mg • Dietary Fiber 12 Gm • Sodium 389 mg • Calcium 155 mg

Braised Artichokes and Peas with Capellini

4 SERVINGS

2 tablespoons butter
1/2 cup chopped scallions
2 ounces (1/8 pound)
  prosciutto, slivered (optional)
1 1/4 cups chicken stock or
  canned broth
6 artichoke hearts, cooked and
  halved (page 21), or 9-ounce
  package frozen artichoke
  hearts

1 1/2 cups shelled peas or
  1 10-ounce package frozen
  petit peas
2 teaspoons cornstarch
Salt and freshly ground black
  pepper
2 tablespoons chopped fresh
  flat-leaf parsley
8 ounces (1/2 pound) capellini
Freshly grated Romano cheese

Heat the butter in a large skillet and sauté the scallions until they are sizzling. Add the prosciutto, if using, and continue sautéing for 3 minutes. Add 1 cup of the stock and the artichokes. Cover and cook 3 minutes, or if using frozen artichokes, until they are almost tender (consult package directions); cut them in half.

Add the peas, breaking them up if frozen, cover, and cook 3 minutes.

Blend the cornstarch into the remaining 1/4 cup of stock, add it to the simmering vegetables, and stir constantly until the mixture bubbles and thickens. Season with salt and pepper to your taste, and cook 3 minutes longer. Stir in the parsley.

Meanwhile, cook the capellini according to package directions and drain. Spoon it into a large serving dish and toss with the vegetables and sauce, letting most of the artichoke hearts remain on top of the dish. Pass the cheese at the table.

Kilocalories 358 Kc • Protein 14 Gm • Fat 8 Gm • Percent of calories from fat 19% • Cholesterol 16 mg • Dietary Fiber 8 Gm • Sodium 327 mg • Calcium 68 mg

Spicy Baked Artichoke Hearts with Couscous

---

4 SERVINGS

1 cup couscous (raw)
2 Anaheim chilies, seeded
  and diced
2 tablespoons olive oil, plus
  more for drizzling
6 artichoke hearts, cooked and
  halved (page 21), or 9-ounce
  package frozen artichoke
  hearts

1 large egg
2 tablespoons water
$1/2$ teaspoon salt
$1/4$ teaspoon cayenne pepper
$1/4$ teaspoon ground coriander
1 cup seasoned dried bread
  crumbs
2 tablespoons grated Parmesan
  cheese

Prepare couscous according to the basic recipe (page 12), or follow package directions, using a flavorful chicken broth rather than water.

In a small skillet, sauté the chilies in the 2 tablespoons oil until tender, about 5 minutes. Mix the chilies into the couscous.

Preheat the oven to 400 degrees F.

If using frozen artichoke hearts, cook them according to package directions, but undercook them slightly. Cool them until they can be handled; cut them in half. In a soup bowl, beat the egg with the water and seasonings. Pour the crumbs onto a sheet of waxed paper and mix them with the cheese. Using 2 forks, dip each artichoke into the egg and then the crumbs. Lay them on an oiled baking sheet and drizzle each one with a little oil.

Bake the artichokes on the top shelf until crusty and golden-brown, 20 minutes. If necessary, reheat the couscous in a double boiler over boiling water, about 15 minutes, or in a microwave-safe casserole in the microwave, about 2 minutes. Fluff well with two forks, breaking up any lumps. Arrange the couscous on a platter, topped with the artichokes.

Kilocalories 417 Kc • Protein 14 Gm • Fat 10 Gm • Percent of calories from fat 22% • Cholesterol 56 mg • Dietary Fiber 7 Gm • Sodium 764 mg • Calcium 112 mg

Artichoke Hearts with Red Bell Pepper Sauce and Penne

---■---

4 SERVINGS

It's easy to make your own roast peppers, and you can't beat that home-made flavor. Simply char the peppers on all sides under a broiler. Put them into a covered casserole for a few minutes to allow the steam to loosen the skins. Peel and seed the peppers, and proceed with the recipe.

2 tablespoons olive oil
1 cup finely chopped onion
2 garlic cloves, minced
1 cup chicken or
   vegetable stock
$^1/_2$ cup dry white wine (or
   substitute another $^1/_2$ cup
   stock)
1 large roasted red bell pepper
   (from a jar or homemade—
   see page 260)

1 tablespoon tomato paste
$^1/_4$ teaspoon salt
$^1/_4$ teaspoon freshly ground
   black pepper
$^1/_8$ teaspoon cayenne pepper
6 artichoke hearts, cooked and
   halved (page 21), or 9-ounce
   package frozen artichoke
   hearts
8 ounces ($^1/_2$ pound) penne

In a medium-size skillet, heat the oil and sauté the onion and garlic until soft but not brown, 3 to 5 minutes. Add the stock and wine; boil rapidly until reduced to 1 cup, about 3 minutes. Purée the mixture with the red bell pepper, tomato paste, and seasonings. Return the sauce to the skillet and continue to cook over low heat, stirring often, for about 3 minutes.

Warm the artichoke hearts in a small skillet with 1 tablespoon water. If the artichoke hearts are frozen, cook them according to package directions; cut them in half. Keep them warm. Meanwhile, cook the penne according to package directions and drain. In a large serving dish, toss the penne with the sauce and artichoke hearts.

Kilocalories 357 Kc • Protein 12 Gm • Fat 8 Gm • Percent of calories from fat 20% • Cholesterol 0 mg • Dietary Fiber 6 Gm • Sodium 410 mg • Calcium 59 mg

Artichokes with Porcini Mushrooms and Rigatoni

■
---

4 SERVINGS

Richly flavored porcini mushrooms add an exotic note to an easy dish, but only dried porcini are available in the United States. If you wish, you can substitute 1 cup fresh diced portobello mushrooms, sautéed. The flavor will not be as intense.

½ cup dried porcini mushrooms
1 cup very hot water
3 tablespoons olive oil
1 teaspoon minced garlic
2 cups canned tomatoes in purée, chopped
4 fresh basil leaves, chopped, or ¼ teaspoon dried
½ teaspoon salt
¼ teaspoon freshly ground black pepper

¼ teaspoon crushed red pepper flakes
6 artichoke hearts, cooked and halved (page 21), or 1 9-ounce package frozen artichoke hearts, thawed to separate
1 tablespoon minced fresh flat-leaf parsley
8 ounces (½ pound) rigatoni
Freshly grated Asiago cheese

Soak the mushrooms in the hot water for 30 minutes. Drain, reserving the liquid. Rinse each mushroom under running water to remove all grit. Drain and chop the reconstituted mushrooms. Put a paper coffee filter in a medium-size strainer and strain the reserved mushroom liquid.

Heat the oil in a 10- or 12-inch skillet and sauté the garlic just until it sizzles. Add the tomatoes, basil, salt, black and red pepper, diced mushrooms, and reserved soaking liquid. Bring to a boil, reduce the heat to medium-high, and cook until slightly thickened, about 10 minutes, stirring often. Add the artichoke hearts. Reduce the heat to a bare simmer and cook 5 minutes, or if using frozen artichokes, until they are tender. Add the parsley.

Meanwhile, cook the rigatoni al dente according to package directions and drain. Stir the rigatoni into the simmering sauce and remove it from the heat. Cover and keep warm for a minute or so.

Stir and serve with grated cheese.

Kilocalories 390 Kc • Protein 12 Gm • Fat 11 Gm • Percent of calories from fat 25% • Cholesterol 0 mg • Dietary Fiber 8 Gm • Sodium 383 mg • Calcium 70 mg

Artichoke Hearts and Black Olives in Tomato Sauce with Spaghetti

6 SERVINGS

2 tablespoons olive oil
2 flat anchovies (optional)
1 garlic clove, minced
1 28-ounce can imported
  Italian plum tomatoes
  with juice
$1/2$ cup black olives
1 tablespoon chopped fresh
  basil, or 1 teaspoon dried
1 tablespoon chopped fresh
  marjoram, or $1/2$ teaspoon
  dried oregano
$1/2$ teaspoon salt

$1/4$ teaspoon freshly ground
  black pepper
6 artichoke hearts, cooked and
  quartered (page 21), or
  1 9-ounce package frozen
  artichoke hearts, cooked and
  quartered
$1/4$ cup chopped fresh flat-leaf
  parsley
1 pound spaghetti
3 tablespoons freshly grated
  Romano cheese, plus more
  to pass

Heat the oil in a large skillet and gently warm the anchovies until they begin to dissolve, about 3 minutes. Add the garlic and sauté until it's softened and fragrant, 2 minutes. Add the tomatoes, olives, basil, marjoram or oregano, salt, and pepper. Cook uncovered, stirring often, until reduced to a sauce consistency, 30 to 35 minutes. Stir in the artichokes and parsley. Cook 2 minutes longer.

Cook the spaghetti according to package directions and drain. Spoon it into a large serving dish, and toss with the sauce and 3 tablespoons cheese. Pass more cheese at the table.

Kilocalories 415 Kc • Protein 13 Gm • Fat 9 Gm • Percent of calories from fat 20% • Cholesterol 3 mg • Dietary Fiber 6 Gm • Sodium 714 mg • Calcium 93 mg

Artichoke and Pasta Salad

◼

4 SERVINGS

6 artichoke hearts, or 9-ounce package frozen artichoke hearts
1 cup diced fennel or celery
1 large tomato, diced
2 tablespoons chopped fresh flat-leaf parsley

1 garlic clove, halved
$1/4$ cup olive oil
2 tablespoons red wine vinegar
$1/2$ teaspoon salt
$1/4$ teaspoon pepper
6 ounces (about $1/3$ pound) mezzani rigati

Prepare and cook the artichokes (page 21 for fresh artichokes; follow package directions for frozen). Drain, cool, and cut them in half.

Combine the artichoke hearts, fennel, tomato, parsley, garlic, olive oil, vinegar, and seasonings in a salad dish. Allow the mixture to marinate at room temperature for half an hour, stirring occasionally. Remove and discard the garlic.

Cook the mezzani rigati according to package directions. Drain and rinse under cold water.

Add the cooked pasta to the salad and toss well before serving.

Kilocalories 343 Kc • Protein 8 Gm • Fat 16 Gm • Percent of calories from fat 40% • Cholesterol 0 mg • Dietary Fiber 6 Gm • Sodium 460 mg • Calcium 54 mg

Asparagus,
Herald of Spring

———■———

Along with the joy of spring comes the joy of fresh asparagus to dispel the winter vegetable doldrums. These elegantly slender stalks, although practically fat-free, are plentiful in the antiaging antioxidant vitamins A and C to tone up your body for spring activities. Asparagus is also an excellent source of folic acid, the important B vitamin that helps prevent certain birth defects, and potassium for heart health.

Shop for asparagus with bright green stalks and closed lavender-tinted tops. Like watercress, asparagus will keep best if stored as it if were a bunch of flowers. Remove a half inch from the ends of the stalks and stand them upright in an inch of water in your refrigerator. The stalks will then absorb the moisture, staying fresh and perky for two or three days.

No need to buy a fancy asparagus steamer! Just steam the stalks in a skillet, as described in the following recipe.

Easy Steamed Asparagus

———■———

Wash the asparagus and trim off the woody ends. Pour $1/2$ cup water into a 12-inch skillet, lay the asparagus in the pan, cover, and bring to a boil. Reduce the heat and simmer, covered, until tender-crisp, about 3 minutes, or until very tender, 5 minutes.

Asparagus Soup with Tortellini

―――――――――――― ■ ――――――――――――

6 SERVINGS

Although easily made, this soup has a surprisingly rich flavor to brighten up a rainy spring day.

1 pound fresh asparagus, trimmed
3 tablespoons olive oil
1 cup well-washed, sliced leeks, or ½ cup chopped onion
3 tablespoons all-purpose flour

8 cups chicken or vegetable stock, or canned broth
8 ounces (½ pound) cheese tortellini
About ½ teaspoon salt
Freshly ground pepper

Cut off the top 2 inches of each asparagus stalk and blanch them in boiling salted water for 2 minutes. Drain and rinse in cold water. Reserve the tips. Cut the remaining stalks into 1-inch pieces.

In a large pot, heat the oil and slowly sauté the leeks or onion until softened and lightly colored, 5 minutes. Add the flour and cook, stirring often, for 3 minutes. Add the asparagus stalks and stock, and bring the soup to a boil. Reduce the heat and simmer over low heat for 10 to 15 minutes.

Meanwhile, cook the tortellini separately according to package directions and drain. Add the tortellini and reserved asparagus tips to the soup. Taste the soup; add salt and pepper to your taste.

Kilocalories 182 Kc • Protein 9 Gm • Fat 9 Gm • Percent of calories from fat 47% • Cholesterol 2 mg • Dietary Fiber 3 Gm • Sodium 809 mg • Calcium 58 mg

Asparagus and Sun-dried Tomatoes with Linguine

2 ENTRÉE SERVINGS

1 pound fresh asparagus, trimmed

$^1/_2$ cup chicken stock or canned broth

2 tablespoons oil from sun-dried tomatoes

1 tablespoon chopped fresh flat-leaf parsley

$^1/_2$ teaspoon dried basil

$^1/_4$ teaspoon salt

Freshly ground black pepper

8 ounces ($^1/_2$ pound) linguine

$^1/_2$ cup oil-packed sun-dried tomatoes, slivered

Steam the asparagus, using the directions on page 29, substituting the chicken stock for water. Do not drain. Season the asparagus with the oil, parsley, basil, salt, and pepper to your taste. Push the stalks to one side of the pan. Keep warm.

Meanwhile, cook the linguine according to package directions and drain. Stir the pasta into the pan juices in the empty side of the skillet.

Transfer the linguine to a warm platter by carefully tipping the skillet. Follow with the asparagus, which should then be on top. Arrange the sun-dried tomatoes over all.

Kilocalories 663 Kc • Protein 23 Gm • Fat 20 Gm • Percent of calories from fat 26% • Cholesterol 0 mg • Dietary Fiber 8 Gm • Sodium 592 mg • Calcium 91 mg

Asparagus with Spinach Fettuccine

---

4 SERVINGS

1 pound fresh asparagus,
  trimmed
$^{1}/_{2}$ cup vegetable stock or
  canned broth
3 tablespoons melted butter
2 tablespoons chopped fresh
  herbs such as cilantro, basil,
  and/or snipped chives

$^{1}/_{4}$ teaspoon salt
Freshly ground black pepper
12 ounces ($^{3}/_{4}$ pound) fresh or
  dried spinach fettuccine
3 tablespoons coarsely grated
  or slivered Parmesan cheese

Steam the asparagus, using the directions on page 29, substituting the vegetable stock for water. Do not drain. Season the asparagus with the butter, herbs, and salt and pepper to your taste. Push the stalks to one side of the pan. Keep warm.

Meanwhile, cook the fettuccine according to package directions and drain. Stir the pasta into the pan juices in the empty side of the skillet.

Transfer the fettuccine to a warm platter by carefully tipping the skillet. Follow with the asparagus, which should then be on top. Sprinkle with the cheese, and serve at once.

Kilocalories 386 Kc • Protein 16 Gm • Fat 15 Gm • Percent of calories from fat 33% • Cholesterol 128 mg • Dietary Fiber 6 Gm • Sodium 551 mg • Calcium 136 mg

Stir-fried Asparagus and Red Bell Pepper with Vermicelli

---

4 SERVINGS

2 tablespoons olive oil
1 pound fresh asparagus, trimmed, cut into 2-inch pieces
1 red bell pepper, seeded and cut into 2-inch strips
1 garlic clove, minced

$1/4$ teaspoon salt
Freshly ground black pepper
$1/2$ cup chicken stock or canned broth
8 ounces ($1/2$ pound) vermicelli
$1/4$ cup coarsely shredded Asiago cheese (optional)

Heat the oil in a skillet and stir-fry the asparagus and red pepper until they are tender-crisp, about 3 minutes. Add the garlic during the last minute. Remove from the heat and season with salt and pepper to your taste. Add the stock.

Meanwhile, cook the vermicelli according to package directions, drain, and spoon it into a large serving dish. Add the asparagus mixture and cheese. Toss well to blend the vegetables with the pasta.

Kilocalories 307 Kc • Protein 11 Gm • Fat 8 Gm • Percent of calories from fat 24% • Cholesterol 0 mg • Dietary Fiber 4 Gm • Sodium 259 mg • Calcium 37 mg

ASPARAGUS, HERALD OF SPRING

33

Asparagus with Basil Pesto and Tagliatelle

---

4 SERVINGS

1 pound fresh asparagus, preferably thin stalks, trimmed
12 ounces (³⁄₄ pound) tagliatelle (or linguine)

¹⁄₃ cup basil pesto (from a jar, or see page 9 for basic recipe)

Steam the asparagus, using the directions on page 29. Meanwhile, cook the tagliatelle according to package directions and drain. Toss the tagliatelle with the pesto on a large serving platter. Rewarm the asparagus if necessary, and arrange the stalks over the pasta.

NOTE: This makes a very pretty presentation, but it's messy to eat. If you'd rather be neat, after steaming the asparagus, cut it into 2-inch lengths and toss it together with the pesto and pasta.

Kilocalories 463 Kc • Protein 16 Gm • Fat 14 Gm • Percent of calories from fat 27% • Cholesterol 1 mg • Dietary Fiber 5 Gm • Sodium 144 mg • Calcium 74 mg

Asparagus and Egg Sauce with Fusilli

---

2 LUNCHEON ENTRÉE SERVINGS

When the fresh vegetable is not in season, keep some frozen asparagus in your freezer and you'll always be able to whip up this lovely luncheon dish.

10 ounces fresh asparagus, trimmed, or 9- or 10-ounce package frozen asparagus cuts
1 tablespoon butter
2 large shallots, minced
1½ tablespoons superfine flour, such as Wondra

Scant ¼ teaspoon salt
⅛ teaspoon white pepper
⅛ teaspoon dry mustard
1 cup milk (whole milk is best in this recipe)
1 hard-boiled egg, chopped
8 ounces (½ pound) fusilli (or any corkscrew-shaped pasta)

Cook the fresh asparagus (page 29) and cut it into 1-inch pieces. If using frozen asparagus, cook it according to package directions and drain. In either case, reserve 2 tablespoons of the cooking water.

In a saucepan, heat the butter and sauté the shallots until they are softened and fragrant, 3 minutes. Whisk the flour and seasonings into the milk. Add the milk mixture and reserved asparagus cooking water to the saucepan and cook over medium-high heat, stirring constantly, until the sauce bubbles and thickens. Simmer over low heat for 3 minutes, stirring occasionally. Remove from the heat. Stir in the asparagus and egg.

Meanwhile, cook the fusilli according to package directions and drain. In a large serving dish, combine the fusilli with the asparagus sauce.

Kilocalories 642 Kc • Protein 26 Gm • Fat 15 Gm • Percent of calories from fat 21% • Cholesterol 139 mg • Dietary Fiber 6 Gm • Sodium 467 mg • Calcium 211 mg

ASPARAGUS, HERALD OF SPRING

Asparagus, Chicken, and Penne Casserole

1 pound fresh asparagus, trimmed

2 cups milk (whole or low-fat)

1 cup chicken stock or canned broth (or use the broth left from cooking the chicken)

$1/4$ cup superfine flour, such as Wondra

$1/4$ cup nonfat dry milk

$1/4$ teaspoon dried tarragon

$1/2$ teaspoon salt

$1/4$ teaspoon white pepper

5 tablespoons grated Parmesan cheese

8 ounces ($1/2$ pound) penne

1 whole chicken breast, cooked, skinned, and cut into chunks (about 2 cups) (see Note)

$1/2$ cup fresh bread crumbs

Steam the asparagus, using the directions on page 29. Cut the cooked asparagus into 2-inch pieces.

In a medium saucepan, combine the liquid milk and stock, and whisk in the flour, dry milk, tarragon, salt, and pepper. Bring to a boil over medium heat, stirring constantly until the mixture bubbles and thickens. Simmer for 3 minutes, stirring occasionally. Remove from the heat and stir in 3 tablespoons of the cheese.

Preheat the oven to 350 degrees F.

Cook the penne according to package directions and drain. Spoon it into a $2^{1}/2$-quart gratin pan or casserole. Stir in half the sauce. Layer the asparagus and chicken on top and pour the remaining sauce over all. Sprinkle with the fresh bread crumbs and remaining 2 tablespoons of cheese. Bake the casserole for 30 minutes, or until bubbling throughout and golden on top.

NOTE: This is a great recipe for using leftover chicken. If that's not available, however, cook the breast as follows: Combine the chicken, 1 cup water, a few herbs of your choice (such as parsley and thyme or sage), and 1 chicken bouillon cube or $1/4$ teaspoon salt. Bring to a simmer, cover, and cook over very low heat 20 to 25 minutes for a bone-in breast, 12 to 15 minutes for boneless, or until just cooked through.

Kilocalories 467 Kc • Protein 33 Gm • Fat 9 Gm • Percent of calories from fat 18% • Cholesterol 62 mg • Dietary Fiber 4 Gm • Sodium 658 mg • Calcium 302 mg

Asparagus, Green Pepper, and Radish Stir-fry with Fresh Asian Noodles

4 SERVINGS

Stir-fry ingredients can always be varied according to what you have on hand. Optional additions might include thinly sliced celery, baby zucchini, cabbage, or seeded, chunked cucumber.

1 pound fresh asparagus, trimmed, cut diagonally into 2-inch lengths
1 large green bell pepper, seeded and diced
8 large radishes, thinly sliced
1 sweet onion, such as Vidalia, thinly sliced

1 12-ounce (3/4 pound) package fresh Asian noodles
2 tablespoons vegetable oil, plus more if needed
2 tablespoons naturally brewed soy sauce, plus more to pass
2 teaspoons oyster sauce

Prepare all the vegetables before beginning the stir-fry.

Bring water to boil for the noodles (see package directions).

Meanwhile, heat 2 tablespoons of the oil in a large skillet or wok and stir-fry the asparagus and green pepper until tender-crisp, about 3 minutes. Remove the vegetables with a slotted spoon.

If necessary, add a little more oil to the pan and stir-fry the radishes and onion until tender-crisp, about 2 minutes. Return the asparagus and green pepper to the skillet and season the vegetables with soy sauce and oyster sauce.

Cook the Asian noodles according to package directions and drain. (Be aware that fresh noodles take only a few minutes to cook.) In a large serving dish, toss the noodles with the vegetable mixture. Pass more soy sauce at the table.

Kilocalories 315 Kc • Protein 9 Gm • Fat 16 Gm • Percent of calories from fat 43% • Cholesterol 0 mg • Dietary Fiber 5 Gm • Sodium 1271 mg • Calcium 93 mg

Asparagus and Shrimp with Ziti

■

2 ENTRÉE SERVINGS

A lovely celebration dinner for two—elegant and easy.

2 cloves garlic, peeled and
  sliced
2 tablespoons olive oil
8 ounces cooked, shelled,
  cleaned medium shrimp
  (frozen, thawed, or see basic
  recipe, page 14)
2 tablespoons fresh
  lemon juice

2 tablespoons minced fresh
  flat-leaf parsley
Cayenne pepper
10 ounces fresh asparagus,
  trimmed, or a 9- to 10-ounce
  package frozen
  asparagus cuts
8 ounces (¹/₂ pound) ziti

Combine the garlic and oil in a large skillet and warm the mixture at the lowest temperature for 5 minutes. Add the shrimp and continue to warm for 5 minutes. Remove and discard the garlic. Stir in the lemon juice and parsley. Sprinkle with cayenne pepper to your taste.

Meanwhile, cook the fresh asparagus, using the directions on page 29; drain and cut it into 1-inch pieces. If using frozen asparagus, cook it according to package directions.

Cook the ziti according to package directions and drain. Combine the shrimp, asparagus, and ziti in a large serving dish and toss to blend.

Kilocalories 694 Kc • Protein 42 Gm • Fat 17 Gm • Percent of calories from fat 22% • Cholesterol 222 mg • Dietary Fiber 6 Gm • Sodium 280 mg • Calcium 105 mg

Asparagus with Gorgonzola and Farfalle

4 SERVINGS

1 pound fresh asparagus,
  trimmed
2 tablespoons olive oil
1/4 cup chopped shallots
Salt and freshly ground pepper

8 ounces (1/2 pound) farfalle
  (egg bows)
3 ounces Gorgonzola cheese
  (or any blue cheese),
  crumbled

Steam the asparagus, using the directions on page 29. Remove and drain the asparagus.

Dry out the skillet and heat the oil in it. Sauté the shallots until they are golden. Cut the asparagus into 2-inch pieces and return them to the pan. Season with salt and pepper to your taste, keeping in mind that the cheese adds salt. Keep warm.

Meanwhile, cook the farfalle according to package directions. Drain the pasta and spoon it into a large serving dish. Toss with the Gorgonzola. Toss again with the asparagus and shallots.

Kilocalories 385 Kc • Protein 16 Gm • Fat 16 Gm • Percent of calories from fat 38% • Cholesterol 82 mg • Dietary Fiber 3 Gm • Sodium 320 mg • Calcium 135 mg

Asparagus and Pasta Salad with Walnut Vinaigrette

4 SERVINGS

Although the salad itself is quickly prepared, note that the dressing needs to marinate for an hour before serving.

1 pound fresh asparagus, trimmed, cut into 2-inch lengths

8 ounces (1/2 pound) ziti

2 inner celery stalks, with leaves, sliced

1/2 cup walnut halves or pieces

8 to 10 Sicilian green olives, pitted and halved or chopped

4 scallions, chopped (optional)

1/3 cup Walnut Vinaigrette (recipe follows)

Cook the asparagus in a large pot of boiling salted water until just tender, about 3 minutes. Lift it out with a slotted spoon into a colander and rinse it under cold water to stop the cooking. Drain well.

Cook the ziti in the same water. Drain and rinse the ziti under cold water. Spoon it into a salad bowl. Add the asparagus, celery, walnuts, olives, and scallions, if using. Stir in the Walnut Vinaigrette.

The salad is best served immediately at room temperature. If this isn't possible, refrigerate until needed. Taste before serving to see if you want more dressing or salt. Refrigerate leftovers.

Kilocalories 483 Kc • Protein 14 Gm • Fat 24 Gm • Percent of calories from fat 44% • Cholesterol 0 mg • Dietary Fiber 5 Gm • Sodium 231 mg • Calcium 67 mg

Walnut Vinaigrette

Walnut oil is always a nutritious addition to a vinaigrette. It's rich in alpha-linolenic acid, a fatty acid that's an essential "brain food" and also helps us to resist toxins. Walnut oil should be refrigerated after opening.

½ cup olive oil

¼ cup walnut oil

¼ cup red wine vinegar

¼ teaspoon dried tarragon

¼ teaspoon dried chervil

¼ teaspoon salt

¼ teaspoon pepper

¼ teaspoon sugar

1 garlic clove, peeled and sliced

Combine all the ingredients in a jar and allow the mixture to marinate at room temperature for an hour or more. Remove and discard the garlic.

Shake well; the vinegar should be well mixed with the oil before measuring.

Kilocalories 183 Kc • Protein 0 Gm • Fat 20 Gm • Percent of calories from fat 99% • Cholesterol 0 mg • Dietary Fiber 0 Gm • Sodium 73 mg • Calcium 2 mg

ASPARAGUS, HERALD OF SPRING

Asparagus, Tuna, and Gemelli Salad

6 SERVINGS

Italian tuna packed in oil is especially flavorful. Even though the tuna is drained, this salad needs very little additional oil.

1 pound fresh asparagus, trimmed

12 ounces (³/₄ pound) gemelli

1 6- to 7-ounce can imported Italian tuna, packed in oil, drained and chunked

¹/₄ cup finely chopped red onion, or 4 scallions, chopped

¹/₄ cup sliced pitted black olives, or 1 roasted whole red bell pepper (from a jar), diced

3 tablespoons fresh lemon juice

1 to 2 tablespoons extra-virgin olive oil

Salt and freshly ground pepper

Steam the asparagus, using the directions on page 29. Rinse in cold water and cut into 2-inch pieces.

Cook the gemelli according to package directions; drain and rinse in cold water. Put the pasta in a large shallow salad dish and toss with the tuna, onion or scallions, olives or red pepper, lemon juice, and oil. Season to your taste with salt and pepper, keeping in mind that the tuna adds salt.

Just before serving, add the asparagus and toss again.

Kilocalories 319 Kc • Protein 18 Gm • Fat 7 Gm • Percent of calories from fat 19% • Cholesterol 5 mg • Dietary Fiber 3 Gm • Sodium 173 mg • Calcium 31 mg

ASPARAGUS, HERALD OF SPRING

Beans for All Seasons

———————— ◼ ————————

One of the world's most nutritious foods, beans are available all year in one form or another. With fresh green beans abundant in summer, shell beans available in the fall, and the whole panoply of dried and canned beans on stock in winter, you're always able to dish up a helping of iron to enhance energy and B vitamins to build strong nerves with this versatile vegetable. Beans are also a great source of soluble fiber to lower cholesterol. And the protease inhibitors they contain help to block the formation of cancers.

In buying green beans, look for slender and crisp beans without rusty blemishes. Store them in a perforated plastic vegetable bag for up to two days. Frozen beans are a reasonable alternative—but never for salads! Dried beans can be soaked and cooked from scratch, of course, but in the recipes that follow I've taken advantage of the many kinds of canned, cooked beans on the market, a marvelous shortcut that encourages the cook to use them more often. Some of the more exotic types of canned beans, if not in your local supermarket, can be found in natural foods stores where organic produce is featured.

Jamaican Kidney Bean Soup with Ditali

---

6 SERVINGS

There's a powerhouse of vitamin A in this spicy soup!

1 tablespoon olive oil
1 green bell pepper, seeded
  and diced
1 fresh jalapeño chili, seeded
  and minced (wear rubber
  gloves)
1 medium yellow onion,
  chopped
1 clove garlic, minced
6 cups chicken or vegetable
  stock, or canned broth

1 pound sweet potatoes, peeled
  and cut into 1-inch chunks
$^{1}/_{2}$ teaspoon dried thyme
$^{1}/_{2}$ teaspoon salt
$^{1}/_{4}$ teaspoon freshly ground
  black pepper
Few dashes of cayenne pepper
1 15- or 16-ounce can kidney
  beans, rinsed and drained
1 cup ditali

Heat the oil in a large pot and sauté the bell pepper, chili, onion, and garlic until they are softened and fragrant, 3 minutes. Add the stock, sweet potatoes, thyme, salt, and black and cayenne peppers, and simmer until the potatoes are tender, 15 minutes. Add the beans and cook 5 minutes longer. Meanwhile, cook the ditali according to package directions and drain. Stir the pasta into the soup.

Kilocalories 319 Kc • Protein 16 Gm • Fat 5 Gm • Percent of calories from fat 13% • Cholesterol 0 mg • Dietary Fiber 9 Gm • Sodium 680 mg • Calcium 63 mg

Red Lentil Soup with Shells

6 SERVINGS

Red lentils are available in natural foods stores; brown lentils can be substituted.

1 tablespoon olive oil
1 red bell pepper, seeded and diced
1 medium yellow onion, chopped
1 celery stalk, diced
2 garlic cloves, minced
6 cups water
$\frac{1}{2}$ pound red lentils

2 carrots, diced
1 teaspoon ground cumin
1 teaspoon ground coriander
1 teaspoon salt
$\frac{1}{4}$ teaspoon freshly ground black pepper
1 cup very small shells
2 tablespoons minced fresh flat-leaf parsley

In a large pot, heat the oil and sauté the bell pepper, onion, celery, and garlic for 3 minutes. Add the water, lentils, carrots, cumin, coriander, salt, and pepper. Simmer over low heat, stirring often, for 30 minutes. Meanwhile, cook the shells according to package directions and drain. Stir the pasta and parsley into the soup.

Kilocalories 208 Kc • Protein 10 Gm • Fat 3 Gm • Percent of calories from fat 13% • Cholesterol 0 mg • Dietary Fiber 2 Gm • Sodium 413 mg • Calcium 45 mg

BEANS FOR ALL SEASONS

White Kidney Bean and Chicory Soup with Farfallini

---

6 SERVINGS

A hearty soup that goes together in 15 minutes. The mild, sweet white kidney beans complement the stronger flavor of chicory.

2 tablespoons olive oil
3 garlic cloves, minced
8 cups chicken or vegetable stock, or canned broth
1 large head (about 1 pound) chicory (curly endive), well washed, coarsely chopped
1 20-ounce can white kidney beans (cannellini), drained and rinsed

2 tablespoons tomato paste
$^{1}/_{2}$ teaspoon salt
$^{1}/_{4}$ teaspoon freshly ground black pepper
4 ounces ($^{1}/_{4}$ pound) farfallini (tiny egg bows)

Heat the oil in a large pot and sauté the garlic until it's sizzling. Add all the remaining ingredients except the pasta and simmer the soup until the chicory is tender but still green, about 10 minutes. Meanwhile, cook the farfallini according to package directions and drain. Stir the pasta into the soup.

Kilocalories 262 Kc • Protein 15 Gm • Fat 8 Gm • Percent of calories from fat 27% • Cholesterol • 22 mg • Dietary Fiber 8 Gm • Sodium 1113 mg • Calcium 83 mg

Pasta e Fagioli
(Italian Pasta and Bean Soup)

4 SERVINGS

Sliced, cooked Italian sausage, hot or sweet, makes a tasty addition to this substantial soup.

2 tablespoons olive oil
1 carrot, diced
1 small yellow onion, chopped
1 celery stalk, diced
2 garlic cloves, minced
1 16-ounce can imported Italian tomatoes with juice
1/2 teaspoon salt
1/4 teaspoon dried basil
1/4 teaspoon dried oregano
1/4 teaspoon dried rosemary
1/4 teaspoon hot red pepper flakes
1/4 teaspoon freshly ground black pepper

4 cups chicken stock or canned broth
3 cups shelled shell beans (about 2 pounds unshelled), or 1 20-ounce can shell, pinto, or cranberry beans, drained and rinsed
5 to 6 ounces (about 1/3 pound) medium elbows
2 tablespoons minced fresh flat-leaf parsley
Freshly grated Parmesan cheese

Heat the oil in a large pot and sauté the carrot, onion, celery, and garlic until they are softened and fragrant, 3 minutes (the carrot will not get very soft). Add the tomatoes, salt, basil, oregano, rosemary, and both peppers. Simmer for 10 minutes, breaking up the tomatoes. Add the stock and shell beans and simmer 20 minutes, or until quite tender (10 minutes for canned beans). Taste to correct seasonings; you may want more salt.

Meanwhile, cook the pasta according to package directions and drain. Stir the pasta and parsley into the soup. Pass the grated cheese at the table.

Kilocalories 527 Kc • Protein 28 Gm • Fat 10 Gm • Percent of calories from fat 17% • Cholesterol 0 mg • Dietary Fiber 21 Gm • Sodium 983 mg • Calcium 157 mg

Green Beans Provençale with Penne

2 tablespoons olive oil
1 dried hot red chili
1 large garlic clove, minced
1 16-ounce can imported
  Italian tomatoes with juice
1/4 cup sliced pitted black
  olives
1/2 teaspoon dried oregano

1/4 teaspoon salt
1/8 teaspoon ground black
  pepper, or to your taste
3/4 pound fresh green beans,
  cut diagonally into 2-inch
  lengths
8 ounces (1/2 pound) penne

Heat the oil in a large skillet. Add the chili and garlic, and sauté until the garlic is soft and fragrant, about 3 minutes.

Add the tomatoes, black olives, oregano, salt, and pepper, and simmer, uncovered, for 5 minutes. Add the green beans and cover. Cook, stirring often, until the beans are tender, about 8 minutes. Remove the chili.

Meanwhile, cook the penne according to package directions and drain, and spoon it into a large serving dish. Add the green beans and toss them with the pasta.

Kilocalories 344 Kc • Protein 10 Gm • Fat 9 Gm • Percent of calories from fat 24% • Cholesterol 0 mg • Dietary Fiber 6 Gm • Sodium 462 mg • Calcium 78 mg

Italian Green Beans and Peppers with Ruote

4 SERVINGS

2 tablespoons olive oil
2 Italian frying peppers, seeded and diced
$^3/_4$ pound fresh Romano beans (a broad, flat green bean) or 1 10-ounce package frozen Italian green beans, thawed just enough to separate

$^1/_2$ cup chicken stock or canned broth
$^1/_4$ teaspoon dried rosemary
$^1/_4$ teaspoon salt
Freshly ground black pepper
6 ounces (about $^1/_3$ pound) ruote (wagon wheels)

Heat the oil in a skillet and sauté the peppers until they're lightly browned, about 3 minutes. Add the green beans and chicken stock. Cover and cook at a simmer until the green beans are tender, 10 minutes if fresh, 5 if frozen. Season the green beans with the rosemary, salt, and pepper to your taste.

Meanwhile, cook the pasta according to package directions and drain. Spoon it into a serving dish, and toss with the vegetable mixture to blend.

Kilocalories 263 Kc • Protein 8 Gm • Fat 8 Gm • Percent of calories from fat 26% • Cholesterol 0 mg • Dietary Fiber 4 Gm • Sodium 253 mg • Calcium 48 mg

Green Beans and Red Pepper with Shells

—◼—

4 SERVINGS

1/2 pound fresh green beans, cut diagonally into 1-inch pieces
2 tablespoons olive oil
1 large red bell pepper, seeded and cut into 1-inch pieces
2 tablespoons minced shallots
1/4 cup sliced pitted black olives

Salt and freshly ground black pepper
1 tablespoon minced fresh ciliantro, or 1/2 teaspoon dried
6 ounces (about 1/3 pound) medium shells

Parboil the green beans in boiling salted water for 5 minutes. Drain.

Heat the oil in a medium skillet and sauté the red pepper until it begins to soften. At the last minute, add the shallots. Spoon the green beans and olives on top, cover the skillet, and braise over very low heat, stirring often, until the vegetables are tender, 5 to 7 minutes. Salt and pepper the vegetables to your taste. Sprinkle with the cilantro.

Meanwhile, cook the shells according to package directions and drain. Combine the shells with the green beans in a serving dish.

Kilocalories 253 Kc • Protein 7 Gm • Fat 9 Gm • Percent of calories from fat 31% • Cholesterol 0 mg • Dietary Fiber 3 Gm • Sodium 50 mg • Calcium 24 mg

Green Beans and Pesto with Farfalle

4 SERVINGS

A spoonful of pesto imparts the delectable aroma of summer.

1 pound fresh green beans, cut into 1-inch pieces
1 tablespoon olive oil
¼ cup basil pesto (from a jar, or see basic recipe, page 9)

8 ounces (½ pound) farfalle ("butterfly" macaroni, also called "bows")
Freshly grated Parmesan cheese

Cook the green beans in boiling salted water until just tender, about 7 minutes. Drain; add the olive oil. Stir in the pesto.

Meanwhile, cook the farfalle according to package directions. Drain and toss with the green beans. Pass the grated cheese at the table.

Kilocalories 381 Kc • Protein 12 Gm • Fat 16 Gm • Percent of calories from fat 37% • Cholesterol 67 mg • Dietary Fiber 5 Gm • Sodium 113 mg • Calcium 70 mg

Green Beans with Scallion Butter, Pine Nuts, and Spinach Penne

---

4 SERVINGS

2 tablespoons butter
4 scallions, chopped
3/4 pound fresh green beans, cut into 1-inch pieces
1/2 cup chicken stock or canned broth
Salt and freshly ground black pepper

1 tablespoon chopped fresh basil, or 1 teaspoon dried
6 ounces (about 1/3 pound) spinach penne
1/4 cup toasted pine nuts

Melt the butter in a large skillet and sauté the scallions until they are fragrant but not brown, about 3 minutes. Add the green beans and stock. Bring to a boil, reduce the heat, cover, and simmer until tender, about 7 minutes. Season the beans with salt and pepper to your taste and stir in the basil.

Meanwhile, cook the penne according to package directions and drain. Toss the green beans and penne together in a serving dish. Sprinkle with the pine nuts and serve.

Kilocalories 301 Kc • Protein 11 Gm • Fat 13 Gm • Percent of calories from fat 38% • Cholesterol 57 mg • Dietary Fiber 6 Gm • Sodium 152 mg • Calcium 66 mg

Green Beans and Walnuts with Spaghettini

This is a good midwinter dish you can toss together quickly from freezer and pantry stores.

1 cup shelled walnut halves or pieces
2 tablespoons olive oil
1 garlic clove, minced
$^3/_4$ pound fresh Romano beans (a broad, flat green bean), or 1 10-ounce package of frozen Italian green beans, thawed just enough to separate

$^1/_2$ cup chicken stock or canned broth
$^1/_2$ teaspoon dried basil
$^1/_4$ teaspoon salt
Freshly ground black pepper
8 ounces ($^1/_2$ pound) spaghettini
3 tablespoons grated Parmesan cheese, plus more to pass

Put the walnuts into a small saucepan with water to cover. Bring to a boil, remove from the heat, and drain well.

Heat the oil in a large skillet and sauté the garlic until it's fragrant. Add the walnuts and continue sautéing for 1 to 2 minutes, without browning the garlic. Add the green beans and stock, cover, and cook on low until the beans are tender, about 10 minutes for fresh beans, 5 minutes for frozen. Season with basil, salt, and pepper to your taste.

Meanwhile, cook the spaghettini according to package directions. Drain and toss in the skillet with the bean mixture and the 3 tablespoons cheese. Spoon into a serving dish. Pass more cheese at the table.

Kilocalories 509 Kc • Protein 19 Gm • Fat 27 Gm • Percent of calories from fat 46% • Cholesterol 3 mg • Dietary Fiber 6 Gm • Sodium 322 mg • Calcium 118 mg

BEANS FOR ALL SEASONS

Green Beans, Chickpeas, and Anchovies with Tagliatelle

2 tablespoons olive oil
1 small yellow onion, chopped
1 garlic clove, minced
$^{1}/_{2}$ pound fresh green beans,
   trimmed, cut diagonally into
   2-inch pieces
$^{1}/_{2}$ cup water

1 15- to 16-ounce can
   chickpeas, drained
   and rinsed
6 anchovy fillets, chopped
8 ounces ($^{1}/_{2}$ pound) tagliatelle
2 tablespoons chopped fresh
   flat-leaf parsley

Heat the oil in a large skillet and sauté the onion and garlic until translucent but not brown, about 3 minutes. Add the green beans and water; cover and simmer until the beans are almost tender, about 5 minutes. Add the chickpeas and anchovies, and simmer, uncovered, for 5 minutes, stirring often.

   Meanwhile, cook the tagliatelle according to package directions and drain. Combine the tagliatelle and vegetables in a large serving dish and gently toss to combine. Sprinkle with the parsley.

Kilocalories 448 Kc • Protein 16 Gm • Fat 10 Gm • Percent of calories from fat 19% • Cholesterol 5 mg • Dietary Fiber 9 Gm • Sodium 570 mg • Calcium 92 mg

Middle Eastern Chickpeas with Couscous

4 SERVINGS

1 cup couscous, raw
2 tablespoons olive oil
1 large yellow onion, chopped
2 garlic cloves, minced
1 20-ounce can chickpeas,
   drained and rinsed
3/4 cup chicken stock or
   canned broth
1 tablespoon fresh lemon juice

1/4 teaspoon ground coriander
1/4 teaspoon ground cumin
1/4 teaspoon turmeric
1/4 teaspoon ground cinnamon
1/4 teaspoon salt
1/8 teaspoon cayenne pepper,
   or more, to your taste
1/4 cup slivered fresh mint
   leaves for garnish (optional)

Prepare the couscous (see page 12 for basic recipe or follow package directions). Fluff to separate the grains.

Heat the oil in a large skillet and sauté the onion and garlic until they are softened and fragrant, 3 minutes. Add the chickpeas and all the remaining ingredients except the couscous and mint. Simmer the mixture for 10 minutes.

Arrange the couscous on a platter and top with the chickpeas. Garnish with mint, if desired.

Kilocalories 449 Kc • Protein 15 Gm • Fat 9 Gm • Percent of calories from fat 18% • Cholesterol 0 mg • Dietary Fiber 10 Gm • Sodium 703 mg • Calcium 73 mg

Chickpeas with "Straw and Hay"

4 SERVINGS

Paglia e fieno, *or "straw and hay," is the Italian name for a two-color combination of spinach and plain fettuccine. They are sometimes packaged together under the name* fettuccine florentine. *Or you can make your own assortment from a package of each.*

1 20-ounce can chickpeas, drained and rinsed
½ cup chicken stock or canned broth
2 tablespoons olive oil
1 clove garlic, crushed
1 tablespoon chopped fresh rosemary and thyme (combined), or ¼ teaspoon *each* of the dried herbs

Salt and freshly ground black pepper
12 ounces (¾ pound) spinach and plain fettuccine
Grated Romano cheese

Slowly simmer the chickpeas with the stock, oil, garlic, and herbs about 10 minutes. There should be at least ¼ cup broth remaining; if not, add a little more. Remove the garlic. Add salt and pepper to your taste.

Meanwhile, cook the fettuccine according to package directions and drain. On a large serving platter, toss the fettuccine with the chickpeas and pan liquid. Pass the cheese at the table.

Kilocalories 556 Kc • Protein 19 Gm • Fat 11 Gm • Percent of calories from fat 18% • Cholesterol 40 mg • Dietary Fiber 10 Gm • Sodium 512 mg • Calcium 92 mg

Fava Beans, Chard, and Olives with Spaghettini

4 SERVINGS

1/2 pound fresh chard
2 tablespoons olive oil
2 garlic cloves, minced
1/2 cup chicken stock or canned broth
1/4 cup Greek or niçoise olives, pitted
1 16-ounce can fava beans, drained and rinsed

Salt and freshly ground pepper
1 tablespoon minced fresh flat-leaf parsley
2 teaspoons minced fresh thyme, or 1/2 teaspoon dried
8 ounces (1/2 pound) spaghettini
1/4 cup loosely packed, freshly grated Romano cheese

Carefully wash the chard. Drain, then chop the leaves into 2-inch pieces and the stalks into 1-inch pieces.

Heat the oil in a large skillet and sauté the garlic until it's sizzling, about 2 minutes. Add the stock, chard, and olives. Cover and simmer until the chard is tender, 3 to 5 minutes. Add the fava beans, season with salt and pepper to your taste (the olives and cheese add salt), and simmer for 5 minutes. Stir in the parsley and thyme.

Meanwhile, cook the spaghettini according to package directions and drain. Spoon it into a large serving dish and toss with the fava bean mixture and the cheese.

Kilocalories 479 Kc • Protein 23 Gm • Fat 11 Gm • Percent of calories from fat 21% • Cholesterol 7 mg • Dietary Fiber 12 Gm • Sodium 870 mg • Calcium 250 mg

Basque Beans with Penne

■

2 tablespoons olive oil
$^1/_2$ cup chopped red onion
1 fresh Anaheim chili (or any medium-hot chili), seeded and diced
2 garlic cloves, minced
3 cups canned light red kidney beans (pink beans), drained and rinsed
$^1/_2$ cup chicken stock or canned broth

1 tablespoon minced fresh parsley
1 tablespoon minced fresh marjoram, or $^1/_2$ teaspoon dried oregano
$^1/_4$ teaspoon salt
$^1/_4$ teaspoon pepper
8 ounces ($^1/_2$ pound) penne

Heat the oil in a large skillet and slowly sauté the red onion, chili, and garlic until they are softened but not brown, 4 to 5 minutes. Stir in the beans, stock, herbs, and seasonings, and simmer 5 minutes.

Meanwhile, cook the penne according to package directions and drain. Spoon the pasta into a large serving dish, and toss with the bean mixture.

Kilocalories 466 Kc • Protein 19 Gm • Fat 9 Gm • Percent of calories from fat 17% • Cholesterol 0 mg • Dietary Fiber 13 Gm • Sodium 990 mg • Calcium 83 mg

Pinto Bean Skillet Dinner

—■—

4 SERVINGS

A quick bean supper from yesteryear, inspired by a kid pleaser called "American Chop Suey" that dates back to the 1940s.

1 tablespoon olive oil
1 large yellow onion, chopped
1 green bell pepper, seeded and diced
1 celery stalk, diced
1 16-ounce can crushed Italian tomatoes (crushed tomatoes should be quite thick with purée)
2 teaspoons chopped fresh basil, or ¹/₂ teaspoon dried

¹/₂ teaspoon sugar
¹/₂ teaspoon salt
¹/₄ teaspoon ground black pepper
1 20-ounce can pinto beans, drained and rinsed
8 ounces (¹/₂ pound) medium elbows
1 cup shredded longhorn or mild Cheddar cheese

In a large (12-inch) skillet, heat the oil and slowly sauté the onion, bell pepper, and celery until they are softened, 5 minutes. Add the tomatoes, basil, sugar, salt, and pepper. Simmer over low heat for 10 minutes. Add the beans, and simmer 10 minutes longer.

Meanwhile, cook the pasta al dente according to package directions and drain. Stir the elbows into the sauce. Stir over very low heat for 1 minute. Remove from the heat and stir in the cheese. Serve immediately.

Kilocalories 521 Kc • Protein 23 Gm • Fat 15 Gm • Percent of calories from fat 25% • Cholesterol 30 mg • Dietary Fiber 9 Gm • Sodium 1018 mg • Calcium 314 mg

Red Beans and Orzo

Orzo replaces rice in this traditional Southern dish.

2 tablespoons vegetable oil
1 Anaheim chili, or 1 green bell pepper, seeded and chopped
1 small yellow onion, chopped
1 garlic clove, minced
1 cup chicken stock or canned broth
1 cup drained canned tomatoes, chopped

1 tablespoon Worcestershire sauce
$1/2$ teaspoon salt
$1/4$ to $1/2$ teaspoon hot pepper sauce, such as Tabasco
1 20-ounce can red kidney beans, drained and rinsed
6 ounces (about $1/3$ pound) orzo

Heat the oil in a large skillet and sauté the chili, onion, and garlic until softened and fragrant, 3 minutes. Add the stock, tomatoes, Worcestershire, salt, hot pepper sauce, and beans. Simmer, stirring often, for 10 to 15 minutes.

Meanwhile, cook the orzo according to package directions and drain. Spoon it into a large serving dish, and ladle the bean mixture on top.

Kilocalories 375 Kc • Protein 15 Gm • Fat 9 Gm • Percent of calories from fat 20% • Cholesterol 0 mg • Dietary Fiber 11 Gm • Sodium 1027 mg • Calcium 73 mg

Adzuki Beans with Fresh Japanese Noodles

---

4 SERVINGS

Adzuki beans are red Japanese beans, slightly sweet. Canned adzuki can be found in natural foods stores.

1 tablespoon vegetable oil
1 teaspoon sesame oil
1 red bell pepper, seeded and
cut into small triangles
1 bunch scallions, cut
diagonally into 2-inch pieces
2 celery stalks, cut diagonally
into 1/2-inch pieces

2 slices fresh ginger, peeled
and minced
1 16-ounce can adzuki beans,
drained and rinsed
2 tablespoons naturally brewed
soy sauce
6 ounces fresh Japanese
noodles

In a large wok or skillet, heat the two oils and stir-fry the bell pepper, scallions, celery, and ginger until the vegetables are tender-crisp, about 3 minutes. Add the adzuki beans and heat through. Season with soy sauce.

Meanwhile, cook the noodles according to package directions and drain. Spoon them into a large serving dish, and toss with the bean mixture.

Kilocalories 359 Kc • Protein 18 Gm • Fat 5 Gm • Percent of calories from fat 11% • Cholesterol 0 mg • Dietary Fiber 7 Gm • Sodium 637 mg • Calcium 56 mg

Spicy Black Beans and Chilies with Shells

2 tablespoons vegetable oil
1 large yellow onion, chopped
1 large red bell pepper, seeded
  and diced
1 large Anaheim chili, seeded
  and diced
1 jalapeño chili, seeded and
  minced (wear rubber gloves)
1 16-ounce can tomatoes with
  juice, chopped

$\frac{1}{2}$ teaspoon dried cilantro
$\frac{1}{2}$ teaspoon ground coriander
$\frac{1}{2}$ teaspoon salt
1 15- or 16-ounce can black
  beans, drained and rinsed
6 ounces (about $\frac{1}{3}$ pound)
  medium shells
1 cup coarsely grated Monterey
  Jack cheese

Heat the oil in a large skillet and slowly sauté the onion, bell pepper, and chilies until they are soft and tender, 5 to 6 minutes. Add the tomatoes, cilantro, coriander, and salt, and simmer for 5 minutes. Add the black beans and simmer for 5 minutes.

Meanwhile, cook the shells according to package directions and drain. In a large serving dish, toss the shells with the bean mixture. Sprinkle the cheese on top.

Kilocalories 434 Kc • Protein 18 Gm • Fat 17 Gm • Percent of calories from fat 33% • Cholesterol 30 mg • Dietary Fiber 9 Gm • Sodium 901 mg • Calcium 281 mg

Cannellini, Fresh Tomatoes, and Sage with Elbows

4 SERVINGS

2 tablespoons olive oil
1 or 2 garlic cloves, minced
1 20-ounce can cannellini (white kidney beans), drained and rinsed
1/2 cup chicken stock or canned broth
1/2 teaspoon salt
Freshly ground black pepper
1 1/2 cups peeled, seeded, diced fresh tomatoes (about 2 large)

2 tablespoons minced fresh flat-leaf parsley
1/2 tablespoon minced fresh sage, or 1/2 teaspoon crushed dried sage leaves or dried basil
6 ounces (about 1/3 pound) casserole elbows
Freshly grated Parmesan cheese

Heat the oil in a large skillet and sauté the garlic until it's soft and fragrant, about 2 minutes. Add the beans, stock, salt, and pepper to your taste; simmer 2 to 3 minutes. Add the tomatoes and cook just long enough to heat them through, about 5 minutes. Remove the mixture from the heat and stir in the minced herbs.

Meanwhile, cook the elbows according to package directions and drain. Spoon them into a large serving dish, and toss with the bean sauce. Pass the grated cheese at the table.

Kilocalories 351 Kc • Protein 14 Gm • Fat 8 Gm • Percent of calories from fat 21% • Cholesterol 0 mg • Dietary Fiber 9 Gm • Sodium 889 mg • Calcium 55 mg

Cannellini and Escarole with Linguine

---

2 tablespoons olive oil
1 red bell pepper, seeded
   and diced
2 garlic cloves, minced
$1/2$ cup chicken stock or
   canned broth
$1/2$ pound escarole, well
   washed, coarsely chopped
1 tablespoon chopped fresh
   marjoram, or 1 teaspoon
   dried oregano

Salt and freshly ground black
   pepper
Few dashes of hot red pepper
   flakes (optional)
1 15- to 16-ounce can
   cannellini, drained
   and rinsed
8 ounces ($1/2$ pound) linguine
$1/3$ cup coarsely grated Asiago
   cheese

Heat the oil in a large skillet and sauté the bell pepper and garlic until they are sizzling, 2 minutes. Add the stock and escarole; cover and cook until the escarole wilts, 3 to 4 minutes. Add the marjoram or oregano. Add salt, black pepper, and red pepper flakes to your taste. Stir in the beans. Keep this mixture at a very low simmer for 5 minutes.

Meanwhile, cook the linguine according to package directions and drain. Spoon it into a large serving dish and toss with the cheese. When this has slightly melted, toss with the cannellini mixture and serve.

Kilocalories 414 Kc • Protein 17 Gm • Fat 10 Gm • Percent of calories from fat 22% • Cholesterol 5 mg • Dietary Fiber 9 Gm • Sodium 630 mg • Calcium 173 mg

Cannellini with Herb Medley Pesto and Spaghetti

---

4 SERVINGS

8 ounces (¹/₂ pound) spaghetti
¹/₃ cup Herb Medley Pesto (see page 10 for basic recipe), or more to your taste

1 20-ounce can cannellini (white kidney beans), drained, rinsed, and heated

Cook the spaghetti according to package directions and drain. In a large serving dish, toss the spaghetti with the pesto. Spoon the beans on top and toss again.

Kilocalories 452 Kc • Protein 17 Gm • Fat 14 Gm • Percent of calories from fat 28% • Cholesterol 1 mg • Dietary Fiber 9 Gm • Sodium 630 mg • Calcium 97 mg

Green Bean, Onion, and Ziti Salad with Basil

4 SERVINGS

$^1/_2$ pound fresh whole
  green beans
3 tablespoons olive oil
2 tablespoons red wine vinegar
$^1/_2$ Vidalia or any sweet onion,
  sliced and separated
  into rings

About 6 leaves fresh basil,
  coarsely chopped
Salt and freshly ground pepper
  to taste
6 ounces (about $^1/_3$ pound) ziti

Wash the green beans and trim the ends. Cook in a pot of boiling salted water 5 to 7 minutes, or until tender-crisp. Drain.

Combine the oil, vinegar, and onion in a salad bowl. Toss with the green beans and basil. Season with salt and pepper to your taste. Cook the ziti according to package directions; drain and rinse in cold water. Add the ziti to the green bean mixture. Taste to correct the seasoning. You may want more vinegar, salt, or pepper.

OPTIONAL ADDITION: A red bell pepper, seeded and cut into rings, makes a colorful addition.

Kilocalories 274 Kc • Protein 7 Gm • Fat 11 Gm • Percent of calories from fat 35% • Cholesterol 0 mg • Dietary Fiber 3 Gm • Sodium 7 mg • Calcium 34 mg

Green Bean and Pasta Salad with Anchovies

4 SERVINGS

3 tablespoons olive oil
2 tablespoons red wine vinegar
1 garlic clove, peeled and
    crushed
$^1/_2$ pound fresh green beans

3 to 4 anchovy fillets, chopped
Freshly ground black pepper
6 ounces (about
    $^1/_3$ pound) penne

Combine the oil, vinegar, and garlic in a cup. Allow the dressing to marinate at room temperature for a half hour or more. Remove and discard the garlic.

Wash the green beans and cut them diagonally into 2-inch pieces. Cook in a pot of boiling salted water, 5 to 7 minutes, or until tender-crisp. Drain and cool.

Toss the green beans with the dressing, anchovies, and black pepper to your taste. Cook the penne according to package directions; drain and rinse in cold water. Add the penne to the green bean mixture. Taste to correct the seasoning, adding more vinegar if you wish. The anchovies should contribute enough salt to season the salad.

OPTIONAL ADDITIONS: Wedges of yellow or red tomato can be added just before serving.

Kilocalories 274 Kc • Protein 7 Gm • Fat 11 Gm • Percent of calories from fat 36% • Cholesterol 3 mg • Dietary Fiber 3 Gm • Sodium 117 mg • Calcium 38 mg

Fava Beans, Tuna, and Pasta Salad

■

4 SERVINGS

Red onions can be fiery, so taste the onion before starting this salad. If you prefer a milder taste, soak the slices in cold water for a half hour. Drain before using.

1 large red bell pepper
1 large green bell pepper
1 small red onion, thinly sliced
1 20-ounce can fava beans, rinsed and drained
1 7- or 8-ounce can tuna, water packed, drained, and flaked
1/2 cup sliced pitted black olives

2 tablespoons minced fresh flat-leaf parsley
1/3 cup olive oil
2 to 3 tablespoons red wine vinegar
Salt and freshly ground black pepper
6 ounces (about 1/3 pound) medium shells

Lay the peppers on a broiler or flat baking pan. Broil them 4 inches from the heat source, turning them until they are charred a little on each side and are tender enough to collapse when pressed with a fork, 15 to 20 minutes. Put them into a covered 2-quart casserole; the steam they generate will loosen their skins.

When the peppers are cool enough to handle, skin them, discard the seeds and piths, and dice the peppers. Rinse and dry the casserole; put the peppers back into it. Add the onion, beans, tuna, olives, and parsley. Toss them with the olive oil. Add vinegar and salt and pepper to your taste.

Meanwhile, cook the shells according to package directions; drain and rinse in cold water. Stir the shells into the bean mixture. Serve immediately or chill until needed. When ready to serve, toss again and taste to see if the salad needs more oil or vinegar.

Kilocalories 591 Kc • Protein 30 Gm • Fat 22 Gm • Percent of calories from fat 33% • Cholesterol 21 mg • Dietary Fiber 10 Gm • Sodium 623 mg • Calcium 69 mg

Chickpea Salad with Shells

―■―

4 SERVINGS

¼ cup extra-virgin olive oil
3 tablespoons red wine vinegar
½ teaspoon dried oregano
½ teaspoon salt
⅛ teaspoon pepper
⅛ teaspoon sugar
2 medium-size ripe tomatoes, cut into wedges
1 garlic clove, sliced in half and crushed slightly

1 cup small shells
1 20-ounce can chickpeas, drained and rinsed
4 cups torn chilled salad greens
4 hard-boiled eggs, sliced, for garnishing (optional)

In a salad bowl, whisk together the oil, vinegar, oregano, salt, pepper, and sugar. Stir in the tomatoes and garlic. Allow the mixture to marinate for a half hour or so, then remove and discard the garlic.

Cook the shells according to package directions and drain. Rinse them in cold water until they are cool. Stir the shells and chickpeas into the salad mixture. When ready to serve, toss with the greens. Garnish with egg slices, if desired.

Kilocalories 352 Kc • Protein 10 Gm • Fat 16 Gm • Percent of calories from fat 39% • Cholesterol 0 mg • Dietary Fiber 8 Gm • Sodium 726 mg • Calcium 91 mg

Chickpea Salad with Tuna

4 ENTRÉE SERVINGS

Follow the preceding recipe. Add a 7- or 8-ounce can Italian oil-packed tuna, drained and chunked. Stir very gently so as not to shred the tuna. Serve as a main dish with warm whole-grain rolls as an accompaniment—a nice 'n easy summer supper dish!

Kilocalories 451 Kc • Protein 24 Gm • Fat 20 Gm • Percent of calories from fat 39% • Cholesterol 9 mg • Dietary Fiber 8 Gm • Sodium 903 mg • Calcium 98 mg

Fava Bean and Farfalle Salad

Corn bread makes a pleasing accompaniment to this dish.

¹/₄ cup olive oil
Juice of 1 large lemon (about
    ¹/₄ cup)
1 tablespoon chopped fresh
    cilantro
¹/₄ teaspoon salt
Several grinds of black pepper
1 canned jalapeño chili, or
    more to your taste, seeded
    and minced (wear rubber
    gloves)

1 cup chopped celery with
    leaves
1 large tomato, chopped
4 ounces (¹/₄ pound) farfalle
    (egg bows)
1 20-ounce can fava beans,
    rinsed and drained

In a salad bowl, whisk together the oil, lemon juice, cilantro, salt, pepper, and jalapeño chili. Stir in the celery and tomato.

Cook the farfalle according to package directions and drain. Rinse under cold water until cool. Toss the farfalle and fava beans with the other salad ingredients.

Kilocalories 401 Kc • Protein 15 Gm • Fat 16 Gm • Percent of calories from fat 35% • Cholesterol 33 mg • Dietary Fiber 9 Gm • Sodium 545 mg • Calcium 68 mg

Tricolor-Bean and Pasta Salad

8 SERVINGS

Not your usual church supper three-bean salad! Red, white, and black beans combine with shells for an artful presentation.

1 bunch scallions, chopped

1 whole roasted red bell pepper, diced (about ½ cup, from a jar)

¼ cup chopped fresh flat-leaf parsley

1 tablespoon chopped fresh summer savory, or ½ teaspoon dried tarragon

½ cup olive oil

¼ cup red wine vinegar

1 teaspoon salt

¼ teaspoon freshly ground black pepper, or more to your taste

1 16-ounce can cannellini, drained and rinsed

1 16-ounce can black beans, drained and rinsed

1 16-ounce can red kidney beans, drained and rinsed

6 ounces (about ⅓ pound) medium shells

In a very large bowl, combine the scallions, bell pepper, herbs, oil, vinegar, and seasonings. Mix well. Cook the shells according to package directions and drain. Rinse under cold water until cool. Toss with the beans and pasta. Marinate at room temperature for 30 minutes to an hour before serving. (For longer keeping, refrigerate.) Taste to correct seasoning; you may want more vinegar or oil.

Kilocalories 320 Kc • Protein 11 Gm • Fat 14 Gm • Percent of calories from fat 39% • Cholesterol 0 mg • Dietary Fiber 9 Gm • Sodium 803 mg • Calcium 58 mg

Broccoli, Champion of Vegetables

Broccoli holds a top rating among healthful vegetables, perhaps the champion of all. One of the cancer-fighting cruciferous vegetables, it's rich in the antioxidants beta-carotene (about 90 percent of your daily requirement in one helping!) and vitamin C. It's also abundant in heart-protecting potassium, calcium, and fiber, and broccoli contributes a share of thiamin, phosphorus, and iron to your daily intake. As if that weren't enough, it's low in calories, too—only 45 per cup!

Broccoli de rabe, also known as broccoli rape, broccoli raab, broccoli rapini, and Chinese flowering cabbage, is a medium-sharp green with edible leaves, stems, and bud clusters. The latter look like immature broccoli. Rabe contains the same cancer-fighting chemicals and rich supply of beta-carotene, vitamin C, and calcium as broccoli.

Broccoli crowns are the tops of the head with about 3 inches of attached stems.

When other vegetables wane in their off-seasons, it's heartening to note that broccoli is available all year. Look for crisp stalks, not too thick and woody, and a fresh green color; avoid any suggestion of yellowing. Store broccoli or rabe in a perforated plastic vegetable bag in the refrigerator, on the lowest shelf. If the vegetable is quite fresh, it should last for three days.

Versatile broccoli is equally at home in a Mediterranean dish, an Asian stir-fry, or a crispy salad. To avoid any suggestion of strong flavor, never overcook this vital vegetable.

Creamy Broccoli Soup
with Chives and Shells

4 SERVINGS

1$\frac{1}{2}$ cups chopped fresh
  broccoli
4 cups chicken stock or
  canned broth
1 carrot, cut diagonally into
  $\frac{1}{2}$-inch slices
3 tablespoons superfine flour,
  such as Wondra

2 tablespoons nonfat dry milk
$\frac{1}{2}$ teaspoon salt
$\frac{1}{8}$ teaspoon white pepper
1 cup milk (whole or low-fat)
4 ounces ($\frac{1}{4}$ pound) medium
  shells
2 tablespoons snipped fresh
  chives

Peel the broccoli stalks and dice them. Cut the florets in half, or in quarters if they are large.

Bring the stock to a boil and add the carrot. When the stock boils again, reduce the heat and simmer until the carrot is nearly tender, about 10 minutes. Add the broccoli and continue simmering for 3 minutes or until tender.

Stir the flour, dry milk, salt, and white pepper into the liquid milk. Add all at once to the simmering soup and stir constantly until it bubbles and thickens slightly.

Meanwhile, cook the shells separately according to package directions and drain them. Stir the shells and chives into the soup. Taste the soup, adding more salt and pepper if needed.

Kilocalories 230 Kc • Protein 13 Gm • Fat 4 Gm • Percent of calories from fat 17% • Cholesterol 8 mg • Dietary Fiber 3 Gm • Sodium 482 mg • Calcium 126 mg

Broccoli Soup with Sun-dried Tomatoes and Fusilli

6 SERVINGS

5 cups chicken stock or
    canned broth
$1/8$ teaspoon freshly ground
    black pepper
Pinch of dried rosemary
1 large potato, peeled and
    diced

6 sun-dried tomatoes, slivered
About $1/4$ teaspoon salt
4 ounces ($1/4$ pound) fusilli
2 cups cooked, chopped
    broccoli (see Note)

Combine the stock, pepper, rosemary, potato, and sun-dried tomatoes in a large pot. Bring to a boil, reduce the heat, and simmer, covered, until the potato is tender, about 8 minutes. Taste the soup and add salt if necessary.

Meanwhile, cook the fusilli separately according to package directions; drain. (Undercook the pasta a bit because it will continue to cook in the soup.) Stir the pasta and cooked broccoli into the soup and simmer 2 to 3 minutes to develop the flavor.

NOTE: For 2 cups cooked broccoli, separate 2 broccoli crowns into florets with short stalks. Cook in boiling salted water for 3 minutes (or 5 minutes for well cooked). Drain and chop.

Kilocalories 146 Kc • Protein 9 Gm • Fat 2 Gm • Percent of calories from fat 10% • Cholesterol 0 mg • Dietary Fiber 3 Gm • Sodium 516 mg • Calcium 48 mg

Farmhouse Broccoli Soup with Garlic Croutons

■

6 SERVINGS

This is the kind of substantial soup that makes a very comforting supper dish on a cold winter's evening.

1 tablespoon olive oil
1/2 cup chopped shallots
3/4 cup chopped ham or cooked smoked pork shoulder (optional)
6 cups chicken stock or canned broth
2 cups cooked, chopped broccoli (see Note in preceding recipe)

4 ounces (1/4 pound) spaghetti
Salt
Freshly ground black pepper
6 slices French bread
Olive oil for brushing on bread
1 garlic clove, peeled
About 1/4 cup grated Parmesan cheese

Heat the oil in a large pot and sauté the shallots and ham, if using, for 3 to 5 minutes, until the shallots are lightly colored. Add the stock and broccoli, and cook over very low heat to blend flavors while cooking the spaghetti.

Boil a large pot of water separately and add the amount of salt you usually do to cook pasta. Holding the spaghetti strands together in a bunch, break them into 2-inch pieces; cook until tender. Drain and add the spaghetti to the soup. Season with salt and pepper to your taste. (The ham, if used, should make this soup salty enough.)

To make the croutons, brush the bread with olive oil on both sides and rub the slices with garlic. Sprinkle with the cheese. Toast the slices in a toaster oven or cook them under a broiler until golden. Ladle the soup into 6 bowls and top each with a crouton. Serve at once.

Kilocalories 229 Kc • Protein 13 Gm • Fat 6 Gm • Percent of calories from fat 23% • Cholesterol 3 mg • Dietary Fiber 3 Gm • Sodium 655 mg • Calcium 103 mg

Broccoli-Cheddar Soup with Elbows

4 SERVINGS

2 cups chicken or vegetable
  stock, or canned broth
2 cups well-cooked broccoli
  (see Note on page 75)
1/4 cup nonfat dry milk
3 tablespoons superfine flour,
  such as Wondra

1/4 teaspoon salt
1/8 teaspoon pepper
1 quart (4 cups) milk (whole or
  low-fat)
4 ounces Cheddar cheese,
  shredded
1 cup small elbows

Boil the stock uncovered until reduced to 1 cup, about 5 minutes. Purée the broccoli in a food processor, gradually adding the stock through the feed tube.

Whisk the dry milk, flour, salt, and pepper into the liquid milk and pour it into a large saucepan. Cook over medium-high heat until bubbling. Whisk in the broccoli purée. Stir in the cheese and simmer, stirring occasionally, until melted.

Meanwhile, cook the elbows according to package directions. Drain and add them to the soup.

Kilocalories 428 Kc • Protein 24 Gm • Fat 19 Gm • Percent of calories from fat 39% • Cholesterol 63 mg • Dietary Fiber 3 Gm • Sodium 684 mg • Calcium 561 mg

BROCCOLI, CHAMPION OF VEGETABLES

77

Broccoli de Rabe Soup with Egg Noodles

1 tablespoon olive oil
1 garlic clove, minced
1 bunch broccoli de rabe ($^{1}/_{2}$ to
  $^{3}/_{4}$ pound), well washed,
  stemmed, and coarsely
  chopped

6 cups chicken or vegetable
  stock, or canned broth
1 tablespoon tomato paste
Freshly ground black pepper
$^{1}/_{4}$ pound wide egg noodles
Salt

Heat the oil in a large pot and sauté the garlic until it's softened, 3 minutes. Add the rabe, stock, and tomato paste, and pepper to your taste. Bring to a boil, reduce the heat, and simmer, covered, until the rabe is tender, about 15 minutes.

Cook the noodles according to package directions. Drain and stir them into the soup. Taste the soup; add salt if needed.

Kilocalories 145 Kc • Protein 9 Gm • Fat 5 Gm • Percent of calories from fat 29% • Cholesterol 18 mg • Dietary Fiber 2 Gm • Sodium 442 mg • Calcium 36 mg

Broccoli de Rabe Soup with Butternut Squash

6 SERVINGS

Make the rabe and egg noodle soup with the following changes: After sautéing the garlic, add 2 cups butternut squash cubes and $^{1}/_{8}$ teaspoon dried rosemary. Braise, stirring often, for 5 minutes. Add all the other ingredients, except the noodles, and cook as in the preceding recipe. Stir in the noodles.

Kilocalories 172 Kc • Protein 9 Gm • Fat 5 Gm • Percent of calories from fat 24% • Cholesterol 18 mg • Dietary Fiber 3 Gm • Sodium 445 mg • Calcium 64 mg

Stir-fried Broccoli with Shiitake Mushrooms and Vermicelli

―――――――――― ■ ――――――――――

4 SERVINGS

Shiitake mushrooms are one of the foods that boost the immune system.

4 to 6 large dried shiitake
  mushrooms
1 bunch broccoli (1 to
  1¼ pounds)
1 cup chicken stock or
  canned broth
2 tablespoons soy sauce
1 tablespoon oyster sauce
1 tablespoon cornstarch

1 teaspoon sugar
2 tablespoons vegetable oil
1 bunch scallions, sliced
  diagonally into 1-inch pieces
2 slices fresh ginger, peeled
  and minced
8 ounces (½ pound) fresh or
  dried Asian vermicelli or
  American vermicelli

Soak the mushrooms in hot water for a half hour. Drain, discard the stems, and chop the mushrooms.

After washing the broccoli, separate the florets from the stalks. Peel the stalks and slice them into ½-inch pieces. Cut large florets in half. Parboil the broccoli in a large pot of boiling salted water for 1 minute, counting from the time the water returns to a boil. Drain and rinse in cold water.

Mix the stock, soy sauce, oyster sauce, cornstarch, and sugar.

Heat the oil in a large wok or skillet and stir-fry the scallions, ginger, and mushrooms for 3 minutes. Add the broccoli and stir-fry until tender-crisp. Add the stock mixture and cook until the thickened sauce coats the broccoli.

Meanwhile, cook the vermicelli according to package directions and drain. Spoon it into a large serving dish and top with the broccoli.

Kilocalories 331 Kc • Protein 12 Gm • Fat 8 Gm • Percent of calories from fat 20% • Cholesterol 0 mg • Dietary Fiber 4 Gm • Sodium 821 mg • Calcium 59 mg

Spiced Broccoli with Toasted Pine Nuts and Couscous

---

4 SERVINGS

Some favorite North African spices team up with the traditional pasta of that region.

1 cup couscous, raw
1 bunch broccoli (1 to 1¼ pounds)
2 tablespoons olive oil
¼ cup chopped shallots
½ teaspoon ground cumin

½ teaspoon ground coriander
¼ teaspoon ground cardamom
½ teaspoon freshly ground black pepper
¼ cup lightly toasted pine nuts

Prepare couscous (see page 12 for basic recipe or follow package directions). Fluff and separate the grains.

After washing the broccoli, separate the florets from the stalks. Cut the florets into roughly uniform size. Peel the stalks and cut them into 1-inch pieces. Cook the broccoli in a large pot of boiling salted water until tender-crisp, about 3 minutes. Drain well.

In a skillet, heat the oil and sauté the shallots until softened, 3 minutes. Add the broccoli, sprinkle with the cumin, coriander, cardamom, and pepper, and toss to blend. Reheat, if needed, when ready to serve.

Spread the couscous on a platter. Top with the broccoli mixture and sprinkle with pine nuts.

Kilocalories 308 Kc • Protein 9 Gm • Fat 12 Gm • Percent of calories from fat 35% • Cholesterol 0 mg • Dietary Fiber 3 Gm • Sodium 53 mg • Calcium 19 mg

Broccoli with Spinach Fettuccine Alfredo

2 ENTRÉE SERVINGS

2 tablespoons superfine flour, such as Wondra

2 tablespoons nonfat dry milk

¼ teaspoon salt

⅛ teaspoon white pepper

1½ cups whole milk

2 tablespoons light cream cheese (Neufchâtel)

2 tablespoons grated Parmesan cheese

3 cups cooked, chopped broccoli (see Note on page 75)

8 ounces (½ pound) fresh or dried spinach fettuccine

1 whole roasted red bell pepper (from a jar or homemade—see page 260), seeded and diced small

Whisk the flour, dry milk, salt, and pepper into the whole milk and pour it into a large saucepan. Cook over medium-high heat, stirring constantly, until thickened and bubbling. Combine the sauce with the cream cheese and Parmesan cheese in a food processor or blender and blend until smooth. Keep the feed tube covered: hot foods tend to bubble up. Pour the sauce back into the saucepan and add the broccoli. Reheat when ready to serve.

Meanwhile, cook the fettuccine according to package directions and drain. Spoon the pasta into a large serving dish and top with the sauce. Garnish with the roasted pepper.

Kilocalories 623 Kc • Protein 33 Gm • Fat 17 Gm • Percent of calories from fat 24% • Cholesterol 173 mg • Dietary Fiber 13 Gm • Sodium 740 mg • Calcium 506 mg

Broccoli with Fettuccine Roquefort

2 ENTRÉE SERVINGS

Follow the preceding recipe, substituting 1 ounce Roquefort (or any blue cheese) for the Neufchâtel. Use either spinach or regular fettuccine. Toss the pasta and sauce with an additional ounce of Roquefort, crumbled. Omit the roasted pepper; garnish with sliced black olives, if desired.

Kilocalories 629 Kc • Protein 35 Gm • Fat 18 Gm • Percent of calories from fat 25% • Cholesterol 175 mg • Dietary Fiber 12 Gm • Sodium 939 mg • Calcium 585 mg

Broccoli and Pistachios with Spaghetti

—■—

4 SERVINGS

1 bunch broccoli (1 to
 1¼ pounds)
2 tablespoons olive oil
½ cup chopped shallots
1 cup peeled, seeded, chopped
 fresh tomatoes
⅔ cup natural pistachios,
 coarsely chopped

1 tablespoon chopped
 fresh basil
1 teaspoon chopped fresh
 thyme or sage
Salt and freshly ground black
 pepper
8 ounces (½ pound) spaghetti

After washing the broccoli, separate the florets from the stalks. Cut the florets into roughly uniform size. Peel the stalks and cut them into 1-inch pieces. Cook the broccoli in a large pot of boiling salted water until barely tender-crisp, about 2 minutes. Drain well.

In a large skillet, heat the oil and sauté the shallots until they begin to sizzle, 2 minutes. Add the broccoli, tomatoes, pistachios, basil, and thyme or sage. Season with salt and pepper to your taste. Sauté, stirring often, for 3 minutes.

Meanwhile, cook the spaghetti according to package directions and drain. Spoon it into a serving dish and toss with the broccoli mixture.

Kilocalories 434 Kc • Protein 14 Gm • Fat 19 Gm • Percent of calories from fat 39% • Cholesterol 0 mg • Dietary Fiber 7 Gm • Sodium 33 mg • Calcium 72 mg

Broccoli and Anchovies with Ziti

4 SERVINGS

1 pound broccoli crowns
2 tablespoons olive oil
6 to 8 anchovy fillets
1 tablespoon drained, rinsed
   capers

$^1\!/_2$ cup chicken stock or
   canned broth
Hot red pepper flakes
8 ounces ($^1\!/_2$ pound) ziti

Trim and cut the broccoli crowns into florets and $^1\!/_2$-inch slices of stalks. Cook them in a large pot of boiling salted water until they are just tender, about 3 minutes. Drain and cool under running cold water to stop the cooking.

Heat the oil in a skillet and sauté the anchovies over very low heat until they soften, 3 minutes. Some anchovies will dissolve into a sauce, but if they don't dissolve, chop them fine with the point of a paring knife. Add the capers and stock. Toss the broccoli with the anchovy mixture. Sprinkle with red pepper flakes to your taste. Heat through, about 3 minutes.

Meanwhile, cook the ziti according to package directions and drain. Toss the ziti with the broccoli.

Kilocalories 321 Kc • Protein 12 Gm • Fat 8 Gm • Percent of calories from fat 23% • Cholesterol 5 mg • Dietary Fiber 4 Gm • Sodium 428 mg • Calcium 53 mg

BROCCOLI, CHAMPION OF VEGETABLES

Broccoli with Macaroni and Feta Cheese

3/4 cup milk (whole or low-fat)
1 egg
2 tablespoons superfine flour,
  such as Wondra
1/8 teaspoon white pepper
8 ounces (1/2 pound) medium
  elbows

2 cups cooked, chopped
  broccoli (see Note on page 75)
1/2 cup crumbled feta cheese
4 tablespoons grated Parmesan
  cheese

Preheat the oven to 350 degrees F.

In a measuring pitcher or small bowl, beat together the milk, egg, flour, and white pepper until smooth.

Cook the elbows according to package directions, undercooking it slightly, and drain. Combine the broccoli, cooked elbows, feta, and 2 tablespoons of the Parmesan in a 2 1/2-quart casserole. Stir to blend. Pour the milk-egg mixture evenly over the top. Sprinkle the remaining 2 tablespoons of Parmesan over the top. Bake until set, 35 to 40 minutes.

Kilocalories 399 Kc • Protein 20 Gm • Fat 12 Gm • Percent of calories from fat 27% • Cholesterol 91 mg • Dietary Fiber 4 Gm • Sodium 510 mg • Calcium 333 mg

Broccoli-stuffed Shells

4 SERVINGS

A festive holiday dish given a healthy new dimension.

24 or more jumbo pasta shells
1 pound ricotta
1 egg, beaten
1 tablespoon minced fresh
   flat-leaf parsley
1/8 teaspoon white pepper
2 cups cooked, chopped
   broccoli (see Note on page 75)

2 1/2 cups tomato sauce (from a
   jar or see Light Tomato
   Sauce, page 317)
2 tablespoons grated Parmesan
   cheese

Choose a baking dish from which you can serve that will fit the shells in one layer. Cook the shells according to package directions (I usually include a few extra in case of breakage), and rinse them in cold water. Lay them on a sheet of waxed paper.

Mix the ricotta, egg, parsley, and white pepper until well blended. Stir in the broccoli.

Spread 1 cup of the tomato sauce in the bottom of the baking dish. Stuff the shells with the broccoli-ricotta mixture and arrange them upright on the sauce. Pour the remaining tomato sauce over the shells, and sprinkle with the Parmesan. (At this point you can cover and refrigerate the shells, and bake them later.)

Preheat the oven to 350 degrees F.

Cut several long slits in a large piece of foil and cover the baking dish with it, tenting the top so that it does not touch the casserole contents. Bake the casserole for 30 minutes (45 minutes if it has been refrigerated). Remove the foil and bake for 15 more minutes or until the ricotta is set like a custard and no longer runny.

Kilocalories 508 Kc • Protein 26 Gm • Fat 19 Gm • Percent of calories from fat 33% • Cholesterol 90 mg • Dietary Fiber 5 Gm • Sodium 723 mg • Calcium 412 mg

BROCCOLI, CHAMPION OF VEGETABLES

85

Broccoli, Roasted Red Peppers, and Provolone with Linguine

2 ENTRÉE SERVINGS

1 bunch broccoli (1 to 1¼ pounds)
2 tablespoons olive oil
1 garlic clove, minced
2 whole roasted red bell peppers (from a jar or homemade—see page 260), seeded and diced

Salt and freshly ground black pepper
8 ounces (½ pound) fresh or dried linguine
½ cup or more finely diced aged provolone cheese

After washing the broccoli, separate the florets from the stalks. Cut the florets into roughly uniform size. Peel the stalks and cut them into 1-inch pieces. Cook the broccoli in a large pot of boiling salted water until barely tender-crisp, about 2 minutes. Drain the broccoli and rinse it with cold water to stop the cooking action.

In a large skillet, heat the oil and sauté the garlic until it begins to sizzle, 2 minutes. Add the broccoli and roasted peppers. Warm the vegetables over low heat until the garlic is softened but not browned, about 5 minutes. Season with salt and pepper to your taste, keeping in mind that the cheese is salty.

Meanwhile, cook the linguine according to package directions; drain it so that the pasta is still fairly moist. Spoon the linguine into a large serving dish and toss it with the cheese and vegetables.

Kilocalories 651 Kc • Protein 28 Gm • Fat 27 Gm • Percent of calories from fat 36% • Cholesterol 146 mg • Dietary Fiber 11 Gm • Sodium 349 mg • Calcium 355 mg

Broccoli, Walnuts, and Pancetta with Shells

2 ENTRÉE SERVINGS

Pancetta is unsmoked Italian bacon, sold at many supermarket deli counters. It's sliced in thick rounds like Canadian bacon.

1/2 tablespoon olive oil, or
 more if needed
2 thick slices pancetta, diced
1 garlic clove, minced
2 cups cooked broccoli florets
 (see Note on page 75)

1/2 cup walnut halves
Salt and freshly ground black
 pepper
8 ounces (1/2 pound) medium
 shells

Heat the oil in a large skillet and slowly sauté the pancetta until it's golden-brown, 5 minutes. Add the garlic and cook until it's soft and fragrant, but not brown, 3 minutes. Add the broccoli and walnuts. Season with salt and pepper to your taste.

Meanwhile, cook the shells according to package directions; drain briefly to keep the pasta moist. Toss the shells with the broccoli in the skillet to blend the flavors. Spoon into a serving dish.

Kilocalories 742 Kc • Protein 32 Gm • Fat 27 Gm • Percent of calories from fat 31% • Cholesterol 16 mg • Dietary Fiber 8 Gm • Sodium 414 mg • Calcium 95 mg

Creamed Broccoli and Farfalle

■

4 SERVINGS

2 cups chopped, cooked
  broccoli (see Note on page 75)
1 cup whole milk, plus $\frac{1}{2}$ cup
$\frac{1}{4}$ teaspoon salt
$\frac{1}{8}$ teaspoon white pepper
Pinch of nutmeg
2 tablespoons superfine flour,
  such as Wondra

2 tablespoons nonfat dry milk
8 ounces ($\frac{1}{2}$ pound) farfalle
  (egg bows)
2 tablespoons grated Parmesan
  cheese

Preheat the oven to 350 degrees F.

Put the broccoli in a large saucepan. Add 1 cup liquid milk and the seasonings; heat to scalding but don't boil the mixture.

Mix the flour and dry milk with the remaining $\frac{1}{2}$ cup liquid milk, add to the pan, and bring to a boil over medium-high heat, stirring constantly, until thick and bubbling.

Meanwhile, cook the farfalle according to package directions, undercooking it slightly. Drain and spoon the pasta into a 2-quart casserole. Stir in the creamed broccoli, sprinkle with cheese, and bake for 20 to 25 minutes, until bubbling throughout and golden on top.

Kilocalories 328 Kc • Protein 15 Gm • Fat 7 Gm • Percent of calories from fat 19% • Cholesterol 80 mg • Dietary Fiber 3 Gm • Sodium 271 mg • Calcium 190 mg

Broccoli de Rabe, Bell Pepper, and Olives with Cavatelli

4 SERVINGS

3 tablespoons olive oil
1 red bell pepper, seeded and cut into small triangles
2 garlic cloves, minced
1 bunch of broccoli de rabe ($^3/_4$ pound), well washed, stemmed, and coarsely chopped
$^1/_4$ cup chicken stock or canned broth, or water

$^1/_2$ cup pitted black olives, any Greek variety
3 tablespoons freshly grated Romano cheese, plus more to pass
Salt and freshly ground black pepper
8 ounces ($^1/_2$ pound) cavatelli or medium shells

In a 12-inch skillet, heat 2 tablespoons of the oil and sauté the red pepper and garlic until they are somewhat softened but not browned, 3 minutes. Add the rabe and stock. Cover and simmer, stirring often, until the vegetables are tender, 8 to 10 minutes. If the rabe seems too dry, add more stock or water.

Blend in the olives and cheese. Taste the rabe, adding salt and pepper to your taste; remember, the cheese adds salt, too. Remove from the heat, but keep warm.

Cook the cavatelli al dente according to package directions. Drain and toss it with the remaining tablespoon of oil. Combine the cavatelli with the vegetables in the skillet and allow the flavors to mingle just for a minute or two before serving. Pass additional grated cheese at the table.

Kilocalories 368 Kc • Protein 12 Gm • Fat 15 Gm • Percent of calories from fat 35% • Cholesterol 4 mg • Dietary Fiber 4 Gm • Sodium 190 mg • Calcium 94 mg

Broccoli de Rabe and Portobello Mushrooms with Linguine

"Baby portobellos," which are only slightly larger than white mushrooms, are perfect for this dish. Regular portobellos can be substituted; cut the slices in half, or thirds if they are very large.

2 tablespoons olive oil
1 garlic clove, minced
4 to 6 ounces small portobello mushrooms, washed and sliced crosswise, 3 to 4 slices per mushroom
1 bunch broccoli de rabe (³/₄ pound), well washed, stemmed, and cut into thirds

³/₄ cup chicken stock or canned broth, or more as needed
¹/₂ teaspoon salt
Freshly ground black pepper
Several dashes of hot red pepper flakes
8 ounces (¹/₂ pound) linguine

In a large saucepan, heat the oil and sauté the garlic until it is fragrant, about 2 minutes. Add the mushrooms and cook until they begin to brown. Remove the mushrooms with a slotted spoon and reserve them.

Add the rabe and stock to the pan. Bring to a boil, reduce the heat, cover, and simmer until the rabe is tender, about 10 minutes. Add more stock if necessary, maintaining at least ¹/₂ inch of liquid in the pan. Return the mushrooms to the pan during the last few minutes of cooking.

Season the vegetables with salt, black pepper, and red pepper flakes to your taste.

Meanwhile, cook the linguine according to package directions and drain. Spoon the linguine into a large serving dish. Add the rabe and mushrooms, tossing to blend.

Kilocalories 300 Kc • Protein 11 Gm • Fat 8 Gm • Percent of calories from fat 24% • Cholesterol 0 mg • Dietary Fiber 4 Gm • Sodium 457 mg • Calcium 89 mg

Deviled Broccoli de Rabe with Egg Noodles

4 SERVINGS

To be really "deviled," the dry mustard should be fairly fresh. Dry mustard from an old tin will have lost its pungency.

1 bunch broccoli de rabe ($^1/_2$ to $^3/_4$ pound), well washed, stemmed, and cut into thirds
1 cup chicken stock or canned broth
About 1$^1/_2$ cups whole milk
3 tablespoons superfine flour, such as Wondra
2 tablespoons nonfat dry milk
$^1/_2$ teaspoon dry mustard

$^1/_4$ teaspoon salt
$^1/_4$ teaspoon white pepper
8 ounces ($^1/_2$ pound) medium egg noodles
1 cup fresh bread crumbs from 1 slice Italian bread
2 tablespoons grated Parmesan cheese
Cayenne pepper

Preheat the oven to 350 degrees F.

Put the rabe into a large pot with the stock. Bring to a boil, reduce the heat, and simmer until the rabe is tender, about 10 minutes. Drain well, reserving all the liquid.

Measure the liquid and add enough whole milk to make 2 cups liquid. Pour this into the pot and whisk in the flour, dry milk, mustard, salt, and white pepper. Cook over medium-high heat, stirring constantly, until thick and bubbling. Reduce the heat to very low and simmer for 3 minutes, stirring often.

Meanwhile, cook the egg noodles according to package directions and drain. Combine the rabe, sauce, and noodles in a 2-quart gratin dish. Sprinkle with fresh bread crumbs, Parmesan cheese, and cayenne pepper to your taste.

Bake for 30 minutes or until bubbling throughout.

Kilocalories 348 Kc • Protein 16 Gm • Fat 7 Gm • Percent of calories from fat 19% • Cholesterol 68 mg • Dietary Fiber 3 Gm • Sodium 492 mg • Calcium 221 mg

Broccoli de Rabe with Two Cheeses and Spaghetti

4 SERVINGS

Melted mild mozzarella is a nice contrast to the assertive flavor of rabe.

2 tablespoons olive oil
2 to 3 garlic cloves, minced
1 cup chicken stock or canned broth
1 bunch broccoli de rabe (3/4 pound), well washed, stemmed, and cut into thirds

About 1/4 teaspoon salt
Freshly ground black pepper
8 ounces (1/2 pound) spaghetti
1 cup shredded mozzarella cheese
1/4 cup freshly grated Parmesan cheese

Heat the oil in a large pot and sauté the garlic until it is fragrant, about 2 minutes. Add the stock and rabe. Bring to a boil, reduce the heat, and simmer until tender, 8 to 10 minutes. Season with salt and pepper to your taste, keeping in mind that the Parmesan is salty.

Meanwhile, cook the spaghetti according to package directions; drain. Spoon it into a large serving dish, add the rabe and pan juices, and toss the mixture together. Add the mozzarella and Parmesan cheeses and toss again.

Kilocalories 389 Kc • Protein 19 Gm • Fat 14 Gm • Percent of calories from fat 33% • Cholesterol 20 mg • Dietary Fiber 3 Gm • Sodium 582 mg • Calcium 330 mg

Broccoli and Sun-dried Tomatoes with Penne

---◼---

4 SERVINGS

This is one of those versatile vegetable dishes that can be served at room temperature as a salad or as a hot dish, whichever you prefer.

³/₄ **pound broccoli crowns**
3 tablespoons olive oil
1 tablespoon oil from sun-dried tomatoes
1 garlic clove, pressed in a garlic press or finely minced
6 oil-packed sun-dried tomatoes, slivered

8 ounces (¹/₂ pound) penne (or mostaccioli or ziti)
About ¹/₄ teaspoon salt
Freshly ground black pepper
Crushed hot red pepper flakes
Grated Parmesan cheese

Cut the broccoli crowns into florets; peel and cut the stems into ¹/₂-inch slices on the diagonal. This should give you about 4 cups. Cook the broccoli in a large pot of boiling salted water until tender-crisp, about 3 minutes. Drain and rinse under cold water to stop the cooking.

In a large skillet, warm the oils with the garlic and sun-dried tomatoes so that it barely heats without browning. Add the broccoli, and stir to blend.

Meanwhile cook the penne according to package directions. Drain, reserving ¹/₄ cup cooking water. Add the cooking water and salt to the broccoli sauce.

In a large serving dish, toss the penne with the broccoli sauce, adding the black pepper and red pepper flakes to your taste. Blend well so that the crushed red pepper will be mixed throughout.

If you serve this dish as a hot dish, pass grated cheese at the table.

Kilocalories 367 Kc • Protein 10 Gm • Fat 15 Gm • Percent of calories from fat 37% • Cholesterol 0 mg • Dietary Fiber 3 Gm • Sodium 184 mg • Calcium 35 mg

Shrimp and Broccoli Salad with Shells

◼

4 SERVINGS

The dressing for this salad needs to be marinated for an hour, so you may wish to prepare it first.

1 pound medium shrimp, cooked, shelled, and cleaned (see basic recipe on page 14)
1 bunch broccoli (1 to 1¼ pounds)

8 ounces (½ pound) medium shell macaroni
About ¾ cup Greek-style Salad Dressing (recipe follows)

After preparing the shrimp, keep them refrigerated until you are ready to assemble the salad.

Wash the broccoli. Remove and separate the florets with about 2 inches of stalk attached. Peel the remaining stalks and cut them into 2-inch pieces. Cook the broccoli in a large pot of boiling salted water until barely tender-crisp, about 2 minutes. Drain and rinse in cold water. Refrigerate the broccoli.

Cook the pasta according to package directions. Drain and rinse in cold water. Mix the pasta with ½ cup of the dressing. Stir in the shrimp and chill.

Just before serving (to prevent discoloration), stir in the broccoli and about ¼ cup more dressing, or to your taste.

Kilocalories 575 Kc • Protein 29 Gm • Fat 29 Gm • Percent of calories from fat 46% • Cholesterol 175 mg • Dietary Fiber 4 Gm • Sodium 374 mg • Calcium 92 mg

Greek-style Salad Dressing

$^1/_3$ cup fresh lemon juice
1 cup olive oil
1 teaspoon dried oregano
$^1/_2$ teaspoon salt

$^1/_4$ teaspoon freshly ground
black pepper
2 garlic cloves, peeled and
halved

Combine all the ingredients in a pint jar. Cover the jar tightly and shake to blend. Let the mixture stand at room temperature for about an hour to develop its flavor. After that, remove the garlic and refrigerate the dressing.

Kilocalories 242 Kc • Protein 0 Gm • Fat 27 Gm • Percent of calories from fat 98% • Cholesterol 0 mg • Dietary Fiber 0 Gm • Sodium 146 mg • Calcium 5 mg

BROCCOLI, CHAMPION OF VEGETABLES

Asian Broccoli Salad with Radishes, Scallions, and Noodles

4 SERVINGS

1 bunch broccoli (1 to
  1¼ pounds)
Tofu-Garlic Dressing (recipe
  follows)
6 ounces Asian noodles
  or linguine

1 bunch radishes, trimmed and
  thinly sliced
1 bunch scallions, cut
  diagonally into 1-inch lengths

Separate the broccoli florets and stalks. Peel the stalks and slice them into ½-inch pieces. Cut large florets in half. Cook the broccoli in a large pot of boiling salted water until barely tender-crisp, about 2 minutes. Drain well and rinse in cold water.

Make the dressing. Cook the noodles according to package directions. Drain and rinse under cold water. Toss with the dressing. Combine with the broccoli, radishes, and scallions in a large salad dish and toss again. Chill before serving.

Kilocalories 448 Kc • Protein 10 Gm • Fat 28 Gm • Percent of calories from fat 55% • Cholesterol 0 mg • Dietary Fiber 4 Gm • Sodium 297 mg • Calcium 81 mg

Tofu-Garlic Dressing

MAKES ABOUT ¾ CUP (8 2-TABLESPOON SERVINGS)

1 garlic clove, peeled
2 ounces soft tofu
1 to 2 tablespoons soy sauce
3 tablespoons rice vinegar

⅛ teaspoon freshly ground
  pepper
½ cup vegetable oil
  (approximately)

Mince the garlic in a food processor. Blend in all the remaining ingredients except the oil. With the motor running, slowly pour enough oil through the feed tube to make a dressing that is thick and smooth, a little softer than mayonnaise.

Kilocalories 174 Kc • Protein 1 Gm • Fat 19 Gm • Percent of calories from fat 96% • Cholesterol 0 mg • Dietary Fiber 0 Gm • Sodium 173 mg • Calcium 12 mg

Broccoli Salad Niçoise with Mezzani Rigati

6 SERVINGS

1 bunch broccoli (1 to
  1¼ pounds)
4 anchovy fillets, rinsed in
  vinegar and chopped
2 tablespoons chopped pitted
  black olives
2 tablespoons chopped stuffed
  green olives
2 tablespoons chopped
  cornichons (small sour
  pickles)
1 tablespoon drained capers

2 tablespoons minced
  red onion
2 tablespoons minced fresh
  flat-leaf parsley
⅓ cup olive oil
2 to 3 tablespoons tarragon
  vinegar
Freshly ground black pepper
8 ounces (½ pound) mezzani
  rigati or penne or casserole
  elbows

Separate the broccoli florets and stems. Peel the stems and slice them into
½-inch pieces. Cut large florets in half. Parboil the florets and stems in a
large pot of boiling salted water until they are tender-crisp—about 3 minutes, counting from the time the water returns to a boil. Drain and rinse in
cold water. Drain again.

In a salad dish, combine the broccoli, anchovies, olives, cornichons,
capers, red onion, and parsley. Stir in the oil. Sprinkle with vinegar and
pepper to your taste and toss to blend.

Meanwhile, cook the mezzani al dente according to package directions.
Drain and rinse in cold water. Stir the pasta into the broccoli mixture.
Serve immediately or chill until needed. When ready to serve, toss again
and taste, adding more oil or vinegar if needed.

Kilocalories 283 Kc • Protein 8 Gm • Fat 14 Gm • Percent of calories from fat
43% • Cholesterol 2 mg • Dietary Fiber 3 Gm • Sodium 305 mg • Calcium 50 mg

BROCCOLI, CHAMPION OF VEGETABLES

Cabbage and Brussels Sprouts, for Cottages and Castles

Cabbage has a long history as a staple food of farm folk in many lands, whereas brussels sprouts have been the upscale vegetable of royalty. As cruciferous vegetables, both are important anticancer vegetables, recommended by the Surgeon General's report on nutrition as well as many top nutritionists. But that's not all! Not only do they supply the disease-fighting chemicals of the cruciferous kingdom, they are also great sources of vitamin C, a nutrient that's also protective against cancer and the degenerative effects of aging.

Although there's only one variety of brussels sprouts, you'll have plenty of cabbage cousins from which to choose at the market: green cabbage, red cabbage, ruffle-leaved savoy cabbage, lettuce-leafed Chinese cabbage, and juicy white-stemmed bok choy. Look for brightly colored, crisp, compact vegetables with no discolored or yellowing outer leaves. Brussels sprouts have a shorter season, but frozen ones are quite an acceptable substitute, except in stir-fries and salads.

Wrap cabbage or sprouts loosely in paper towels and store in a perforated plastic vegetable bag. Fresh sprouts will keep three days or more. Cabbage has even greater staying power; it remains fresh at least a week, often much longer.

Savoy Cabbage and Double Tomato Soup with Gemellini

6 SERVINGS

6 cups chicken stock or
  canned broth
1 cup peeled, seeded, chopped
  fresh tomatoes
2 tablespoons tomato paste
3 cups coarsely chopped savoy
  cabbage (about $1/2$ of a
  medium head)

$1/2$ cup sun-dried tomatoes,
  snipped into slivers
6 leaves chopped fresh basil, or
  $1/2$ teaspoon dried
$1/2$ teaspoon salt
Freshly ground pepper
1 cup gemellini (very small
  twists)

Combine the stock, tomatoes, tomato paste, cabbage, sun-dried tomatoes, basil, and salt in a large pot. Bring to a boil, reduce the heat, and simmer until the cabbage is tender, about 8 minutes. Add pepper to your taste.

    Meanwhile, cook the gemellini separately according to package directions. Drain and add to the soup.

Kilocalories 136 Kc • Protein 9 Gm • Fat 2 Gm • Percent of calories from fat 13% • Cholesterol 0 mg • Dietary Fiber 3 Gm • Sodium 731 mg • Calcium 34 mg

Sweet-and-Sour Green Cabbage Soup with Egg Noodles

---

6 SERVINGS

Although basically similar to the preceding recipe, this soup, German in origin, tastes quite different from the double-tomato Mediterranean version.

6 cups chicken stock or
  canned broth
1 cup tomato purée
3 cups coarsely chopped green
  cabbage (about ¹/₂ of a
  medium head)
2 tablespoons balsamic vinegar

1 teaspoon brown sugar
¹/₂ teaspoon dried chervil
¹/₂ teaspoon salt
Freshly ground pepper
4 ounces (¹/₄ pound) broad egg
  noodles

Combine the stock, tomato purée, cabbage, vinegar, sugar, chervil, and salt in a large pot. Bring to a boil, reduce the heat, and simmer until the cabbage is tender, about 8 minutes. Add pepper to your taste. Taste to correct seasoning, adding more vinegar or brown sugar as desired.

Meanwhile, cook the egg noodles according to package directions. Drain and add to the soup.

Kilocalories 147 Kc • Protein 9 Gm • Fat 2 Gm • Percent of calories from fat 14% • Cholesterol 18 mg • Dietary Fiber 2 Gm • Sodium 640 mg • Calcium 40 mg

Asian Cabbage Soup with Noodles

◼

6 SERVINGS

6 cups chicken stock or
   canned broth
1/4 teaspoon five-spice powder
   (see Note)
4 cups shredded Chinese
   cabbage (1 small head)

6 scallions, cut into 2-inch
   lengths
1 carrot, thinly sliced
4 ounces (1/4 pound) Asian
   whole wheat angel hair or
   American angel hair

Combine the stock and five-spice powder in a large pot and whisk to blend. Add the cabbage, scallions, and carrot. Bring to a boil, reduce the heat, and simmer until the vegetables are tender, about 10 minutes.

Meanwhile, cook the noodles separately, 5 minutes or until tender; drain. Add the noodles to the soup and serve.

Kilocalories 110 Kc • Protein 9 Gm • Fat 2 Gm • Percent of calories from fat 14% • Cholesterol 0 mg • Dietary Fiber 3 Gm • Sodium 443 mg • Calcium 63 mg

NOTE: Five-spice powder is an Asian seasoning sold in most supermarkets.

Cabbage, Mushroom, and Egg Noodle Casserole

4 SERVINGS

2 tablespoons olive oil
About 6 ounces mushrooms, cleaned and sliced
1 large shallot, minced
1 teaspoon dried tarragon
1½ cups chicken or vegetable stock, or canned broth
4 cups shredded green cabbage (about ½ of a large head)
4 ounces (¼ pound) broad egg noodles

¼ cup superfine flour, such as Wondra
¼ cup nonfat dry milk
¼ teaspoon salt
⅛ teaspoon pepper
⅛ teaspoon dry mustard
1½ cups milk (whole or low-fat)
⅓ cup grated Asiago cheese, or Gruyère
½ cup fresh bread crumbs

Heat the oil in a skillet and fry the mushrooms and shallot over medium-high heat, stirring often, until the mushrooms begin to brown. Remove them to a 2½-quart gratin pan or casserole and sprinkle with tarragon.

Put the stock in the skillet, add the cabbage, and simmer, covered, stirring often, until the cabbage is tender, 5 to 7 minutes. Remove the cabbage with a slotted spoon and add it to the casserole. Reserve the remaining stock in the skillet. Cook the noodles according to package directions and drain, and mix them with the cabbage and mushrooms.

Preheat the oven to 350 degrees F.

Whisk the flour, dry milk, salt, pepper, and mustard into the liquid milk. Add it to the remaining stock in the skillet, and cook, stirring constantly, until the mixture bubbles and thickens. Remove from the heat and stir in all but 1 tablespoon of the cheese. Pour the sauce over the vegetables and noodles; sprinkle with the bread crumbs and the remaining 1 tablespoon cheese.

Bake the casserole for 25 to 30 minutes, until bubbling throughout and golden on top.

Kilocalories 345 Kc • Protein 15 Gm • Fat 15 Gm • Percent of calories from fat 39% • Cholesterol 50 mg • Dietary Fiber 3 Gm • Sodium 428 mg • Calcium 273 mg

Orzo-stuffed Cabbage Leaves

4 SERVINGS

12 large green cabbage leaves
  (outer leaves of 2 cabbages)
2 tablespoons olive oil
1 cup chopped onion
1$^1/_2$ cups cooked orzo ($^1/_2$ cup
  uncooked—prepare
  according to package
  directions)
2 teaspoons chopped fresh
  thyme, or $^1/_2$ teaspoon dried

$^3/_4$ teaspoon salt
$^1/_8$ teaspoon pepper
2 cups tomato purée
2 tablespoons minced fresh
  flat-leaf parsley
2 teaspoons paprika
Several dashes of cayenne
  pepper
1 garlic clove, pressed in a
  garlic press

Blanch the cabbage leaves in boiling salted water for 2 to 3 minutes. Remove with tongs and rinse in cold water. Drain. Trim off the core portion from each leaf—a small wedge-shaped cut at the bottom.

Heat the oil in a large skillet and sauté the onion very slowly until it's golden, 5 to 8 minutes. Remove from the heat and stir in the cooked orzo, thyme, $^1/_4$ teaspoon of the salt, and pepper.

Spoon about 1$^1/_2$ tablespoons orzo filling on each leaf. Roll up the leaves, starting at the core end and folding in the sides to seal them. (If necessary, secure the rolls with toothpicks.) Place the rolls, seam sides down, in a large 2-inch-deep casserole with a cover. (At this point the dish can be refrigerated, covered, for several hours or overnight.)

When ready to cook, preheat the oven to 350 degrees F.

Mix the tomato purée with the parsley, paprika, remaining $^1/_2$ teaspoon salt, cayenne pepper, and garlic, and pour the sauce over the cabbage rolls. Cover and bake 40 minutes, 50 minutes if refrigerated. (Remove any toothpicks before serving.)

Kilocalories 254 Kc • Protein 8 Gm • Fat 8 Gm • Percent of calories from fat 27% • Cholesterol 0 mg • Dietary Fiber 6 Gm • Sodium 580 mg • Calcium 61 mg

Cabbage Roll Soup

Warm leftover cabbage rolls in the tomato sauce. Put 1 roll and a little sauce into each soup plate. With a sharp knife, carefully cut each roll into 4 pieces. Gently pour 1 cup hot chicken or beef broth over each serving. Serve immediately. Toasted caraway rye bread makes a nice accompaniment.

Kilocalories 122 Kc • Protein 7 Gm • Fat 5 Gm • Percent of calories from fat 32% • Cholesterol 5 mg • Dietary Fiber 2 Gm • Sodium 332 mg • Calcium 40 mg

Curried Cabbage and Cashews with Whole Wheat Couscous

◼

4 SERVINGS

Quickly sautéed, tender-crisp cabbage has an entirely different, much lighter flavor than the well-cooked cabbage in soups.

1 cup whole wheat
  couscous, raw
1 tablespoon vegetable oil
4 cups thinly shredded green
  cabbage (about ¹/₂ of a
  large head)

1 tablespoon water
1 teaspoon curry powder
¹/₄ cup unsalted cashews,
  whole or pieces

Prepare the couscous (see page 12 for basic recipe or follow package directions); fluff and separate grains.

Heat the oil in a large skillet and stir-fry the cabbage over medium-high heat until wilted, about 2 minutes. Add the water, cover, and continue cooking over low heat 2 to 3 minutes or until the cabbage is tender-crisp. Toss with the curry until evenly coated.

Top the couscous with the cabbage. Sprinkle with cashews.

Kilocalories 248 Kc • Protein 7 Gm • Fat 8 Gm • Percent of calories from fat 27% • Cholesterol 0 mg • Dietary Fiber 6 Gm • Sodium 23 mg • Calcium 39 mg

Scalloped Cabbage and Tomatoes with Farfalle

4 SERVINGS

2 tablespoons butter
1 cup chopped yellow onion
1 16-ounce can chopped
   tomatoes with juice
3 cups chopped cabbage,
   1-inch chunks (about $^1/_2$ of a
   medium head)
$^1/_2$ teaspoon dried thyme

$^1/_2$ teaspoon sugar
$^1/_2$ teaspoon salt
$^1/_4$ teaspoon pepper
6 ounces (about $^1/_3$ pound)
   farfalle (egg bows)
1 cup fresh bread crumbs,
   toasted, or herb stuffing mix
   (not an instant stuffing mix)

Melt the butter in a large skillet and sauté the onion until softened, 3 minutes. Add the tomatoes, cabbage, thyme, and seasonings. Cover and simmer until the cabbage is tender, 15 minutes.

Meanwhile, cook the farfalle according to package directions, undercooking it slightly, and drain. Preheat the oven to 350 degrees F. Combine the cabbage and farfalle in a 2-quart gratin or other baking dish, and top with the stuffing mix, pressing it down into the sauce. Bake until hot throughout and slightly browned on top, 20 to 25 minutes if the ingredients are still warm.

Kilocalories 327 Kc • Protein 11 Gm • Fat 9 Gm • Percent of calories from fat 25% • Cholesterol 66 mg • Dietary Fiber 5 Gm • Sodium 657 mg • Calcium 51 mg

Cabbage and Potatoes with Mezzani

■

4 SERVINGS

There's something deliciously sinful about combining potatoes and pasta in one dish—but in fact, it's the fat that makes foods fattening. With less than a tablespoon of oil per portion, you can enjoy this dish quite guiltlessly.

3 tablespoons olive oil
2 cooked potatoes, diced (see Note)
3 cups shredded green cabbage (about 1/2 of a medium head)
1 red bell pepper, seeded and slivered
1 garlic clove, minced
1/4 teaspoon salt

Freshly ground black pepper
8 ounces (1/2 pound) mezzani
1/4 cup hot chicken stock or canned broth
1/2 cup finely diced Asiago or provolone cheese
2 tablespoons chopped fresh flat-leaf parsley

Heat 2 tablespoons of the oil in a large skillet and fry the potatoes until they are brown and crispy.

Remove the potatoes and add the remaining tablespoon of oil to the skillet. Stir-fry the cabbage, red pepper, and garlic until the cabbage is tender-crisp, 3 to 5 minutes. Add the salt and ground pepper to your taste.

Meanwhile, cook the mezzani according to package directions and drain. Stir the potatoes, pasta, stock, and cheese into the cabbage. Let the flavors blend for a minute over a warm burner. Garnish with the chopped parsley and serve.

NOTE: This is an ideal way to use leftover boiled potatoes. Otherwise, cook peeled, quartered potatoes in a steamer until tender, about 10 minutes. I usually add a little salt (for flavor) and 1 teaspoon white vinegar (to preserve whiteness) to the water whenever I cook potatoes, whether steamed or boiled.

Kilocalories 444 Kc • Protein 14 Gm • Fat 15 Gm • Percent of calories from fat 31% • Cholesterol 10 mg • Dietary Fiber 4 Gm • Sodium 315 mg • Calcium 152 mg

Cabbage and Shell Bean Stew with Shells

■

4 SERVINGS

Fresh shell beans and fresh tomatoes make this a perfect quick summer-time dish.

2 tablespoons olive oil

2 garlic cloves, minced

1¹/₂ cups fresh shell beans (see Note)

1¹/₂ cups chicken or vegetable stock, or canned broth

1 cup peeled, chopped fresh tomatoes

3 cups chopped cabbage, 1-inch chunks (about ¹/₂ of a medium head)

2 teaspoons chopped fresh thyme, or ¹/₂ teaspoon dried

2 teaspoons chopped fresh marjoram, or ¹/₂ teaspoon dried oregano

¹/₂ teaspoon salt

¹/₄ teaspoon freshly ground pepper

4 ounces (¹/₄ pound) medium shells

2 tablespoons chopped fresh flat-leaf parsley

Heat the oil in a large pot and sauté the garlic until sizzling, about 2 minutes. Add the beans, stock, tomatoes, cabbage, thyme, marjoram or oregano, salt, and pepper. Cover and simmer, stirring often, until the beans are quite tender, 20 to 25 minutes.

Meanwhile, cook the shells according to package directions and drain. Stir them into the finished stew. Sprinkle with parsley.

NOTE: One 16-ounce can of pinto beans, drained and rinsed, can be substituted. If using canned beans, reduce the cooking time to about 15 minutes, just until the cabbage is tender.

Kilocalories 333 Kc • Protein 15 Gm • Fat 9 Gm • Percent of calories from fat 23% • Cholesterol 0 mg • Dietary Fiber 12 Gm • Sodium 469 mg • Calcium 94 mg

Cabbage and Tofu Stew with Noodles

4 SERVINGS

Here's a midwinter vegetable stew. Fortunately, fresh cabbage is available in every season.

2 tablespoons olive oil
1 cup chopped yellow onion
1 green bell pepper, seeded
  and diced
1 1/2 cups chicken or vegetable
  stock, or canned broth
1 16-ounce can chopped
  tomatoes with juice
3 cups chopped cabbage,
  1-inch chunks (about 1/2 of a
  medium head)

1 teaspoon paprika
2 teaspoons chopped fresh
  thyme, or 1/2 teaspoon dried
1/2 teaspoon salt
1/4 teaspoon freshly ground
  pepper
4 ounces firm tofu, diced
4 ounces (1/4 pound) broad egg
  noodles

Heat the oil in a Dutch oven or large pot and sauté the onion and bell pepper until sizzling. Add all the remaining ingredients except the tofu and noodles. Cover and simmer, stirring often, until the cabbage is tender, 15 minutes. Add the tofu and continue to cook over very low heat for 5 minutes.

Meanwhile, cook the noodles according to package directions and drain. Stir them into the finished stew.

Kilocalories 282 Kc • Protein 13 Gm • Fat 12 Gm • Percent of calories from fat 35% • Cholesterol 27 mg • Dietary Fiber 5 Gm • Sodium 657 mg • Calcium 144 mg

Venetian Smothered Cabbage with Spaghetti

4 SERVINGS

2 tablespoons olive oil
1 garlic clove, minced
1 teaspoon fresh rosemary
  leaves, or $1/4$ teaspoon dried
3 to 4 ounces prosciutto,
  slivered

4 cups shredded green cabbage
  (about $1/2$ of a large head)
$1/2$ cup chicken stock or
  canned broth
Salt and freshly ground pepper
8 ounces ($1/2$ pound) spaghetti

Heat the oil in a large skillet and sauté the garlic and rosemary until they are sizzling, about 2 minutes. Immediately add the prosciutto, cabbage, and stock. Cover and cook over very low heat until the cabbage is quite tender, 15 minutes, checking the liquid level from time to time. Season with salt and pepper to your taste (the prosciutto adds salt).

Meanwhile, cook and drain the spaghetti according to package directions. In a large serving dish, toss the pasta with the cabbage.

Kilocalories 312 Kc • Protein 12 Gm • Fat 8 Gm • Percent of calories from fat 23% • Cholesterol 0 mg • Dietary Fiber 3 Gm • Sodium 323 mg • Calcium 50 mg

Creamy Savoy Cabbage with Fettuccine

4 SERVINGS

4 cups shredded savoy
    cabbage (about ½ of a
    large head)
1 cup chicken stock or
    canned broth
3 tablespoons butter
¼ cup chopped shallots
3 tablespoons flour

1½ cups heated milk
½ teaspoon dried dill
½ teaspoon dry mustard
½ teaspoon salt
⅛ teaspoon freshly ground
    black pepper
8 ounces (½ pound) fettuccine

In a large pot, cook the cabbage in the stock until it is tender, 8 to 10 minutes. Drain the cabbage, reserving ½ cup of the liquid.

Heat the butter in a large saucepan and slowly sauté the shallots until they are golden. Add the flour and cook over low heat for 3 minutes, stirring often. Add the heated milk all at once and cook over medium-high heat, stirring constantly, until the sauce bubbles and thickens. Whisk in the reserved liquid, dill, mustard, salt, and pepper. Stir in the cabbage and cook over very low heat for 3 minutes.

Meanwhile, cook and drain the fettuccine according to package directions. In a large serving dish, toss the pasta with the cabbage.

Kilocalories 396 Kc • Protein 14 Gm • Fat 14 Gm • Percent of calories from fat 30% • Cholesterol 37 mg • Dietary Fiber 4 Gm • Sodium 559 mg • Calcium 151 mg

Creamy Savoy Cabbage with Ravioli

4 SERVINGS

Follow the preceding recipe, substituting 1 tablespoon minced fresh basil (1 teaspoon dried) and 1 teaspoon fresh minced rosemary (¼ teaspoon dried) for the dill and mustard. Substitute 2 dozen cheese ravioli, cooked according to package directions, for the fettuccine. Garnish with slivered prosciutto and fresh basil leaves, if desired.

Kilocalories 395 Kc • Protein 16 Gm • Fat 22 Gm • Percent of calories from fat 48% • Cholesterol 61 mg • Dietary Fiber 4 Gm • Sodium 588 mg • Calcium 295 mg

Stir-fried Savoy Cabbage with Peanuts and Rice Stick Noodles

4 SERVINGS

2 tablespoons peanut oil

1 red bell pepper, seeded and cut into small triangles

1 bunch scallions, cut into 2-inch lengths

1 slice fresh ginger, peeled and minced

1 jalapeño chili, seeded and minced (wear rubber gloves)

4 cups shredded savoy cabbage (about $1/2$ of a large head)

2 tablespoons seasoned rice vinegar

1 tablespoon naturally brewed soy sauce, plus more to pass

8 ounces (about $1/2$ pound) rice stick noodles

$1/2$ cup chopped unsalted peanuts

In a large wok or skillet, heat the peanut oil and stir-fry the bell pepper and scallions until tender-crisp, 3 minutes. Remove them with a slotted spoon.

Add the ginger, jalapeño chili, and cabbage, and stir-fry until the cabbage is wilted, about 5 minutes. Return the bell pepper and scallions to the wok. Season the vegetables with the rice vinegar and soy sauce.

Meanwhile, heat a pot of water to the boiling point, remove from the heat, and soak the noodles in it until they are tender, 5 to 7 minutes. Gently toss the vegetables with the noodles. Sprinkle with the peanuts. Pass more soy sauce at the table.

Kilocalories 400 Kc • Protein 6 Gm • Fat 16 Gm • Percent of calories from fat 35% • Cholesterol 0 mg • Dietary Fiber 5 Gm • Sodium 303 mg • Calcium 61 mg

Stir-fried Sesame Chinese Cabbage and Mushrooms with Noodles

4 SERVINGS

1 tablespoon vegetable oil
1 teaspoon sesame oil
1 slice fresh ginger, peeled and minced
1 Anaheim chili, seeded and cut into small triangles
4 ounces fresh brown mushrooms, cleaned and sliced
About 4 cups shredded Chinese cabbage (1 medium head)

2 tablespoons stock, canned broth, or water
1/2 teaspoon sugar
1 tablespoon naturally brewed soy sauce, or more to taste
8 ounces (1/2 pound) fresh Asian noodles
2 tablespoons lightly toasted sesame seeds (see Note page 128)

Heat the oils in a large wok or skillet and stir-fry the ginger, chili, and mushrooms for 1 minute. Add the cabbage and stir-fry for 2 minutes. Add the stock and sugar, cover, and cook until the cabbage is tender-crisp, 3 to 5 minutes. Season with soy sauce to your taste.

Meanwhile, cook the noodles according to package directions and drain. In a large serving dish, toss the noodles with the cabbage. Sprinkle with sesame seeds.

Kilocalories 288 Kc • Protein 9 Gm • Fat 6 Gm • Percent of calories from fat 18% • Cholesterol 0 mg • Dietary Fiber 2 Gm • Sodium 279 mg • Calcium 65 mg

Bok Choy, Bell Peppers, and Chinese Noodles

4 SERVINGS

$^1/_2$ cup chicken stock or
canned broth
$1^1/_2$ tablespoons naturally
brewed soy sauce
1 teaspoon oyster sauce
2 teaspoons cornstarch
1 tablespoon vegetable oil
3 or more slices fresh ginger,
peeled
4 large bok choy stalks (about
$^1/_2$ pound), without leaves,
cut into 2-inch sticks, about
$^1/_4$ inch wide

1 red bell pepper, seeded and
cut into strips
1 green bell pepper, seeded
and cut into strips
1 sweet onion (such as Vidalia),
thinly sliced
6 ounces (about $^1/_3$ pound)
dried Chinese noodles or
American thin linguine

Prepare all the ingredients in advance and have the water boiling for the noodles. Mix the chicken stock with the soy and oyster sauces. Stir the cornstarch into the stock until blended.

Heat the oil in a large skillet or wok. Add the ginger and vegetables and stir-fry until barely tender-crisp, 3 to 5 minutes. Remove the ginger.

Add the chicken stock mixture and bring to a boil. Stir constantly until thickened. Remove from the heat.

Meanwhile, cook the noodles. If the package does not have directions, taste for doneness. Dried noodles the width of thin linguine take about 8 minutes.

Drain the noodles and put them into a large dish. Spoon the vegetable mixture on top and blend some of the sauce into the noodles.

Kilocalories 139 Kc • Protein 4 Gm • Fat 4 Gm • Percent of calories from fat 24% • Cholesterol 0 mg • Dietary Fiber 2 Gm • Sodium 479 mg • Calcium 51 mg

Bok Choy with Chilies and Shrimp

4 SERVINGS

Follow the preceding recipe, substituting 1 Anaheim chili, seeded and chunked, and 1 jalapeño chili, seeded and minced (wear rubber gloves), for the bell peppers. Omit the onion. Add 2 cups cooked, shelled, deveined shrimp (see basic recipe page 14) during the last minute of stir-frying the vegetables.

Kilocalories 195 Kc • Protein 20 Gm • Fat 5 Gm • Percent of calories from fat 22% • Cholesterol 156 mg • Dietary Fiber 1 Gm • Sodium 636 mg • Calcium 72 mg

German-style Red Cabbage (Rötkohl) with Gemelli

4 SERVINGS

2 tablespoons butter
2 yellow onions, chopped
4 cups shredded red cabbage
  (1 medium head)
1 cup chicken stock or
  canned broth

$1/4$ cup red wine vinegar
2 tablespoons brown sugar
$1/4$ teaspoon salt
$1/8$ teaspoon pepper
8 ounces ($1/2$ pound) gemelli or
  rotelle

Heat $1^1/2$ tablespoons of the butter in a 4-quart pot and sauté the onions until translucent, about 5 minutes. Add the cabbage and continue to sauté 5 minutes longer.

Add the stock, vinegar, sugar, salt, and pepper. Bring to a boil, reduce the heat, and simmer, covered, for 25 to 30 minutes, stirring often.

Meanwhile, cook the gemelli according to package directions and drain. Spoon the pasta into a large serving dish and toss it with the remaining $1/2$ tablespoon of butter. Ladle the cabbage on top.

Kilocalories 348 Kc • Protein 10 Gm • Fat 8 Gm • Percent of calories from fat 19% • Cholesterol 16 mg • Dietary Fiber 4 Gm • Sodium 331 mg • Calcium 72 mg

Braised Sprouts, Mushrooms, and Red Pepper with Rigatoni

4 SERVINGS

An attractively chunky side dish. To make a more substantial version, add 1 cup chunked cooked chicken or turkey to make 2 entrée servings.

10 ounces fresh brussels
  sprouts
2½ tablespoons olive oil
8 ounces whole button
  mushrooms, cleaned
1 red bell pepper, seeded
  and diced

2 garlic cloves, minced
Salt and freshly ground pepper
6 ounces (about ⅓ pound)
  rigatoni

Clean the sprouts and cut an X in the bottom of each core. Drop them into a pot of boiling salted water and blanch them until just tender, 6 to 10 minutes, depending on the size. Drain.

Heat the oil in a large skillet and fry the mushrooms and red peppers until they are beginning to brown. At the last minute, add the garlic.

Add the sprouts and braise the vegetables together for about 3 minutes or until the sprouts, too, begin to brown. Salt and pepper the vegetables to your taste.

Meanwhile, cook the rigatoni according to package directions. Drain the pasta and combine it with the vegetables in a serving dish.

Kilocalories 281 Kc • Protein 9 Gm • Fat 10 Gm • Percent of calories from fat 30% • Cholesterol 0 mg • Dietary Fiber 5 Gm • Sodium 21 mg • Calcium 40 mg

Sprouts with Poppy Seeds and Shells

4 SERVINGS

Serve warm as a side dish or at room temperature as a salad.

1 pound fresh brussels sprouts
3 tablespoons olive oil
3 garlic cloves, minced
2 tablespoons fresh lemon
  juice (¹/₂ large lemon)

1 tablespoon poppy seeds
Salt and freshly ground pepper
6 ounces (about ¹/₃ pound)
  large shells

Clean the sprouts and cut an X in the bottom of each core. Drop them into a pot of boiling salted water and blanch them until just tender, 6 to 10 minutes, depending on the size. Drain. When cool enough to handle, cut the sprouts into halves.

Heat the oil in a large skillet and sauté the garlic until it is softened and fragrant. Add the sprouts, lemon juice, and poppy seeds. Season with salt and pepper to your taste. Heat to blend flavors, about 3 minutes.

Meanwhile, cook the shells according to package directions and drain. In a large serving dish, toss the sprouts with the shells.

Kilocalories 307 Kc • Protein 9 Gm • Fat 12 Gm • Percent of calories from fat 35% • Cholesterol 0 mg • Dietary Fiber 7 Gm • Sodium 28 mg • Calcium 84 mg

Sprouts, Carrots, and Pine Nuts with Ziti

■

4 SERVINGS

The sweetness of carrots complements the strong flavor of sprouts.

3 tablespoons olive oil
1 pound fresh brussels sprouts, quartered and cored
1 large carrot, diced very small
1/2 green bell pepper, diced very small

2 to 3 tablespoons water, if needed
2 garlic cloves, minced
1/4 cup pine nuts
Salt and freshly ground pepper
6 ounces (about 1/3 pound) ziti

Heat the oil in a large skillet and stir-fry the sprouts, carrot, and pepper, stirring constantly, until the sprouts are tender-crisp and lightly colored, 4 to 5 minutes. (If the sprouts are not yet tender, add 2 to 3 tablespoons water, as needed. The steam generated in the hot pan will finish cooking the sprouts.) Add the garlic and pine nuts during the last minute of the cooking time. Season with salt and pepper to your taste.

Meanwhile, cook the ziti according to package directions; drain and toss with the sprouts.

Kilocalories 355 Kc • Protein 11 Gm • Fat 17 Gm • Percent of calories from fat 39% • Cholesterol 0 mg • Dietary Fiber 7 Gm • Sodium 34 mg • Calcium 60 mg

Brussels Sprouts and Chicken with Mezzani

---

4 SERVINGS

A perfect way to use the last of a roast chicken (or turkey). I usually make a broth from the carcass plus a few vegetables, sage, and thyme.

10 ounces fresh or frozen brussels sprouts
2 tablespoons olive oil
1 garlic clove, chopped
3/4 cup well-flavored chicken stock or canned broth
2 cups cooked chicken chunks (see basic recipe, page 17)

Salt, if needed
Several dashes of cayenne pepper
8 ounces (1/2 pound) mezzani
1/4 cup freshly grated Parmesan cheese

If you're using fresh sprouts, clean and trim them. Cut an X in the core of each. Cook them in boiling salted water until tender, 8 to 10 minutes. If you're using frozen sprouts, cook them according to package directions. Drain the sprouts.

In a 10- to 12-inch skillet, heat the oil and sauté the garlic until it's fragrant. Add the sprouts and continue sautéing for 1 to 2 minutes. Add the stock, chicken, salt (if the stock is not sufficiently flavorful), and cayenne pepper.

Meanwhile, cook the mezzani according to package directions and drain. Stir the pasta into the sprouts and chicken; allow the flavors to blend for a minute or so.

Just before serving, stir in the cheese.

Kilocalories 449 Kc • Protein 34 Gm • Fat 13 Gm • Percent of calories from fat 26% • Cholesterol 63 mg • Dietary Fiber 4 Gm • Sodium 246 mg • Calcium 118 mg

Cabbage Slaw with Gemellini

■

4 SERVINGS

3 tablespoons mayonnaise
2 tablespoons cider vinegar
1 tablespoon minced fresh dill,
  or 1 teaspoon dried
1/2 teaspoon celery salt
1/4 teaspoon caraway seeds
1/4 teaspoon white pepper

4 cups finely shredded green
  cabbage (about 1/2 of a large
  head)
1/2 cup minced sweet onion,
  such as Vidalia, or scallions
4 ounces (1/4 pound) gemellini
  (very small twists)

Whisk together the mayonnaise, vinegar, dill, celery salt, caraway seeds, and white pepper. Spoon the dressing into a large bowl. Add the cabbage and onion, and toss to blend. Allow the mixture to marinate in the refrigerator for 1 hour or more.

Cook the gemellini according to package directions and drain. Toss with the slaw. Taste to correct the seasoning. You may want more mayonnaise or vinegar.

Kilocalories 207 Kc • Protein 5 Gm • Fat 9 Gm • Percent of calories from fat 38% • Cholesterol 8 mg • Dietary Fiber 3 Gm • Sodium 74 mg • Calcium 44 mg

Brussels Sprouts Salad with Shells and Russian Dressing

■

6 SERVINGS

1 pound fresh brussels sprouts
Double batch of Light Russian
Dressing (see page 12 for
basic recipe)

8 ounces ($^1/_2$ pound) large
shells

Clean the sprouts and cut an X in the bottom of each core. Drop them into a pot of boiling salted water and blanch them until just tender, 6 to 10 minutes, depending on the size. Drain. When cool enough to handle, cut the sprouts into halves. Mix them with the dressing.

Meanwhile, cook the shells according to package directions and drain. Rinse them in cold water and toss them with the salad.

Kilocalories 283 Kc • Protein 9 Gm • Fat 10 Gm • Percent of calories from fat 30% • Cholesterol 3 mg • Dietary Fiber 4 Gm • Sodium 456 mg • Calcium 85 mg

Brussels Sprouts Salad with Cavatelli and Honey-Mustard Vinaigrette

6 SERVINGS

Follow the preceding recipe, substituting 1 batch Honey-Mustard Vinaigrette (see page 11 for basic recipe) for the Light Russian Dressing and cavatelli for the shells. Add $^1/_2$ cup chopped sweet or red onion.

Kilocalories 328 Kc • Protein 6 Gm • Fat 19 Gm • Percent of calories from fat 51% • Cholesterol 0 mg • Dietary Fiber 3 Gm • Sodium 130 mg • Calcium 37 mg

Carrots to Count On

———————————— ■ ————————————

Carrots can be counted on to brighten up the produce counter all year long, offering a bountiful supply of beta-carotene, cheerfully evident in this vegetable's bright orange color. Carrots may be the most common of vegetables, but they are uncommonly nutritious—fairly bursting with antioxidant power to avert diseases and the signs of aging.

Although rarely paired with pasta, carrots have a special sweetness that combines well with the tomato's acidic bite or the strong flavors of many greens in a vegetable sauce. In addition, the lycopene in tomatoes enhances the absorption of carrots' beta-carotene.

Fresh carrots taste best when purchased in unpackaged bunches sporting fresh green tops, not disguised in orange plastic bags. If packaged carrots are the only ones available, however, peer through the plastic to be sure that the tops are not moldy or sprouting leaves and the tips are not sprouting threads of roots. This useful vegetable will keep for weeks in the refrigerator in perforated plastic bags, so you can buy several pounds when you find carrots of good quality.

Ginger-scented Carrot Soup with Elbows

■

6 SERVINGS

2 tablespoons butter
$^1/_4$ cup chopped shallots
2 slices fresh ginger, peeled
  and minced (about
  1 tablespoon)
1 pound carrots, sliced
6 cups vegetable or chicken
  stock, or canned broth
2 tablespoons tomato paste

$^1/_4$ cup superfine flour, such as
  Wondra
$^1/_4$ teaspoon salt
$^1/_8$ teaspoon white pepper
2 cups whole milk
1 cup small elbows
Snipped chives for garnishing
  (optional)

Melt the butter in a large pot and sauté the shallots and ginger until soft and fragrant, about 3 minutes. Add the carrots, stock, and tomato paste, and bring to a boil. Reduce the heat, cover, and simmer the soup until the carrots are tender, about 10 minutes.

Remove the carrots with a slotted spoon and purée them in a food processor or blender, adding about 1 cup of the soup liquid. Return them to the pot. Whisk the flour and seasonings into the milk and add the mixture all at once to the simmering soup. Cook, stirring, until bubbling, then continue cooking for 3 minutes.

Meanwhile, cook the elbows according to package directions and drain. Stir them into the soup. If desired, garnish each portion with chives.

Kilocalories 245 Kc • Protein 8 Gm • Fat 7 Gm • Percent of calories from fat 26% • Cholesterol 22 mg • Dietary Fiber 3 Gm • Sodium 297 mg • Calcium 131 mg

Sliced Carrot Soup with Stellini

■

4 SERVINGS

2 tablespoons olive oil
1 onion, chopped
1 celery stalk, sliced diagonally
2 large carrots, sliced
  diagonally
6 cups chicken or vegetable
  stock, or canned broth

1 tablespoon tomato paste
Pinches of dried rosemary,
  dried sage, and dried thyme
2/3 cup stellini ("little stars";
  tubettini can be substituted)

In a large pot, heat the oil and slowly sauté the onion and celery until soft and fragrant, 5 minutes. Add the carrots, stock, tomato paste, and herbs. Bring to a boil, reduce the heat, and simmer for 5 minutes. Add the stellini and continue cooking until the carrots and pasta are tender, about 3 minutes.

Kilocalories 219 Kc • Protein 11 Gm • Fat 9 Gm • Percent of calories from fat 38% • Cholesterol 0 mg • Dietary Fiber 3 Gm • Sodium 665 mg • Calcium 41 mg

Coriander-scented Carrot Stew with Shells

---

4 SERVINGS

Serve this chunky vegetable stew in bowls, with crusty rye bread and a good cheese on the side.

2 to 3 leeks (1 bunch)
2 tablespoons vegetable oil
1 green bell pepper, seeded and diced
2 celery stalks, sliced
3½ cups vegetable or chicken stock, or canned broth
½ pound peeled baby carrots
¾ pound yellow potatoes, such as Yukon Gold, peeled and cut into 1-inch chunks

1 teaspoon ground coriander
½ teaspoon salt
¼ teaspoon freshly ground black pepper
3 tablespoons flour
½ cup water
4 ounces (¼ pound) medium shells
¼ cup chopped fresh flat-leaf parsley

Trim off and discard the tough green part of the leeks. Cut them in half lengthwise. Soak and rinse well under cold running water to remove all grit. Cut them into halves again lengthwise, and into ½-inch slices crosswise. Shake them dry in a towel.

Heat the oil in a large pot and slowly sauté the leeks, green pepper, and celery until lightly browned, 10 minutes. Add the stock, carrots, potatoes, and seasonings, and simmer the soup until the vegetables are quite tender, 15 minutes. Combine the flour and water in a jar and shake until blended. Pour the flour mixture into the simmering stew and stir constantly until bubbling. Simmer 5 more minutes.

Meanwhile, cook the pasta according to package directions and drain. Stir the shells and parsley into the soup.

Kilocalories 303 Kc • Protein 7 Gm • Fat 8 Gm • Percent of calories from fat 22% • Cholesterol 0 mg • Dietary Fiber 6 Gm • Sodium 436 mg • Calcium 79 mg

Carrots Alfredo with Spinach Fettuccine

---

4 SERVINGS

A low-fat alternative to traditional Alfredo sauce.

4 carrots, sliced
1 tablespoon butter
1 large shallot, minced
2 tablespoons superfine flour, such as Wondra
2 tablespoons nonfat dry milk
1/4 teaspoon salt
1/8 teaspoon white pepper

1 1/2 cups whole milk
2 tablespoons light cream cheese (Neufchâtel)
2 tablespoons grated Parmesan cheese
8 ounces (1/2 pound) spinach fettuccine

Put the carrots in a medium-size saucepan with water to cover. Boil them until tender, 8 to 10 minutes. Drain.

Heat the butter in a large skillet and sauté the shallot until softened and fragrant, about 2 minutes. Whisk the flour, dry milk, salt, and pepper into the liquid milk and pour it into the skillet. Cook over medium-high heat, stirring constantly, until thickened and bubbling. Combine the sauce with the cream cheese and Parmesan cheese in a food processor or blender, and blend until smooth, taking care since hot foods tend to bubble up. Pour the sauce back into the skillet and add the carrots. Reheat when ready to serve.

Meanwhile, cook the fettuccine according to package directions; drain. Spoon the pasta into a large serving dish and top with the sauce.

Kilocalories 367 Kc • Protein 14 Gm • Fat 10 Gm • Percent of calories from fat 25% • Cholesterol 79 mg • Dietary Fiber 6 Gm • Sodium 353 mg • Calcium 208 mg

Stir-fry Carrots and Snow Peas with Chinese Noodles

For a more substantial dish, add 1 cup of any kind of cooked meat, slivered, during the last minute of stir-frying. You can substitute sugar snap peas for snow peas, but you'll need to remove the strings as well as the stems.

1 tablespoon vegetable oil
1 teaspoon sesame oil
2 carrots, cut diagonally into
    very thin slices
1 bunch scallions, cut into
    2-inch pieces
About 1 1/2 cups fresh snow
    peas, stem tips removed
1 tablespoon naturally brewed
    soy sauce

4 ounces (1/4 pound) fresh or
    dried Chinese noodles or
    American thin linguine
1/4 cup hot chicken stock or
    canned broth
1 tablespoon lightly toasted
    sesame seeds (see Note)

Heat the vegetable and sesame oils in a large wok or skillet and stir-fry the vegetables until tender-crisp, 3 to 5 minutes. Season with the soy sauce.

Cook the Chinese noodles according to package directions and drain. Spoon them into a serving dish and toss with the hot stock. Top with the stir-fried vegetables. Sprinkle with the sesame seeds. Pass more soy sauce at the table.

NOTE: Toast sesame seeds (without oil) in a small skillet over low heat, stirring constantly. As soon as they are golden, remove them from the heat.

Kilocalories 399 Kc • Protein 13 Gm • Fat 12 Gm • Percent of calories from fat 26% • Cholesterol 0 mg • Dietary Fiber 7 Gm • Sodium 882 mg • Calcium 129 mg

Baby Carrots with Rigatoni

The intense flavor of fresh parsley is brought out when you use quite a lot of it, not just the usual sprinkle.

2 tablespoons olive oil
2 leeks, white part only, well
  washed, chopped small
1 green bell pepper, seeded
  and diced small
1 pound peeled baby carrots

1 cup chicken stock or
  canned broth
8 ounces (1/2 pound) rigatoni
1/4 cup chopped fresh flat-leaf
  parsley

In a large saucepan, heat the oil and very slowly sauté the leeks with the green pepper, 5 to 7 minutes. Add the carrots and stock, bring to a boil, reduce the heat, and simmer, covered, until the carrots are tender, 10 minutes.

Meanwhile, cook the rigatoni according to package directions; drain. Toss together the rigatoni, carrots, pan juices, and parsley in a large serving dish.

Kilocalories 380 Kc • Protein 11 Gm • Fat 8 Gm • Percent of calories from fat 20% • Cholesterol 0 mg • Dietary Fiber 6 Gm • Sodium 186 mg • Calcium 86 mg

Baby Carrots with Scallions and Spinach Fusilli

---

4 SERVINGS

1 pound peeled baby carrots
1 cup chicken stock or
  canned broth
4 scallions with green tops,
  chopped

8 ounces (¹/₂ pound) spinach
  fusilli or regular rotelle
1 cup shredded mozzarella
  cheese

Combine the carrots and stock in a saucepan and bring to a boil. Reduce the heat and simmer, covered, until the carrots are tender, about 10 minutes. Remove from the heat and stir in the scallions.

Meanwhile, cook the fusilli according to package directions; drain. In a large serving dish, toss the carrots with the fusilli. Stir in the mozzarella and serve.

Kilocalories 347 Kc • Protein 18 Gm • Fat 7 Gm • Percent of calories from fat 20% • Cholesterol 70 mg • Dietary Fiber 7 Gm • Sodium 340 mg • Calcium 249 mg

Creamed Carrots with Cilantro and Farfalle

4 SERVINGS

1 tablespoon butter
1 tablespoon olive oil
2 shallots, chopped
2 cups carrots, sliced
    diagonally into ¹/₂-inch pieces
    (about 2 large carrots)
³/₄ cup chicken stock or
    canned broth
2 tablespoons superfine flour,
    such as Wondra

¹/₄ teaspoon salt
¹/₈ teaspoon white pepper
1 cup whole milk
3 tablespoons chopped fresh
    cilantro, or 1 teaspoon dried
2 cups (about ¹/₃ pound)
    farfalle (egg bows)

Heat the butter and oil in a large saucepan and sauté the shallots until they are softened, 3 minutes. Add the carrots and stock. Bring to a boil, reduce heat, and simmer, with the cover ajar, until the carrots are tender, 8 to 10 minutes.

Whisk the flour, salt, and pepper into the milk and pour the mixture into the simmering carrots. Stir constantly until the sauce bubbles and thickens. Simmer 3 minutes, stirring occasionally. Remove from the heat and stir in the cilantro.

Meanwhile, cook the farfalle according to package directions and drain. Combine the carrots, sauce, and pasta in a serving dish and stir to blend.

Kilocalories 287 Kc • Protein 9 Gm • Fat 11 Gm • Percent of calories from fat 34% • Cholesterol 60 mg • Dietary Fiber 2 Gm • Sodium 313 mg • Calcium 95 mg

Creamed Carrots and Peas with Shells

4 SERVINGS

Follow the preceding recipe, reducing the carrots to 1¹/₂ cups. When the carrots are tender, stir in 1 cup frozen peas and continue as directed. (The heat from the sauce will cook them.)

Substitute parsley and a pinch of dried mint for the cilantro. Substitute medium shells for the farfalle.

Kilocalories 306 Kc • Protein 11 Gm • Fat 10 Gm • Percent of calories from fat 28% • Cholesterol 16 mg • Dietary Fiber 5 Gm • Sodium 306 mg • Calcium 109 mg

Orzo Pilaf with Carrots, Raisins, and Ginger

■

4 SERVINGS

2 tablespoons olive oil

2 tablespoons minced shallots

8 ounces ($1/2$ pound) orzo

2 large cooked carrots (see
  Note), coarsely chopped
  (about $1^1/2$ cups)

$1/2$ cup golden raisins

1 tablespoon chopped
  crystalized ginger, or
  $1/2$ teaspoon ground ginger

$1/4$ teaspoon salt

$1/8$ teaspoon white pepper

$1/2$ cup chicken stock or
  canned broth

Nonfat plain yogurt as an
  accompaniment

Preheat the oven to 350 degrees F. Combine the oil and shallots in a 2-quart casserole and put it into the heating oven until the shallots are sizzling, 2 to 3 minutes. Remove the casserole.

Meanwhile, cook the orzo al dente according to package directions, drain, and mix into the shallots and oil. Stir in the carrots, raisins, and seasonings. Pour the chicken stock over all. Bake the casserole, covered, for 20 to 25 minutes. Fluff the orzo with a fork. Serve with yogurt as a topping.

NOTE: Boil the carrots in salted water until tender, 7 to 10 minutes.

Kilocalories 362 Kc • Protein 9 Gm • Fat 8 Gm • Percent of calories from fat 20% • Cholesterol 0 mg • Dietary Fiber 5 Gm • Sodium 220 mg • Calcium 31 mg

Carrots and Escarole with Spaghetti

---

4 SERVINGS

1 bunch escarole (¹/₂ to
  ³/₄ pound)
2 tablespoons olive oil
2 garlic cloves, chopped
3 large carrots, coarsely
  chopped
³/₄ cup chicken stock or
  canned broth

Salt and freshly ground black
  pepper
Hot red pepper flakes
8 ounces (¹/₂ pound) spaghetti
Freshly grated Parmesan
  cheese

Carefully wash the escarole and cut the leaves into thirds.

Heat the oil in a 12-inch skillet and sauté the garlic until softened, 3 minutes. Add the escarole, carrots, and stock. Bring to a boil, reduce the heat, and simmer, covered, until the vegetables are tender, 10 minutes. Add salt, black pepper, and red pepper flakes to your taste.

Meanwhile, cook the spaghetti according to package directions and drain. Spoon it into a large serving dish and toss with the vegetables. Serve in pasta bowls. Pass the grated cheese at the table.

Kilocalories 312 Kc • Protein 10 Gm • Fat 8 Gm • Percent of calories from fat 23% • Cholesterol 0 mg • Dietary Fiber 5 Gm • Sodium 116 mg • Calcium 59 mg

Carrots and Green Beans with Mustard-Shallot Sauce and Egg Noodles

———■———

4 SERVINGS

3 carrots, cut into $1/2$-inch slices diagonally
$1/2$ pound fresh green beans, cut into 1-inch pieces diagonally
$1/4$ cup chopped shallots

$1^1/2$ cups chicken stock or canned broth
1 tablespoon cornstarch
1 tablespoon Dijon mustard
8 ounces ($1/2$ pound) medium egg noodles

Combine the carrots, green beans, shallots, and 1 cup of the stock in a saucepan and bring to a boil. Reduce the heat and simmer, covered, until the vegetables are tender, 8 to 10 minutes. Whisk together the remaining $1/2$ cup of stock, cornstarch, and mustard until blended, and pour all at once into the simmering vegetables. Cook, stirring constantly, until the mixture is bubbling and thickened. Simmer 3 minutes.

Meanwhile, cook the egg noodles according to package directions and drain. Spoon them into a large serving dish and top with the vegetable mixture.

Kilocalories 287 Kc • Protein 12 Gm • Fat 3 Gm • Percent of calories from fat 11% • Cholesterol 54 mg • Dietary Fiber 5 Gm • Sodium 214 mg • Calcium 67 mg

Carrot-Tomato Casserole with Mezzani

4 SERVINGS

1 tablespoon olive oil
1 tablespoon butter
1 large onion, chopped
1 16-ounce can Italian plum
  tomatoes with juice
3 medium carrots, coarsely
  chopped
$1/2$ teaspoon dried oregano
$1/2$ teaspoon dried thyme

$1/2$ teaspoon salt
$1/4$ teaspoon freshly ground
  pepper
Pinch of ground cloves
2 tablespoons chopped fresh
  flat-leaf parsley
8 ounces ($1/2$ pound) mezzani
1 cup feta cheese, diced

Heat the oil and butter in a large skillet and gently sauté the onion and carrots until soft and fragrant. Add the tomatoes, dried herbs, salt, pepper, and cloves. Simmer, stirring often and breaking up the tomatoes, until the carrots are tender and the tomatoes have reached a sauce consistency, 10 to 15 minutes. Stir in the parsley.

Preheat the oven to 350 degrees F.

Cook the mezzani according to package directions, undercooking it slightly, and drain. Combine with the carrot-tomato sauce and the feta cheese in a 2-quart gratin dish or casserole. Bake for 25 to 30 minutes.

Kilocalories 507 Kc • Protein 18 Gm • Fat 21 Gm • Percent of calories from fat 37% • Cholesterol 65 mg • Dietary Fiber 6 Gm • Sodium 1305 mg • Calcium 393 mg

Noodle Kugel with Carrots and Apricots

---

6 SERVINGS

This traditional Jewish sweet noodle dish can be served as an entrée accompaniment or as a dessert.

3 tablespoons vegetable oil	¹/₄ teaspoon ground nutmeg
8 ounces (¹/₂ pound) broad egg noodles, flat, not curly	¹/₈ teaspoon salt
3 eggs	1 cup grated carrots
¹/₂ cup apple juice	¹/₂ cup slivered dried apricots
¹/₄ cup brown sugar	2 tablespoons dry unflavored bread crumbs

Preheat the oven to 375 degrees F and brush a 2-quart casserole with some of the oil.

Cook the noodles according to package directions. While they are cooking, beat together the eggs, apple juice, brown sugar, nutmeg, and salt. Drain the noodles and mix them with the egg mixture, remaining oil, carrots, and apricots. Spoon the mixture into the prepared casserole. Sprinkle with the bread crumbs and bake for 30 to 40 minutes or until browned and set. If the top becomes too brown before the casserole has set, cover it loosely with aluminum foil. Let rest 10 minutes before serving.

Kilocalories 313 Kc • Protein 9 Gm • Fat 10 Gm • Percent of calories from fat 29% • Cholesterol 158 mg • Dietary Fiber 3 Gm • Sodium 180 mg • Calcium 49 mg

Carrot and Couscous Salad with a Moroccan Flavor

6 SERVINGS

1 cup couscous (raw)
1 pound carrots, julienned
1/3 cup extra-virgin olive oil
1/4 cup fresh lemon juice
2 garlic cloves, pressed in a garlic press
2 tablespoons minced fresh flat-leaf parsley
1 tablespoon chopped fresh mint, or 1/2 teaspoon dried

1/4 teaspoon hot pepper sauce, such as Tabasco
1/2 teaspoon salt
1/4 teaspoon freshly ground black pepper
1/4 teaspoon ground cumin
1/4 teaspoon ground coriander
1/8 teaspoon ground cinnamon

Prepare the couscous (see page 12 for basic recipe or follow package directions); fluff and separate the grains. There should be no lumps in the couscous.

Put the carrots in a saucepan with water to cover and boil until tender, 5 to 8 minutes. Drain and cool.

Mix together the oil, lemon juice, garlic, parsley, mint, hot pepper sauce, salt, pepper, cumin, coriander, and cinnamon. In a salad dish, combine the couscous, carrots, and dressing; toss well. Marinate at room temperature for a half hour or so. Taste to correct seasonings; you may want more oil, lemon juice, hot pepper sauce, salt, or pepper. Refrigerate leftovers.

Kilocalories 243 Kc • Protein 4 Gm • Fat 12 Gm • Percent of calories from fat 43% • Cholesterol 0 mg • Dietary Fiber 5 Gm • Sodium 228 mg • Calcium 29 mg

Cauliflower,
a Dense Bouquet of Flavor

Cauliflower's white buds nestled in green leaves look like a bouquet, and its name does indeed mean "flower of the cabbage." Like broccoli, cauliflower is a cancer-fighting cruciferous vegetable rich in the protective chemical sulforaphane. One cup of cauliflower provides 100 percent of the RDA for the antioxidant vitamin C. Cauliflower is also a good source of folate, a vitamin that helps prevent birth defects.

Shop for a head of cauliflower that's creamy white with no brown discoloration or black speckles. The leaves surrounding a cauliflower are a clue to its freshness; they should be crisp and green, not wilted and yellow. Cauliflower keeps well for two to three days, stored in a perforated plastic vegetable bag in the refrigerator.

A bay leaf added to the pot seems to diminish the pungent aroma of cooking cauliflower and also adds a pleasing taste. For a sweet, fresh flavor, don't overcook this nutritious vegetable, especially if it will be subject to additional cooking in a casserole or skillet dish.

Broccoflower, a cross between cauliflower and broccoli with a purple-green head, can be substituted for regular cauliflower in most recipes.

Curried Cauliflower Soup with Orzo

— ■ —

6 SERVINGS

1 medium head cauliflower
  (1 to 1½ pounds)
6 cups water
1 teaspoon salt
2 tablespoons butter
1 garlic clove, minced
3 tablespoons superfine flour,
  such as Wondra

3 tablespoons nonfat dry milk
2 teaspoons curry powder
½ teaspoon cumin
2 cups whole milk
1 cup orzo

Trim the cauliflower and break it into florets; cut any extralarge florets in half. Bring the water to a boil in a large pot, add the cauliflower and salt, and cook until the vegetable is tender enough to purée, 4 to 5 minutes. Drain in a colander, catching and reserving the cooking liquid in a bowl.

Reserve 2 cups of the cooked florets. In a food processor, purée the remaining cauliflower with 1 cup of the reserved cooking liquid. In the pot used for cooking the cauliflower, melt the butter and sauté the garlic until it is fragrant. Add the puréed cauliflower and the remaining cooking liquid, and bring to a simmer. Whisk the flour, dry milk, curry powder, and cumin into the liquid milk. Add it all at once to the simmering soup and stir constantly until it bubbles and thickens. Add the reserved florets. Cook 3 minutes, stirring occasionally.

Meanwhile, cook the orzo according to package directions and drain. Stir it into the soup.

Kilocalories 258 Kc • Protein 10 Gm • Fat 8 Gm • Percent of calories from fat 26% • Cholesterol 22 mg • Dietary Fiber 4 Gm • Sodium 503 mg • Calcium 136 mg

Cauliflower Soup with Ditali

8 SERVINGS

Sautéing the vegetables before boiling makes this soup especially flavorful.

1 medium head cauliflower
   (1 to 1½ pounds)
2 tablespoons olive oil
1 large leek, chopped (white
   part only)
1 carrot, chopped small
1 cup finely chopped celery
1 bay leaf
2 tablespoons water
8 cups chicken stock or
   canned broth

¼ cup all-purpose flour
½ teaspoon salt
⅛ teaspoon pepper
2 tablespoons snipped fresh
   chives
2 tablespoons chopped fresh
   flat-leaf parsley
4 ounces (¼ pound) ditali

Trim the cauliflower and break it into florets; cut any extralarge florets in half.

Heat the oil in a large pot and sauté the leek, carrot, and celery for 3 minutes. Add the cauliflower, bay leaf, and water. Cover and continue braising over very low heat until tender, stirring often to prevent sticking, about 12 minutes.

Reserve 1 cup stock and add the rest to the vegetables. Bring the soup to a simmer. Combine the flour, salt, pepper, and reserved cup of stock in a jar, cover, and shake until blended. Add all at once to the simmering soup. Stir constantly until the soup bubbles and thickens slightly. Reduce the heat and cook 5 minutes, stirring often. Remove the bay leaf. Stir in the chives and parsley.

Meanwhile, cook the ditali according to package directions. Drain and stir into the soup.

Kilocalories 165 Kc • Protein 9 Gm • Fat 5 Gm • Percent of calories from fat 28% • Cholesterol 0 mg • Dietary Fiber 3 Gm • Sodium 609 mg • Calcium 45 mg

Cauliflower with Peanut Sauce and Asian Noodles

1 medium head cauliflower
(1 to 1½ pounds)
2 tablespoons smooth peanut butter
2 tablespoons naturally brewed soy sauce
1 tablespoon rice vinegar
⅔ cup (approximately) vegetable or chicken stock, or canned broth

1 tablespoon vegetable oil
1 bunch scallions, cut diagonally into 1-inch pieces
1 red bell pepper, seeded and cut into small triangles
6 ounces (about ⅓ pound) dried Asian medium noodles or American linguine
½ cup chopped peanuts

Trim the cauliflower and break it into florets; cut any extralarge florets in half.

Whisk together the peanut butter, soy sauce, and rice vinegar until blended. Add 1 to 2 tablespoons stock if the sauce seems too thick.

Heat the oil in a large wok or skillet and stir-fry the scallions and red pepper until tender-crisp, 2 minutes. Remove the vegetables with a slotted spoon. Add the cauliflower and ½ cup stock, cover, and simmer until tender-crisp, 3 minutes. Stir in the sauce and the stir-fried vegetables.

Meanwhile, cook the noodles according to package directions and drain. If no directions are given on the package, boil them in salted water, taste-testing for tenderness. Dried noodles cook in about 10 minutes. Spoon the noodles into a large serving dish and top with the cauliflower mixture. Sprinkle with peanuts. Pass more soy sauce at the table.

Kilocalories 382 Kc • Protein 10 Gm • Fat 17 Gm • Percent of calories from fat 38% • Cholesterol 0 mg • Dietary Fiber 6 Gm • Sodium 813 mg • Calcium 59 mg

Cauliflower with Anchovies and Fusilli

4 SERVINGS

1 medium head cauliflower
(1 to 1½ pounds)
2 tablespoons olive oil
1 garlic clove, pressed in a
garlic press
4 flat anchovy fillets
1 dried hot red chili
1½ cups peeled, chopped fresh
tomatoes (about 2 medium
tomatoes) or canned crushed
Italian tomatoes

1 tablespoon drained capers
2 teaspoons minced fresh
marjoram, or ½ teaspoon
dried oregano
¼ teaspoon freshly ground
black pepper
2 tablespoons chopped fresh
flat-leaf parsley
8 ounces (½ pound) fusilli (or
rotelle)

Trim leaves and stalk from the cauliflower and separate into florets. Cook in boiling salted water until tender-crisp, about 3 minutes; drain and rinse with cold water.

Heat the olive oil in a large skillet and sauté the garlic, anchovy, and chili over very low heat, stirring occasionally, until the anchovy has dissolved into the oil. (If the heat is too high, the anchovy will crisp instead of softening, in which case you will have to chop it into small pieces.)

Add the tomatoes, capers, marjoram or oregano, and black pepper. Simmer, uncovered, stirring occasionally, for 10 minutes. Remove the chili pod and discard. Add the cauliflower and heat through. Stir the parsley into the sauce.

Meanwhile, cook the fusilli according to package directions. Drain and spoon into a large serving dish. Toss with the cauliflower.

Kilocalories 325 Kc • Protein 11 Gm • Fat 9 Gm • Percent of calories from fat 23% • Cholesterol 3 mg • Dietary Fiber 5 Gm • Sodium 329 mg • Calcium 55 mg

Golden Saffron Cauliflower with Pine Nuts and Gemelli

---

4 SERVINGS

Even though saffron seems expensive, you need to buy only a quarter ounce at a time. Just a pinch or two will season a dish with its subtly exotic flavor.

2 pinches saffron
½ cup warm chicken stock or canned broth
1 medium head cauliflower (1 to 1½ pounds)
1 tablespoon olive oil
1 garlic clove, finely minced

¼ cup pine nuts
8 ounces (½ pound) gemelli
¼ cup freshly grated Romano cheese
Several sprigs fresh flat-leaf parsley, chopped

Add the saffron to the warm stock and let it soften for at least 20 minutes.

Trim leaves and stalk from the cauliflower, and separate it into florets. Cook in boiling salted water until tender, about 3 minutes; drain, reserving the cooking water. Cut the florets in half. In a large skillet, heat the oil and sauté the garlic with the pine nuts, until the nuts are golden but not browned. Add the cauliflower and saffron-stock mixture. Stir to coat the florets with the golden broth.

Meanwhile, cook the gemelli according to package directions in the reserved water. Drain the pasta, spoon it into a large serving dish, and toss with the cauliflower. Add the cheese and parsley.

Kilocalories 353 Kc • Protein 15 Gm • Fat 12 Gm • Percent of calories from fat 29% • Cholesterol 7 mg • Dietary Fiber 5 Gm • Sodium 177 mg • Calcium 116 mg

Cauliflower au Gratin with Tomatoes and Elbows

4 SERVINGS

This is a real family pleaser, even for those who are less than wild about cauliflower.

1 small head cauliflower (about 1 pound)
1/2 cup milk (whole or low-fat)
2 tablespoons superfine flour, such as Wondra
1 cup tomato sauce (from a jar or see Light Tomato Sauce, page 317)

1 cup small elbows
1 cup coarsely grated provolone cheese
1 cup fresh bread crumbs, made in a food processor from 1 slice Italian bread

Trim the leaves and stalk from the cauliflower and separate into florets. Cook in boiling salted water until tender, about 3 minutes; drain. Cut the florets in half.

Combine the milk and flour in a saucepan and bring the mixture to a boil, stirring constantly until bubbling. The sauce will be quite thick. Whisk in the tomato sauce over medium heat until the mixture is smooth, 3 minutes.

Preheat the oven to 350 degrees F. Cook the elbows according to package directions, undercooking it slightly, and drain. In a 2-quart gratin pan, combine the elbows, cauliflower, and sauce. Stir in 3/4 cup of the cheese. Top with bread crumbs and the remaining 1/4 cup cheese. Bake the casserole, uncovered, on the middle shelf for 30 minutes.

Kilocalories 296 Kc • Protein 16 Gm • Fat 10 Gm • Percent of calories from fat 28% • Cholesterol 24 mg • Dietary Fiber 5 Gm • Sodium 563 mg • Calcium 296 mg

Curried Cauliflower with Egg Noodles

4 SERVINGS

1 medium head cauliflower (1 to 1½ pounds)
2¼ cups milk (whole or low-fat)
¼ cup nonfat dry milk

¼ cup superfine flour, such as Wondra
2 teaspoons curry powder
8 ounces (½ pound) fine egg noodles

Trim the leaves and stalk from the cauliflower, and separate into florets. Cook in boiling salted water until tender, about 3 minutes; drain. Cut the florets in thirds, or quarters if they are large.

In a medium-size saucepan, blend the liquid milk, dry milk, flour, and curry powder. Cook over medium heat, stirring constantly, until thick and bubbling.

Preheat the oven to 350 degrees F. Cook the egg noodles according to package directions (undercook slightly). Drain and combine with the cauliflower in a 2-quart gratin dish or casserole. Pour the sauce over all. Bake for 30 minutes or until bubbling throughout.

Kilocalories 364 Kc • Protein 16 Gm • Fat 7 Gm • Percent of calories from fat 18% • Cholesterol 73 mg • Dietary Fiber 5 Gm • Sodium 122 mg • Calcium 231 mg

Cauliflower with Toasted Crumbs and Spinach Penne

4 SERVINGS

1 medium head cauliflower
(1 to 1½ pounds)
3 tablespoons olive oil
1 garlic clove, minced
1½ cups fresh bread crumbs,
made in a food processor
from about 1½ slices Italian
bread

2 tablespoons grated Parmesan
cheese
Salt and freshly ground black
pepper
8 ounces (½ pound) spinach
penne or regular penne

Trim the leaves and stalk from the cauliflower, and separate into florets. Cook in boiling salted water until tender, about 3 minutes. Drain, reserving ¼ cup of the water. Keep the vegetable warm in the same pan over very low heat.

Heat the oil in a large skillet and sauté the garlic until it's softened and fragrant, about 2 minutes. Add the bread crumbs and stir-fry until they are golden. Remove from the heat and add the cheese. Season with salt and pepper to your taste.

Meanwhile, cook the penne according to package directions; drain. Spoon the pasta into a large serving dish and toss with the cauliflower and reserved cooking water. Add the toasted crumbs, toss again, and serve immediately.

Kilocalories 235 Kc • Protein 7 Gm • Fat 12 Gm • Percent of calories from fat 46% • Cholesterol 21 mg • Dietary Fiber 5 Gm • Sodium 153 mg • Calcium 80 mg

CAULIFLOWER, A DENSE BOUQUET OF FLAVOR

Dutch-Treat Cauliflower with Egg Noodles

4 SERVINGS

1 medium head cauliflower
(1 to 1½ pounds)
3 tablespoons butter
3 tablespoons all-purpose flour
2 cups heated low-fat milk
2 tablespoons snipped fresh
chives
½ teaspoon salt

¼ teaspoon white pepper
1 cup diced Gouda cheese (3 to
4 ounces)
6 ounces (about ⅓ pound)
broad egg noodles
2 tablespoons dry bread or
cracker crumbs

Trim the leaves and stalk from the cauliflower and separate into florets. Cook in boiling salted water until tender, about 3 minutes. Drain, reserving ½ cup of the water.

Melt the butter in a saucepan and stir in the flour. Cook the roux for 3 minutes, stirring often; do not brown it. Pour in the hot milk all at once and cook over medium-high heat, stirring constantly, until bubbling and thickened. Simmer over low heat for 5 minutes. Whisk in the reserved cooking water, chives, salt, and pepper. Remove from the heat and stir in the cheese.

Preheat the oven to 350 degrees F. Cook the egg noodles according to package directions and drain. Combine the cauliflower, sauce, and egg noodles in a 2-quart gratin dish or casserole. Sprinkle with the crumbs and bake until bubbling throughout and golden on top, 30 minutes.

Kilocalories 589 Kc • Protein 29 Gm • Fat 31 Gm • Percent of calories from fat 46% • Cholesterol 145 mg • Dietary Fiber 4 Gm • Sodium 1029 mg • Calcium 638 mg

Cavolfiore al Pomodoro
(Italian-style Broccoflower with Tomatoes and Ziti)

4 SERVINGS

If this basic dish were prepared in the Sicilian manner (with a strong North African influence), it would include capers, raisins, and pine nuts—along with more pepper. Broccoli or cauliflower may be substituted.

1 medium head broccoflower (1 to 1½ pounds)
2 tablespoons olive oil
1 garlic clove, minced
1 onion, chopped
1½ cups peeled, chopped fresh or canned Italian plum tomatoes
½ cup pitted black olives
½ teaspoon salt

¼ teaspoon freshly ground black pepper
Tomato juice, broth, or water, if needed
2 tablespoons minced fresh flat-leaf parsley
8 ounces (½ pound) ziti
¼ cup freshly grated Romano cheese

Trim the broccoflower and break it into florets; they will have slightly longer stems than cauliflower. Cut any extralarge florets in half lengthwise through the stem. Cook the broccoflower in boiling salted water until tender-crisp, about 4 minutes; drain.

Heat the oil in a large skillet and sauté the garlic and onion until they are softened but not brown. Add the tomatoes, olives, salt, and pepper. Simmer 10 minutes, uncovered, stirring often. If the sauce gets too dry, add a little tomato juice, broth, or water.

Add the broccoflower and parsley; stir and simmer 2 minutes. Remove from the heat.

Meanwhile, cook the ziti according to package directions and drain. Spoon the pasta into a large serving dish and toss with the broccoflower mixture and the cheese. Pass more cheese at the table.

Kilocalories 381 Kc • Protein 14 Gm • Fat 12 Gm • Percent of calories from fat 27% • Cholesterol 7 mg • Dietary Fiber 7 Gm • Sodium 504 mg • Calcium 138 mg

CAULIFLOWER, A DENSE BOUQUET OF FLAVOR

Broccoflower and Bell Pepper Salad with Penne

4 SERVINGS

Serving a Mediterranean salad at room temperature seems to bring out the rich flavor of the cooked vegetables.

1 medium head broccoflower (1 to 1½ pounds)
3 tablespoons olive oil
1 large red bell pepper, seeded and cut into strips
1 garlic clove, minced
¼ cup minced red onion

2 tablespoons red wine vinegar
1 tablespoon minced fresh flat-leaf parsley
¼ teaspoon salt
⅛ teaspoon pepper
6 ounces (about ⅓ pound) penne

Trim the broccoflower and break it into florets; they will have slightly longer stems than cauliflower. Cut any extralarge florets in half lengthwise through the stem. Cook the broccoflower in boiling salted water until tender-crisp, about 3 minutes; drain and rinse in cold water.

Heat the oil in a large skillet and sauté the red pepper until lightly brown and tender. Add the garlic during the last minute. Combine the broccoflower, red pepper, onion, vinegar, parsley, salt, and pepper in a large serving dish.

Cook the penne according to package directions and drain. Rinse in cold water and stir into the salad. Serve the salad at room temperature.

Kilocalories 293 Kc • Protein 9 Gm • Fat 11 Gm • Percent of calories from fat 33% • Cholesterol 0 mg • Dietary Fiber 5 Gm • Sodium 176 mg • Calcium 51 mg

Cauliflower and Shrimp Salad with Shells

6 SERVINGS

1 medium head cauliflower
  (1 to 1$\frac{1}{2}$ pounds)
$\frac{1}{2}$ cup plain nonfat yogurt
$\frac{1}{4}$ cup mayonnaise
3 tablespoons chili sauce
Hot pepper sauce, such as
  Tabasco, to taste
$\frac{1}{2}$ cup sliced stuffed green
  olives

$\frac{1}{3}$ cup chopped scallions with
  green tops
6 ounces (about $\frac{1}{3}$ pound)
  medium shells
2 cups cooked, shelled,
  deveined shrimp (see page 14
  for basic recipe)

Trim the cauliflower and break it into florets; cut any extralarge florets in half. Cook the cauliflower in boiling salted water until tender-crisp, about 3 minutes. Drain; rinse with cold water.

Whisk together the yogurt, mayonnaise, chili sauce, and hot pepper sauce to your taste. Stir in the olives and scallions.

Meanwhile, cook the shells according to package directions; drain and rinse with cold water.

Combine the cauliflower, shrimp, shells, and dressing in a large salad bowl. Toss gently to blend. Chill until ready to serve.

Kilocalories 269 Kc • Protein 15 Gm • Fat 10 Gm • Percent of calories from fat 34% • Cholesterol 90 mg • Dietary Fiber 3 Gm • Sodium 373 mg • Calcium 78 mg

CAULIFLOWER, A DENSE BOUQUET OF FLAVOR

Simple Celery
and Exotic Fennel

Big on flavor and fiber but low in fat and calories, celery and fennel make refreshing snacks as well as versatile ingredients. Although similar in crunchiness, they are different in taste: Fennel has the flavor of licorice or anise, which is why this bulbous vegetable is sometimes called anise. Anise, however, is an herb, a different plant entirely.

Ancient Asian healers used celery to control high blood pressure, and modern science has confirmed that it contains a chemical compound that reduces blood pressure by relaxing the smooth muscle lining of the blood vessels, allowing blood to flow more freely. Fennel is especially high in the antioxidant vitamins A and C.

Celery is available all year, but fennel is more commonly seen in the fall and winter months. Look for crisp vegetables with fresh-looking leaves and no rust at the core. Pale celery is less stringy than very green celery. The feathery leaves of fennel may be dried to use as an herb.

To store celery, cut and wash it, and wrap in a kitchen towel covered with a plastic bag. It will keep this way in the refrigerator for up to a week. Fennel turns brown easily, so it's best to wash and cut it just before cooking; for a salad, immediately toss it with oil or a vinaigrette after cutting.

Cream of Celery Soup with Orecchiette

4 SERVINGS

2 tablespoons butter
3 cups chopped celery
1 yellow onion, chopped
2½ cups chicken or vegetable stock, or canned broth
3 cups low-fat milk
¼ cup nonfat dry milk

2 tablespoons superfine flour, such as Wondra
½ teaspoon salt
¼ teaspoon white pepper
1 cup orecchiette
¼ cup chopped celery leaves

In a large pot, melt the butter and sauté the celery and onion until lightly colored. Add the stock and simmer until the vegetables are very tender, 15 minutes. Purée the soup in a food processor and return it to the pot. Add 2 cups of the liquid milk and heat, but do not boil.

Whisk the dry milk, flour, salt, and pepper into the remaining cup of liquid milk and pour the mixture all at once into the soup. Cook over medium heat, stirring, until the mixture bubbles and thickens slightly. Reduce the heat to very low and simmer the soup for 5 minutes.

Meanwhile, cook the orecchiette according to package directions and drain. Stir the pasta and celery leaves into the soup. Taste to correct the seasonings, adding more salt if needed.

Kilocalories 315 Kc • Protein 15 Gm • Fat 11 Gm • Percent of calories from fat 32% • Cholesterol 30 mg • Dietary Fiber 3 Gm • Sodium 806 mg • Calcium 302 mg

Fennel and Porcini Soup with Egg Noodles

6 SERVINGS

$^1/_2$ cup dried porcini
  mushrooms
$1^1/_4$ cups very hot water
2 tablespoons olive oil
1 fennel bulb (about 1 pound),
  cored and chopped into
  1-inch pieces
4 ounces fresh white or brown
  mushrooms, cleaned and
  sliced
1 yellow onion, chopped

1 garlic clove, minced
1 16-ounce can Italian plum
  tomatoes with juice, chopped
4 cups chicken or vegetable
  stock, or canned broth
$^1/_4$ teaspoon salt
$^1/_8$ teaspoon pepper
4 ounces ($^1/_4$ pound) medium
  egg noodles
2 tablespoons chopped fresh
  flat-leaf parsley

Soak the dried mushrooms in the hot water for 30 minutes. Drain, reserving the liquid. Rinse each mushroom under running water to remove all grit. Drain and chop the reconstituted mushrooms. Put a paper coffee filter into a medium-size strainer and strain the reserved mushroom liquid.

Heat the oil in a large pot and sauté the fennel, fresh mushrooms, and onion until they begin to brown, 5 to 8 minutes. Add the garlic during the last minute.

Add the reconstituted porcini mushrooms, reserved soaking liquid, tomatoes, stock, salt, and pepper, and simmer the soup for 20 to 25 minutes.

Cook the egg noodles according to package directions and drain. Stir the egg noodles and parsley into the soup. Taste to correct seasonings, adding more salt or pepper if desired.

Kilocalories 204 Kc • Protein 9 Gm • Fat 7 Gm • Percent of calories from fat 28% • Cholesterol 18 mg • Dietary Fiber 5 Gm • Sodium 571 mg • Calcium 86 mg

Fennel and Leek Soup with Farfallini

■

4 SERVINGS

3 to 4 leeks (1 bunch)
2 small fennel bulbs (about
  2 pounds)
2 tablespoons olive oil
1 sprig fresh thyme
6 cups chicken or vegetable
  stock, or canned broth

2 tablespoons tomato paste
$^1\!/_2$ teaspoon salt
$^1\!/_4$ teaspoon freshly ground
  pepper
$^3\!/_4$ cup farfallini (tiny egg bows)
2 tablespoons finely minced
  fresh flat-leaf parsley

Trim off and discard the tough green part of the leeks. Cut them in half lengthwise. Soak and rinse well under cold running water to remove all grit. Cut them into quarters lengthwise and into $^1\!/_2$-inch slices crosswise. Shake them dry in a towel. Chop the fennel bulbs into 1-inch pieces.

Heat the oil in a large pot and slowly sauté the leeks and fennel until they just begin to brown, 8 to 10 minutes. Strip the leaves from the thyme sprig and add them while the vegetables are braising.

Add the stock, tomato paste, salt, and pepper, and simmer the soup for 25 to 30 minutes.

Meanwhile, cook the farfallini according to package directions and drain. Stir the pasta and parsley into the soup.

Kilocalories 338 Kc • Protein 15 Gm • Fat 11 Gm • Percent of calories from fat 28% • Cholesterol 25 mg • Dietary Fiber 9 Gm • Sodium 1076 mg • Calcium 195 mg

Braised Celery, Scallions, and Fresh Sage with Penne

4 SERVINGS AS A SIDE DISH

2 tablespoons butter
1 tablespoon olive oil
1 bunch scallions, chopped
3 cups diagonally sliced celery
   with leaves
1/2 cup broth or water
1/4 cup dry vermouth or
   white wine

8 leaves fresh sage, chopped,
   or 1 teaspoon dried leaves
Freshly ground black pepper
Salt
8 ounces (1/2 pound) penne
1/4 cup grated Parmesan cheese

Heat the butter and oil in a large skillet. Sauté the scallions and celery over medium heat, stirring frequently, until they are lightly browned. Add the broth and wine, and continue to cook until the vegetables are tender, about 10 minutes. Stir in the sage and lots of black pepper. Add salt if desired (celery is naturally salty).

Meanwhile, cook the penne al dente according to package directions and drain. Stir the penne into the sauce in the skillet. Stir in the cheese and toss well. Keep warm for a minute or two before serving, to blend the flavors.

Kilocalories 363 Kc • Protein 11 Gm • Fat 12 Gm • Percent of calories from fat 30% • Cholesterol 20 mg • Dietary Fiber 3 Gm • Sodium 293 mg • Calcium 133 mg

Braised Celery and Ham with Penne

2 ENTRÉE SERVINGS

Follow the preceding recipe. Braise 1 cup or more diced ham with the shallots and celery.

Kilocalories 836 Kc • Protein 39 Gm • Fat 28 Gm • Percent of calories from fat 30% • Cholesterol 79 mg • Dietary Fiber 6 Gm • Sodium 1515 mg • Calcium 271 mg

Stir-fried Celery, Baby Zucchini, and Shiitake Mushrooms with Fresh Asian Noodles

Recent studies have indicated that shiitake mushrooms may enhance the immune system.

3 to 4 dried shiitake mushrooms
1 cup very hot water
1 tablespoon vegetable oil
1 teaspoon sesame oil
2 cups diagonally, thinly sliced celery
1/2 pound baby zucchini, thinly sliced
4 scallions, thinly sliced

3/4 cup chicken stock or canned broth
2 tablespoons naturally brewed soy sauce
1 teaspoon oyster sauce
2 teaspoons cornstarch
7 to 8 ounces fresh Asian noodles or fresh American thin linguine

Soak the mushrooms in the hot water for a half hour or so. Drain; remove and discard the stems. Chop the mushrooms.

In a large wok or skillet, heat the oils and stir-fry the celery, zucchini, and scallions until they are tender-crisp, 3 minutes. Add the reconstituted mushrooms.

In a small pitcher or a cup, combine and blend the stock, soy sauce, oyster sauce, and cornstarch. Pour all at once into the wok and cook, stirring, until the sauce is thick and the vegetables are glazed.

Cook the noodles according to package directions and drain. Spoon them into a large serving dish and top with the celery mixture.

Kilocalories 192 Kc • Protein 6 Gm • Fat 6 Gm • Percent of calories from fat 25% • Cholesterol 15 mg • Dietary Fiber 1 Gm • Sodium 759 mg • Calcium 54 mg

Creamy Braised Celery with Dill and Mezzani

---■---

4 SERVINGS

2 tablespoons butter
3 cups sliced celery
$^1/_2$ cup chicken stock or
  canned broth
2 tablespoons chopped
  fresh dill
2 tablespoons nonfat dry milk
$1^1/_2$ tablespoons superfine
  flour, such as Wondra

$^1/_4$ teaspoon salt
Several grinds of pepper
1 cup whole milk
1 tablespoon fresh lemon juice
8 ounces ($^1/_2$ pound) mezzani
Sprigs of fresh dill and carrot
  curls for garnish (optional)

Melt the butter in a large skillet and sauté the celery until slightly softened, 3 minutes. Add the stock, cover, and simmer until the vegetable is tender, 10 minutes. Add the dill.

Blend the dry milk, flour, salt, and pepper into the liquid milk, and pour the mixture into the skillet. Cook, stirring constantly, until the mixture bubbles and thickens. Stir in the lemon juice. Simmer over low heat 5 minutes.

Meanwhile, cook the mezzani according to package directions and drain. Spoon the pasta into a large serving dish and toss with the celery mixture. Garnish with sprigs of dill and carrot curls, if desired.

Kilocalories 334 Kc • Protein 11 Gm • Fat 9 Gm • Percent of calories from fat 25% • Cholesterol 25 mg • Dietary Fiber 3 Gm • Sodium 377 mg • Calcium 133 mg

SIMPLE CELERY AND EXOTIC FENNEL

159

Celery Stew with Elbows

—■—

4 SERVINGS

Serve this as a vegetarian entrée with a crusty rye bread and a wedge of Monterey Jack cheese on the side.

2 tablespoons olive oil
3 cups diagonally sliced celery
2 Anaheim chilies, seeded and diced
1 cup chopped onion
1 garlic clove, minced
4 large fresh tomatoes, chopped
2 tablespoons chopped fresh cilantro, or 1 teaspoon dried

1 teaspoon chili powder
1/2 teaspoon salt
Freshly ground black pepper to taste
1/4 cup broth or water, if needed
1 20-ounce can pinto beans, drained and rinsed
1 cup small elbows

Heat the oil in a large skillet and sauté the celery, chilies, and onion until softened, 5 minutes. Add the garlic during the last minute. Add the tomatoes, cilantro, and seasonings, cover, and simmer until the celery is tender, 10 to 15 minutes. If the tomatoes are not juicy, you may have to add 1/4 cup broth or water.

Add the beans and cook over very low heat to combine the flavors. Meanwhile, cook the elbows according to package directions and drain. Stir them into the stew.

Kilocalories 331 Kc • Protein 12 Gm • Fat 8 Gm • Percent of calories from fat 22% • Cholesterol 0 mg • Dietary Fiber 10 Gm • Sodium 858 mg • Calcium 113 mg

Celery and Peas au Gratin with Orzo

4 SERVINGS

2 tablespoons butter
3 cups chopped celery
$^1/_2$ cup chicken stock or canned broth
1 cup fresh shelled or frozen petit peas, thawed to separate
3 tablespoons nonfat dry milk
$3^1/_2$ tablespoons superfine flour, such as Wondra
$^1/_4$ teaspoon salt
$^1/_8$ teaspoon white pepper
2 cups low-fat milk
1 cup shredded sharp Cheddar cheese
1 cup orzo
2 tablespoons seasoned dry bread crumbs

Melt the butter in a large skillet and sauté the celery until slightly softened, 3 minutes. Add the stock, cover, and simmer until the vegetable is tender, 10 minutes. Add the peas.

Blend the dry milk, flour, salt, and pepper into the liquid milk, and pour the mixture into the skillet. Cook, stirring constantly, until the mixture bubbles and thickens. Simmer over low heat 5 minutes. Remove from the heat and stir in the cheese.

Preheat the oven to 350 degrees F. Cook the orzo according to package directions, undercooking it slightly, and drain. Spoon the orzo into a 2-quart gratin pan or baking dish and combine with the celery mixture. Top with the bread crumbs. Bake the dish until bubbling throughout, 20 to 25 minutes.

Kilocalories 520 Kc • Protein 23 Gm • Fat 19 Gm • Percent of calories from fat 33% • Cholesterol 55 mg • Dietary Fiber 6 Gm • Sodium 716 mg • Calcium 421 mg

SIMPLE CELERY AND EXOTIC FENNEL

161

Braised Celery with Anchovies, Basil, and Spaghettini

---

4 SERVINGS

The combination of lots of fresh basil and anchovies is reminiscent of Thai cuisine, although Thai cooks would use nam pla, *a fish sauce, in place of anchovies.*

2 tablespoons olive oil
3 cups sliced celery with leaves
1 garlic clove, minced
6 anchovy fillets, chopped
1/2 cup chicken stock or
   canned broth

Freshly ground black pepper
1/4 cup fresh basil leaves,
   slivered
12 ounces (3/4 pound)
   spaghettini

Heat the oil in a large skillet and sauté the celery over medium heat, stirring frequently, until yellowed, 5 minutes. Add the garlic and anchovies during the last minute. Don't brown the garlic.

Add the stock and continue to cook, covered, until the celery is tender, about 10 minutes. Season with pepper to your taste and sprinkle with the basil.

Meanwhile, cook the spaghettini according to package directions and drain. In a large serving dish, toss the pasta with the celery mixture.

Kilocalories 408 Kc • Protein 14 Gm • Fat 9 Gm • Percent of calories from fat 20% • Cholesterol 5 mg • Dietary Fiber 4 Gm • Sodium 358 mg • Calcium 72 mg

Braised Fennel, Shallots, and Bell Peppers with Fresh Linguine

4 SERVINGS

3 tablespoons olive oil
¼ cup chopped shallots
2 red bell peppers, seeded and diced
1 fennel bulb (about 1 pound), cored and diced
Salt and freshly ground black pepper

½ cup chicken stock or canned broth
2 tablespoons chopped fresh flat-leaf parsley
12 ounces (¾ pound) fresh linguine
¼ cup freshly grated Romano cheese

Heat the oil in a large skillet and sauté the shallots and red peppers for 3 minutes. Add the fennel, cover, and cook, stirring often, until the vegetables are tender and lightly browned, about 10 minutes. Add salt and pepper to your taste. Stir in the stock and parsley; continue to cook over very low heat for 5 minutes.

Meanwhile, cook the linguine according to package directions and drain. In a large serving dish, toss the linguine with the fennel and cheese.

Kilocalories 487 Kc • Protein 16 Gm • Fat 14 Gm • Percent of calories from fat 26% • Cholesterol 6 mg • Dietary Fiber 6 Gm • Sodium 252 mg • Calcium 176 mg

SIMPLE CELERY AND EXOTIC FENNEL

Braised Fennel-Tomato Sauce with Ziti

◼

4 SERVINGS

2 tablespoons olive oil
1 cup fresh bread crumbs, made in a food processor from 1 slice Italian bread
1 fennel bulb (about 1 pound), cored and chopped into 1-inch pieces
1 garlic clove, minced
1 16-ounce can Italian plum tomatoes, drained and chopped

¼ teaspoon dried oregano
¼ teaspoon salt
Several grindings of black pepper
8 ounces (½ pound) ziti
2 to 3 tablespoons freshly grated Parmesan cheese
1 tablespoon minced fresh flat-leaf parsley

Heat 1 tablespoon of the oil in a large skillet and stir-fry the bread crumbs until they are golden. Remove and reserve them.

Heat the remaining tablespoon of oil and stir-fry the fennel until it begins to turn golden, 5 minutes. Add the garlic and sauté 1 minute longer.

Add the tomatoes, oregano, salt, and pepper, and continue to cook, uncovered, stirring occasionally, until the fennel is tender and the tomato liquid is mostly evaporated, 10 minutes.

Meanwhile, cook the ziti according to package directions, drain, and mix with the fennel in a large serving dish. Sprinkle with the bread crumbs, cheese, and parsley and toss well.

Kilocalories 371 Kc • Protein 11 Gm • Fat 9 Gm • Percent of calories from fat 22% • Cholesterol 2 mg • Dietary Fiber 6 Gm • Sodium 514 mg • Calcium 143 mg

Braised Fennel with Sun-dried Tomatoes and Penne

4 SERVINGS

2 tablespoons olive oil
1 tablespoon oil from sun-dried tomatoes
2 medium fennel bulbs (about 1 1/2 pounds), cored and chopped
1 garlic clove, minced
1/4 cup chicken stock or canned broth
1/3 cup slivered sun-dried tomatoes packed in oil

2 tablespoons chopped fresh flat-leaf parsley
8 ounces (1/2 pound) penne, cooked
1 to 2 tablespoons coarsely chopped fennel leaves (they are feathery, like dill)
Freshly grated Parmesan cheese

Heat the olive oil and tomato oil in a large skillet and sauté the fennel until it's tender and golden-brown, 10 minutes. Add the garlic during the last minute. Add the stock, tomatoes, and parsley, and allow the mixture to marinate while cooking the penne.

Cook the penne according to package directions and drain. Spoon it into a large serving dish and toss with the sauce. Sprinkle with chopped fennel leaves. Pass the grated cheese at the table.

Kilocalories 376 Kc • Protein 10 Gm • Fat 13 Gm • Percent of calories from fat 29% • Cholesterol 0 mg • Dietary Fiber 7 Gm • Sodium 145 mg • Calcium 105 mg

SIMPLE CELERY AND EXOTIC FENNEL

165

Celery Pasta Salad with Honey-Mustard Vinaigrette

2 cups diagonally sliced celery
1 red bell pepper, seeded and
  cut into small triangles
1 small zucchini (about
  $1/4$ pound), thinly sliced
8 radishes, sliced
$1/2$ cup Honey-Mustard
  Vinaigrette, or more (see page
  11 for basic recipe)

Several sprigs of parsley,
  chopped
4 ounces ($1/4$ pound) medium
  shells

Combine the celery, bell pepper, zucchini, and radishes with the dressing and parsley. Cook the shells according to package directions and drain. Rinse them in cold water. Stir the pasta into the salad. Chill until ready to serve. Toss the salad and taste it to see if you want more dressing.

Kilocalories 326 Kc • Protein 5 Gm • Fat 23 Gm • Percent of calories from fat 61% • Cholesterol 0 mg • Dietary Fiber 3 Gm • Sodium 190 mg • Calcium 38 mg

Fennel, Apple, and Walnut Pasta Salad

4 SERVINGS

This salad has its "roots" in the Waldorf Salad of yesteryear. Using fennel instead of celery adds a subtly different flavor, and the traditional mayonnaise has been considerably lightened with nonfat yogurt.

$\frac{1}{2}$ **cup nonfat plain yogurt**
$\frac{1}{4}$ **cup mayonnaise**
2 teaspoons minced fresh chervil, or $\frac{1}{2}$ **teaspoon dried**
$\frac{1}{4}$ **teaspoon salt**
$\frac{1}{4}$ **teaspoon white pepper**

1 fennel bulb (about 1 pound)
1 large tart red apple, such as McIntosh
$\frac{3}{4}$ **cup walnut halves or pieces**
1 cup small elbows

In a large salad bowl, whisk together the yogurt, mayonnaise, chervil, salt, and pepper until well blended. Core and chop the fennel bulb, stirring it into the dressing as you work. Save some of the feathery leaves for garnish. Leaving the apple unpeeled, core and dice it, and stir it into the dressing. This will keep the fennel and apple from turning brown. Stir in the walnuts.

Meanwhile, cook the elbows according to package directions and drain. Rinse them in cold water and toss them with the salad. Garnish with the reserved fennel leaves.

Kilocalories 422 Kc • Protein 12 Gm • Fat 25 Gm • Percent of calories from fat 52% • Cholesterol 11 mg • Dietary Fiber 7 Gm • Sodium 303 mg • Calcium 136 mg

Corn, a Noble Native

A gift from the Native Americans, corn is a complex carbohydrate food for sustained energy. It's high in fiber and potassium, making it healthy for the heart and the digestion. Fresh corn contains more vitamin C than frozen corn, but the latter is still a quality product as a substitute in regions where fresh corn is available only as a late summer and early fall treat. Yellow corn adds the bonus of beta-carotene to fight cancer.

The sugar in fresh sweet corn is quickly converted to starch, so two cardinal rules prevail: Keep the corn refrigerated and cook it as soon as possible. Look for ears whose silk is soft and golden-brown, not dry and brittle. The kernels at the tips should be smaller than the rest but not shriveled; if they are fully mature, the ear may be overripe and tough.

After husking corn, remove all the silk with a dry vegetable brush. To cut whole raw kernels from the cob, hold the ear upright and run a sharp knife down the length of it. Leave one-eighth inch of pulp and be gentle so that you don't get part of the cob in the bargain.

When boiling corn, don't salt the water, which would toughen the kernels; cooking time is 4 to 7 minutes, depending on size. Or steam corn in 1 inch of water (my preferred method) for 6 to 10 minutes.

New England Corn Chowder with Shells

---◾---

4 SERVINGS

Slightly mashing the potato gives the chowder a creamier texture.

1 tablespoon butter
$^1/_4$ cup chopped shallots
$^1/_2$ green bell pepper,
  seeded and diced small
1 celery stalk, diced small
2 cups fresh corn kernels or
  frozen, thawed to separate
1 large potato, peeled
  and diced
$^1/_2$ cup water
$^1/_2$ teaspoon salt

2 tablespoons superfine flour,
  such as Wondra
Few dashes of white pepper
  and cayenne pepper
2 cups milk (whole milk
  is best)
1 sprig fresh thyme, chopped
  (remove any woody stem), or
  $^1/_4$ teaspoon dried
1 cup small shell pasta

In a large saucepan, melt the butter and sauté the shallots, green pepper, and celery until softened, about 3 minutes. Add the corn, potato, water, and salt. Bring to a boil, reduce the heat, and simmer, covered, for 10 minutes, or until the potato is tender. Mash some of the potato slightly.

Blend the flour, white pepper, and cayenne into the milk. Add the thyme. Pour the mixture into the pan. Bring to a boil, stirring constantly. Lower the heat and simmer 2 minutes, stirring occasionally. Keep warm.

Meanwhile, cook the shells according to package directions and drain. Add them to the chowder and serve.

Kilocalories 317 Kc • Protein 11 Gm • Fat 8 Gm • Percent of calories from fat 21% • Cholesterol 25 mg • Dietary Fiber 4 Gm • Sodium 399 mg • Calcium 170 mg

Jalapeño and Corn Chowder with Orecchiette

4 SERVINGS

1 tablespoon olive oil
1/2 cup chopped yellow onion
1/2 cup diced red bell pepper
1 to 2 fresh or canned jalapeño
  chilies, seeded and minced
  (wear rubber gloves)
1 celery stalk, sliced
2 cups fresh corn kernels or
  frozen, thawed to separate
1 cup vegetable or chicken
  stock, or canned broth

2 tablespoons superfine flour,
  such as Wondra
2 teaspoons minced fresh
  cilantro, or 1/2 teaspoon dried
1/2 teaspoon salt
Several dashes of white pepper
  and cayenne pepper
2 cups milk (whole milk
  is best)
1 1/2 cups orecchiette

In a large saucepan, heat the oil and sauté the onion, pepper, chilies, and celery until softened, about 3 minutes. Add the corn and stock. Bring to a boil, reduce the heat, and simmer, covered, for 3 minutes, or until the corn is almost tender.

Blend the flour, cilantro, salt, white pepper, and cayenne into the milk. Pour the mixture into the pan. Bring to a boil, stirring constantly. Lower the heat and simmer 5 minutes, stirring occasionally. Keep warm.

Meanwhile, cook the orecchiette according to package directions and drain. Add them to the chowder.

Kilocalories 368 Kc • Protein 13 Gm • Fat 8 Gm • Percent of calories from fat 20% • Cholesterol 17 mg • Dietary Fiber 4 Gm • Sodium 504 mg • Calcium 162 mg

Fresh Succotash with Elbows

■

4 SERVINGS

Crumbled crisply cooked bacon or coarsely grated longhorn cheese can be sprinkled on each serving as a garnish.

About 2 cups shell beans, shelled (1½ pounds unshelled)
1 cup chicken or vegetable stock, or canned broth
2 tablespoons vegetable oil
1 green bell pepper, seeded and diced
¼ cup minced shallots

2 cups fresh corn kernels
1 teaspoon minced fresh tarragon, or ¼ teaspoon dried
1 teaspoon minced fresh thyme, or ¼ teaspoon dried
¼ teaspoon white pepper
¼ teaspoon salt
1½ cups small elbows

Put the shelled beans in a pot with the stock. Bring to a boil, reduce the heat, and simmer, covered, until tender, 20 to 25 minutes.

Heat the oil in a large skillet and sauté the green pepper and shallots until they are soft and fragrant, about 5 minutes. Add the corn, tarragon, thyme, white pepper, and salt. Add the shell beans and their broth to the corn mixture. Simmer until the corn is tender, 5 minutes.

Meanwhile, cook the elbows according to package directions, drain, and stir them into the corn and beans.

Kilocalories 452 Kc • Protein 20 Gm • Fat 8 Gm • Percent of calories from fat 16% • Cholesterol 0 mg • Dietary Fiber 15 Gm • Sodium 262 mg • Calcium 78 mg

Shrimp Succotash with Shells

---

4 ENTRÉE SERVINGS

This main-dish succotash can be quickly assembled by using frozen cooked, cleaned shrimp. You can thaw them in minutes by placing them in a strainer and running tepid water over them. To cook and clean raw shrimp, see page 14 for the basic recipe.

2 tablespoons olive oil
4 scallions, cut into 1-inch pieces
$1/2$ cup diced celery
$3/4$ cup clam broth (bottled) or vegetable broth
2 cups fresh corn kernels or frozen, thawed to separate
1 16-ounce can light kidney beans, drained and rinsed

$1/2$ pound cooked, shelled, deveined shrimp
1 tablespoon chopped cilantro, or $1/2$ teaspoon dried
$1/8$ to $1/4$ teaspoon cayenne pepper
1 cup very small shells

Heat the oil in a skillet and sauté the scallions and celery until they begin to soften, 3 minutes. Add the broth and corn. Bring to a simmer and cook 5 minutes, or until the corn is tender. Add the beans and shrimp. Season with cilantro and cayenne, and continue cooking for 3 minutes to blend the flavors.

Meanwhile, cook the shells according to package directions and drain. Stir them into the succotash.

Kilocalories 386 Kc • Protein 24 Gm • Fat 8 Gm • Percent of calories from fat 19% • Cholesterol 112 mg • Dietary Fiber 9 Gm • Sodium 635 mg • Calcium 72 mg

Scalloped Corn and Tomatoes with Ditali

4 SERVINGS

1 tablespoon olive oil
4 scallions, chopped
2 cups fresh corn kernels or
  frozen, thawed to separate
1/2 cup chicken stock or
  canned broth
3 tablespoons superfine flour,
  such as Wondra
1/4 teaspoon salt
1/8 teaspoon white pepper
1 1/2 cups milk (whole or
  low-fat)

1 cup peeled, seeded, chopped
  fresh tomatoes
3 to 4 leaves fresh sage,
  chopped, or a pinch of
  ground sage
1 cup ditali
1 cup corn bread or herb
  stuffing mix (not an instant
  stuffing mix)

Preheat the oven to 350 degrees F.

Heat the oil in a large saucepan and sauté the scallions until they begin to soften, 3 minutes. Add the corn and stock. Bring to a simmer. Whisk the flour, salt, and pepper into the milk, and pour the mixture into the simmering corn. Stir constantly until the sauce bubbles and thickens. Simmer 3 minutes, stirring occasionally. Remove from the heat and stir in the tomatoes and sage.

Cook the ditali according to package directions, undercooking it slightly, and drain. Combine the corn mixture and pasta in a baking dish and stir to blend. Top with the stuffing mix, pressing it down slightly into the sauce. Bake for 20 to 25 minutes.

Kilocalories 343 Kc • Protein 12 Gm • Fat 8 Gm • Percent of calories from fat 20% • Cholesterol 12 mg • Dietary Fiber 4 Gm • Sodium 435 mg • Calcium 138 mg

Macaroni and Cheese with Corn

— ■ —

6 SERVINGS

A comfort food casserole to soothe the soul after a stressful day.

2 cups low-fat milk
$1/4$ cup nonfat dry milk
3 tablespoons superfine flour,
  such as Wondra
$1/4$ teaspoon dry mustard
$1/4$ teaspoon salt
$1/8$ teaspoon white pepper
$1^1/2$ cups shredded sharp
  Cheddar cheese

2 cups fresh corn kernels or
  frozen, thawed to separate
1 whole roasted pepper, diced
  (from a jar)
8 ounces ($1/2$ pound) medium
  elbows

Preheat the oven to 350 degrees F.

Pour the milk into a saucepan and whisk in the dry milk, flour, and seasonings. Cook over medium-high heat, stirring constantly, until the mixture bubbles and thickens. Remove from the heat and stir in the cheese. When it has melted, stir in the corn and roasted pepper.

Meanwhile, cook the elbows according to package directions, undercooking it slightly, and drain. Combine the corn mixture and elbows in a $2^1/2$-quart gratin pan or casserole. Bake until bubbling throughout, 20 to 25 minutes.

Kilocalories 356 Kc • Protein 17 Gm • Fat 11 Gm • Percent of calories from fat 28% • Cholesterol 36 mg • Dietary Fiber 2 Gm • Sodium 331 mg • Calcium 324 mg

Crustless Corn Quiche

■

Here's a festive way to use up a cup of leftover macaroni. The cheese and crumbs make a no-work crust.

$^1/_2$ **tablespoon soft butter**
1 cup coarsely grated Monterey Jack cheese
2 cups fresh bread crumbs made in a food processor from Italian white bread, slightly toasted
1 cup cooked corn kernels
1 cup slightly undercooked small elbows or any small macaroni

$^1/_4$ **cup finely chopped green bell pepper**
2 tablespoons finely chopped onion
3 eggs
1 cup milk (whole or low-fat)
$^1/_4$ **teaspoon salt**
$^1/_8$ **teaspoon white pepper**

Preheat the oven to 350 degrees F.

Butter a 10- or 9-inch pie pan and sprinkle $^1/_2$ cup of the cheese on the bottom. Sprinkle 1 cup of the crumbs over the cheese. Add the corn, elbows, bell pepper, and onion. Beat together the eggs, milk, and seasonings. Pour the mixture evenly over the vegetables and pasta. Top with the remaining 1 cup of crumbs and $^1/_2$ cup of cheese, pressing them down slightly with the back of a spoon.

Bake in the middle of the oven for 25 to 30 minutes, or until a knife inserted near the center comes out clean. Let stand for 10 minutes before cutting.

Kilocalories 222 Kc • Protein 12 Gm • Fat 11 Gm • Percent of calories from fat 42% • Cholesterol 129 mg • Dietary Fiber 2 Gm • Sodium 320 mg • Calcium 215 mg

Corn and Pastina Pudding

---

4 SERVINGS

1/2 cup pastina

2 cups fresh corn kernels or
frozen, thawed to separate

1 cup milk (whole milk is best)

1 1/2 tablespoons superfine
flour, such as Wondra

1/4 teaspoon salt

1/8 teaspoon white pepper

2 tablespoons snipped
fresh chives or chopped
scallion tops

1 tablespoon butter, melted

Preheat the oven to 325 degrees F.

Cook the pastina according to package directions, undercooking it slightly, and drain. Mix it with the corn.

Blend together the milk, flour, salt, and pepper. Stir in the corn mixture, chives, and melted butter. Pour into a buttered 1 1/2-quart casserole. Bake for 50 to 60 minutes, until set.

Kilocalories 241 Kc • Protein 8 Gm • Fat 6 Gm • Percent of calories from fat 20% • Cholesterol 16 mg • Dietary Fiber 3 Gm • Sodium 211 mg • Calcium 77 mg

Corn with Spanish Sauce and Farfallini

4 SERVINGS

2 cups fresh corn kernels or
   frozen, thawed to separate
$1/2$ cup chicken stock or
   canned broth

Freshly ground black pepper
1 cup farfallini (tiny egg bows)
1 cup Spanish Sauce, heated
   (see page 13 for basic recipe)

Simmer the corn in the stock until tender, 5 to 7 minutes. Do not drain. Season with pepper to your taste.

Meanwhile, cook the farfallini according to package directions; drain. Combine the corn and farfallini in a medium-size serving dish. Top with the sauce.

Kilocalories 163 Kc • Protein 6 Gm • Fat 4 Gm • Percent of calories from fat 18% • Cholesterol 9 mg • Dietary Fiber 4 Gm • Sodium 381 mg • Calcium 40 mg

Creamed Corn with Spinach Rotelle

4 SERVINGS

1 tablespoon olive oil
2 scallions, chopped
2 cups fresh corn kernels or
   frozen, thawed to separate
$1/2$ cup chicken stock or
   canned broth
$1^1/2$ tablespoons superfine
   flour, such as Wondra

$1/4$ teaspoon salt
$1/8$ teaspoon white pepper
1 cup whole milk
1 tablespoon snipped fresh
   chives
6 ounces (about $1/3$ pound)
   spinach rotelle

Heat the oil in a large saucepan and sauté the scallions for 3 minutes. Add the corn and stock. Bring to a boil, reduce the heat, and simmer, covered, for 5 minutes.

Whisk the flour, salt, and pepper into the milk and pour the mixture into the simmering corn. Stir constantly until the sauce bubbles and thickens. Simmer 5 minutes over very low heat, stirring occasionally. Remove from the heat and stir in the chives.

Meanwhile, cook the rotelle according to package directions and drain. Combine the corn mixture and pasta in a serving dish and stir to blend.

Kilocalories 293 Kc • Protein 11 Gm • Fat 7 Gm • Percent of calories from fat 22% • Cholesterol 44 mg • Dietary Fiber 4 Gm • Sodium 260 mg • Calcium 100 mg

Sautéed Corn with Couscous

4 SERVINGS

1 cup couscous, raw
2 tablespoons olive oil
1 garlic clove, minced
1 celery stalk, diced
2 cups fresh corn kernels or frozen, thawed to separate

1½ cups peeled, chopped plum tomatoes, fresh or canned
2 teaspoons chili powder
1 teaspoon ground cumin

Prepare the couscous (see page 12 for basic recipe or follow package directions); fluff and separate grains as instructed in the basic recipe.

Heat the oil in a large skillet and sauté the garlic and celery until softened and translucent, 3 minutes. Add the corn, tomatoes, chili powder, and cumin. Sauté until the corn is tender and the tomatoes slightly thickened, about 5 minutes.

To serve, spread the couscous on a platter and mound the corn sauce on top.

Kilocalories 342 Kc • Protein 12 Gm • Fat 8 Gm • Percent of calories from fat 21% • Cholesterol 0 mg • Dietary Fiber 6 Gm • Sodium 251 mg • Calcium 35 mg

Corn and Orzo Pancakes

MAKES **16** PANCAKES

Serve them for brunch with ricotta cheese or salsa.

$^1/_3$ **cup orzo**
2 cups fresh, tender corn
   kernels or frozen, thawed
$^3/_4$ **cup all-purpose flour**
2 tablespoons sugar
4 teaspoons baking powder
$^1/_2$ **teaspoon salt**
$^1/_8$ **teaspoon cayenne pepper**

$1^1/_4$ **cups yellow cornmeal**
2 eggs
1 cup milk (whole or low-fat)
$^1/_4$ **cup vegetable oil, plus more**
   for frying
2 tablespoons snipped fresh
   chives, or $^1/_4$ **cup chopped**
   scallion tops

Cook the orzo according to package directions and drain. Mix it with the corn.

Sift the flour, sugar, baking powder, salt, and cayenne pepper into a large bowl. Stir in the cornmeal.

In a small bowl, lightly beat the eggs. Whisk in the milk and $^1/_4$ cup oil. Stir in the chives. Stir the liquid ingredients into the dry until just blended. Fold in the corn and orzo.

In a large skillet, nonstick or well-seasoned cast iron, heat a small amount of oil. Spoon batter by $^1/_4$ cupful, 3 or 4 at a time, into the hot pan; flatten slightly with the back of a spoon. Fry the cakes slowly until bubbles appear; turn. Cook until golden on both sides. Repeat with the remaining batter, adding more oil as needed. Keep cooked cakes warm in an oven set on the lowest heat.

Kilocalories 147 Kc • Protein 4 Gm • Fat 5 Gm • Percent of calories from fat 29% • Cholesterol 29 mg • Dietary Fiber 2 Gm • Sodium 190 mg • Calcium 63 mg

Corn and Tomato Salad with Rotelle

4 SERVINGS

This summery salad is best made with fresh corn.

4 large ears fresh corn
2 large vine-ripened tomatoes (1 pound), chopped
1/4 cup finely chopped red onion
1/4 cup extra-virgin olive oil
2 tablespoons red wine vinegar

1/4 cup slivered fresh basil leaves, or 1 cup chopped celery stalks and leaves (preferably, tender inner stalks)
1/4 teaspoon salt
1/8 teaspoon pepper
1/4 pound (4 ounces) rotelle

Husk the corn and remove the silk. Pour 1 inch of water into a large pot, add the ears, and bring to a boil. Cover and steam for 6 minutes or until tender. Remove and cool the corn.

With a sharp knife, cut the kernels off the ears of corn and let them cool slightly. Combine the corn kernels, tomatoes, and onion in a serving dish. Add all the remaining ingredients, except the pasta, and toss well. Allow the mixture to marinate at room temperature while cooking the rotelle according to package directions.

Drain and rinse the rotelle in cold water. Stir the pasta into the vegetable mixture and serve at room temperature.

Kilocalories 336 Kc • Protein 7 Gm • Fat 15 Gm • Percent of calories from fat 39% • Cholesterol 0 mg • Dietary Fiber 4 Gm • Sodium 171 mg • Calcium 19 mg

Corn and Green Bean Salad

4 SERVINGS

Boil 1/2 pound green beans in salted water for 5 minutes, or until tender-crisp, and substitute them for the tomatoes in the preceding recipe. Add 1 pimiento, from a jar, cut into strips.

Kilocalories 332 Kc • Protein 7 Gm • Fat 15 Gm • Percent of calories from fat 38% • Cholesterol 0 mg • Dietary Fiber 5 Gm • Sodium 167 mg • Calcium 40 mg

Corn and Black Bean Salad with Gemelli

3 tablespoons olive oil
1 Anaheim chili, seeded
and diced
1 small fresh jalapeño chili,
seeded and minced (wear
rubber gloves)
2 cups fresh corn kernels or
frozen, thawed to separate

1 cup gemelli
1 16-ounce can black beans,
drained and rinsed
$^1/_2$ cup chopped fresh cilantro
or flat-leaf parsley
$^1/_4$ cup lime juice
Salt and freshly ground pepper

Heat 1 tablespoon of the oil in a large skillet and sauté the chilies and corn over very low heat until the vegetables are tender-crisp, 3 to 5 minutes. Cool.

Cook the gemelli according to package directions, drain, and rinse in cold water.

In a salad bowl, combine the corn mixture, gemelli, beans, cilantro, lime juice, the remaining 2 tablespoons of oil, and salt and pepper to your taste. Toss well to blend. Serve at room temperature.

Kilocalories 323 Kc • Protein 11 Gm • Fat 11 Gm • Percent of calories from fat 27% • Cholesterol 0 mg • Dietary Fiber 8 Gm • Sodium 273 mg • Calcium 57 mg

Eggplant,
a Seductive Mediterranean

With its glossy rich color and smooth seductive shape, eggplant is pretty enough to be a table centerpiece, yet versatile enough when cooked to replace meat in many a vegetarian entrée. It's a good source of fiber to help lower cholesterol and provides potassium for a healthy heart. In addition, eggplant contains phytochemicals that protect against cancer.

It takes experience to size up eggplants in the market and select a fresh, firm, yet ripe vegetable. Look for impeccable sheen and smoothness. Press the flesh gently. It should yield slightly, yet spring back to its original shape. Eggplant does not keep well. Store it on the least cool shelf of the refrigerator (probably the bottom shelf or a crisper drawer) and use it as soon as possible.

Although it contains virtually no fat itself, thirsty eggplant absorbs more fat in cooking than any other vegetable. Salting and draining, however, make the flesh denser and less absorbent. Cubed eggplant can be cooked in a minimum of oil if stir-fried with alacrity. Broiling is another low-fat method of cooking eggplant that is used in many of the following recipes.

Eggplant and Mushrooms with Shells

---

4 SERVINGS

An easy buffet dish that can be served at room temperature. As part of a buffet with other foods, any dish will yield more servings, perhaps twice as many, as it will for a family dinner.

1 medium eggplant (1 to 1¼ pounds)

2 tablespoons olive oil, plus more if needed

1 large red bell pepper, seeded and cut into small triangles

6 ounces mushrooms, cleaned and sliced

1 to 2 garlic cloves, minced

1 teaspoon dried oregano

¼ teaspoon salt, or more, to your taste

Several grinds of black pepper

2 tablespoons minced fresh flat-leaf parsley

1 tablespoon balsamic vinegar

8 ounces (½ pound) medium shells

Peel and slice the eggplant. Salt the slices and allow them to drain in a colander for a half hour or more. Rinse, drain, and pat the eggplant slices dry in a towel. Dice the slices.

Heat 2 tablespoons of oil in a large nonstick skillet and sauté the bell pepper, mushrooms, and garlic for about 3 minutes. Add the eggplant and continue frying until it begins to soften. Season the mixture with the oregano, salt, and pepper. Cover and cook over very low heat until the vegetables are quite tender, 20 to 30 minutes, adding more oil if needed. Stir in the parsley and vinegar.

Meanwhile, cook the shells according to package directions and drain. Toss the shells with the eggplant mixture in a large serving dish. Serve warm or at room temperature.

Kilocalories 327 Kc • Protein 9 Gm • Fat 8 Gm • Percent of calories from fat 23% • Cholesterol 0 mg • Dietary Fiber 5 Gm • Sodium 153 mg • Calcium 21 mg

Herbed Baby Eggplants
on a Bed of Couscous

■

4 SERVINGS

1 cup couscous, raw
1 teaspoon minced garlic
1 teaspoon chopped
  fresh oregano, or
  ¹/₄ teaspoon dried
1 teaspoon chopped fresh
  basil, or ¹/₄ teaspoon dried
1 teaspoon chopped fresh dill,
  or ¹/₄ teaspoon dried

¹/₄ teaspoon salt
¹/₄ teaspoon freshly ground
  pepper
3 tablespoons olive oil
4 baby eggplants (about
  1 pound total)
2 tablespoons red wine vinegar
2 tablespoons minced fresh
  flat-leaf parsley

Prepare couscous (see page 12 for basic recipe or follow package directions); cool and separate the grains as instructed. When ready to serve, reheat over hot water or in a microwave-safe casserole in the microwave. Fluff well with two forks, breaking up any lumps.

Mix the garlic, herbs (except parsley), and seasonings with the oil and let the mixture stand at room temperature while preparing the eggplant. Remove the stem ends from each eggplant and cut the eggplants in half lengthwise. Cut slits in the flesh, keeping the skin intact. Salt the eggplants and drain for a half hour or more. Rinse and pat them dry.

Preheat the oven to 400 degrees F. Arrange the eggplant halves, cut sides up, in a baking dish and pour the seasoned oil over them so that it drizzles into the slits. Bake until browned and tender, about 30 minutes. Sprinkle the halves with vinegar and parsley and serve them on a platter of warmed couscous.

Kilocalories 317 Kc • Protein 7 Gm • Fat 11 Gm • Percent of calories from fat 30% • Cholesterol 0 mg • Dietary Fiber 5 Gm • Sodium 202 mg • Calcium 25 mg

Eggplant Verde with Gemelli

1 medium eggplant (1 to
  1¼ pounds)
3 tablespoons olive oil
1 green bell pepper, seeded
  and diced
¼ cup chopped shallots
1 garlic clove, minced
1 cup vegetable or chicken
  stock, or canned broth

½ teaspoon salt
¼ teaspoon pepper
3 tablespoons basil pesto (from
  a jar or see page 9 for basic
  recipe)
3 ounces (½ pound) gemelli or
  penne

Peel and slice the eggplant. Salt the slices and allow them to drain in a colander for a half hour or more. Rinse, drain, and pat the eggplant slices dry in a towel. Dice the slices.

Heat the oil in a large skillet and sauté the green pepper, shallots, and garlic until sizzling. Add the eggplant and sauté over low heat, stirring often, until it begins to soften, 5 minutes. Add the stock, salt, and pepper, and simmer with cover ajar, stirring occasionally, until the eggplant is tender and the sauce is thickened, 20 to 25 minutes. Stir in the pesto.

Meanwhile, cook the gemelli according to package directions and drain. Spoon it into a large serving dish and toss with the eggplant sauce.

Kilocalories 413 Kc • Protein 10 Gm • Fat 19 Gm • Percent of calories from fat 40% • Cholesterol 1 mg • Dietary Fiber 5 Gm • Sodium 592 mg • Calcium 42 mg

Eggplant, Sun-dried Tomatoes, and Black Olives with Rotelle

4 SERVINGS

1 medium eggplant (1 to 1¼ pounds)

2 tablespoons olive oil, or more as needed

1 garlic clove, minced

¼ cup slivered sun-dried tomatoes

1 cup vegetable or chicken stock, or canned broth

⅓ cup loosely packed, whole pitted black olives

Salt and freshly ground black pepper

8 ounces (½ pound) rotelle

2 tablespoons chopped fresh flat-leaf parsley

3 tablespoons freshly grated, loosely packed Romano cheese

Peel and slice the eggplant. Salt the slices and allow them to drain in a colander for a half hour or more. Rinse, drain, and pat the eggplant slices dry in a towel. Cut the slices into ½-inch strips.

In a 12-inch skillet, heat the oil until it's quite hot and stir-fry the eggplant over medium-high heat until it begins to soften, 3 minutes. Add the garlic and cook 1 minute. Add the sun-dried tomatoes, stock, black olives, and salt and pepper to your taste. (You may not need any salt, since the tomatoes, olives, stock, and cheese all add salt.) Simmer over low heat, uncovered, stirring often, until the eggplant is tender, about 10 minutes. Most of the liquid will be absorbed.

Meanwhile, cook the rotelle al dente according to package directions and drain. Spoon the pasta into the skillet, toss with the eggplant mixture, and cook over very low heat for 1 minute. Sprinkle with the parsley and cheese.

Kilocalories 352 Kc • Protein 10 Gm • Fat 11 Gm • Percent of calories from fat 28% • Cholesterol 4 mg • Dietary Fiber 5 Gm • Sodium 437 mg • Calcium 65 mg

Eggplant Caponata with Farfalle

—■—

6 SERVINGS

Caponata is a relish with a piquant sweet-and-sour flavor.

1 medium eggplant (1 to
 1¼ pounds)
2 tablespoons olive oil, or
 more as needed
1 green bell pepper, seeded
 and diced
2 celery stalks, sliced
2 garlic cloves, minced
1 16-ounce can Italian plum
 tomatoes, chopped,
 with juice
12 green Sicilian olives, pitted
 and halved
2 tablespoons red wine vinegar

1 tablespoon drained capers
1 teaspoon sugar
2 teaspoons chopped
 fresh oregano, or
 ½ teaspoon dried
½ teaspoon salt
¼ teaspoon freshly ground
 black pepper
Few dashes hot red pepper
 flakes
2 tablespoons minced fresh
 flat-leaf parsley
12 ounces (¾ pound) farfalle
 (egg bows)

Peel and slice the eggplant. Salt the slices and allow them to drain in a colander for a half hour or more. Rinse, drain, and pat the eggplant slices dry in a towel. Dice the slices.

In a 12-inch skillet, heat the oil until it's quite hot and stir-fry the eggplant over medium-high heat until it begins to soften. If you stir constantly, you will need less oil, but if the pan gets too dry, add a bit more. Add the green pepper, celery, and garlic. Stir-fry for 2 minutes.

Add all the remaining ingredients except the parsley and pasta. Simmer the caponata with cover ajar, stirring often, until the eggplant is very tender but still holds its shape, 30 minutes. Add the parsley. Taste to correct the seasonings; you may want more vinegar or hot red pepper.

Meanwhile, cook the farfalle according to package directions, drain, and spoon it into a large serving dish. Pour the caponata over the top and serve.

Kilocalories 328 Kc • Protein 10 Gm • Fat 9 Gm • Percent of calories from fat 25% • Cholesterol 54 mg • Dietary Fiber 5 Gm • Sodium 655 mg • Calcium 50 mg

Japanese Eggplant with Noodles

4 SERVINGS

½ cup chicken or vegetable stock, or canned broth
1 tablespoon naturally brewed soy sauce
2 teaspoons sugar
1 teaspoon cornstarch
2 tablespoons vegetable oil
4 ounces ground turkey, lean
Pinch of anise seed or fennel seed
4 small Japanese eggplants or 4 baby eggplants (¾ pound total), unpeeled, cut into quarters lengthwise

2 green bell peppers, seeded and cut into strips
4 scallions, cut into 1-inch lengths
1 tablespoon fresh ginger, peeled and minced
8 ounces (½ pound) fresh Japanese noodles

Stir together the stock, soy sauce, sugar, and cornstarch until they are blended.

Heat 1 tablespoon of the oil in a large wok or skillet and stir-fry the ground meat with the anise seed until it's no longer pink, 2 minutes.

Add the remaining tablespoon of oil, eggplant, green peppers, scallions, and ginger. Continue stir-frying until the vegetables are tender-crisp, 4 to 6 minutes. Blend the cornstarch mixture again and add it to the wok. Stir constantly until the mixture thickens. Simmer 2 minutes, stirring often. Keep warm.

Cook the noodles according to package directions and drain. Spoon them into a large serving dish, and top with the vegetable mixture.

Kilocalories 380 Kc • Protein 18 Gm • Fat 10 Gm • Percent of calories from fat 23% • Cholesterol 27 mg • Dietary Fiber 4 Gm • Sodium 467 mg • Calcium 32 mg

Eggplant and Ziti Casserole

■

This is a basic, useful kind of casserole that you can prepare early in the day and refrigerate until you're ready to cook.

1 garlic clove, finely minced
¼ cup olive oil
1 medium eggplant (1 to
   1¼ pounds)
8 ounces (½ pound) ziti

1½ cups thin tomato sauce
   (from a jar or see Marinara
   Sauce page 318)
3 tablespoons grated Romano
   cheese

Mix the garlic with the olive oil and allow it to marinate for 30 minutes or more.

Slice the eggplant, unpeeled, into ½-inch slices. Salt the slices and let them drain in a colander for a half hour or more. Rinse off the salt and press the slices dry between paper towels.

Preheat the broiler 5 minutes.

Brush the eggplant slices on both sides with the garlic oil. (Any leftover oil will be delicious in a vinaigrette.)

Lay the slices on an oiled baking sheet and broil them 6 inches below the heat source until they are browned and tender but not mushy, about 7 minutes on each side.

Cook the ziti according to package directions, undercooking it slightly, and drain. Mix the ziti with 1 cup of the tomato sauce.

Preheat the oven to 350 degrees F. Oil a 2-quart gratin pan and make a layer of half the eggplant. Spread all the ziti over the eggplant. Top with the remaining eggplant and the remaining ½ cup sauce.

Sprinkle the casserole with the cheese. Bake for 30 minutes, or 40 to 45 minutes if it was refrigerated before baking.

Kilocalories 428 Kc • Protein 10 Gm • Fat 19 Gm • Percent of calories from fat 41% • Cholesterol 4 mg • Dietary Fiber 5 Gm • Sodium 352 mg • Calcium 73 mg

Eggplant with Creamy Ricotta and Shells

6 SERVINGS

1 medium eggplant (1 to
1¼ pounds)
3 tablespoons olive oil
1 green bell pepper, seeded
and diced
1 garlic clove, minced
1 dried hot red chili
2 anchovies, chopped
(optional)
1 16-ounce can imported
Italian plum tomatoes with
juice
1 tablespoon balsamic vinegar

2 teaspoons minced fresh
oregano, or ½ teaspoon dried
¼ to ½ teaspoon salt (the
lesser amount if using
anchovies)
¼ teaspoon black pepper
¼ cup chopped fresh flat-leaf
parsley
12 ounces (¾ pound) medium
shells
⅓ cup part-skim ricotta cheese
2 tablespoons grated Parmesan
cheese

Peel and slice the eggplant. Salt it and allow it to drain in a colander for a half hour or more. Rinse, drain, and pat the eggplant slices dry in a towel. Dice the slices.

Heat the olive oil in a large skillet. Add the eggplant cubes and green pepper, and sauté the vegetables, stirring frequently (to keep the eggplant from soaking up all the oil) until they begin to brown. Add the garlic, chili, and anchovies, if using, and sauté for a minute or two longer.

Add the tomatoes, vinegar, oregano, salt, and pepper. Cover and cook on low for 20 minutes, stirring often and breaking up the tomatoes, until the eggplant is quite tender. Remove from the heat and stir in the parsley.

Meanwhile, cook the shells according to package directions. Drain and spoon them into a large warm serving dish. Toss them with the ricotta and 2 tablespoons of the grated cheese until blended.

Remove the chili from the eggplant and add the eggplant to the shells, tossing gently. Pass additional grated cheese at the table.

Kilocalories 349 Kc • Protein 11 Gm • Fat 10 Gm • Percent of calories from fat 24% • Cholesterol 5 mg • Dietary Fiber 5 Gm • Sodium 319 mg • Calcium 108 mg

Baked, Stuffed Eggplant with Orzo

4 SERVINGS

1 large eggplant ($1^1/_4$ to $1^1/_2$ pounds)
3 tablespoons olive oil
1 small yellow onion, chopped
1 green pepper, seeded and diced
1 garlic clove, minced
$1^1/_2$ cups canned tomatoes, chopped

1 tablespoon chopped fresh flat-leaf parsley
1 tablespoon chopped fresh oregano, or 1 teaspoon dried
$^1/_2$ teaspoon salt
$^1/_4$ teaspoon pepper
$^3/_4$ cup orzo
About $^1/_2$ cup shredded mozzarella cheese

Remove the eggplant stem and cut the eggplant in half lengthwise. Scoop out the flesh (a serated grapefruit spoon works well) and reserve, leaving about a $^3/_4$-inch shell. Salt the shells and drain them upside down for 30 minutes. Rinse and pat dry. Preheat the broiler. Brush the eggplant shells with a little of the oil, put them on a baking sheet, and broil them 8 inches below the heat source, cut sides up, until they begin to brown, 8 to 10 minutes.

Dice the reserved eggplant pulp. In a large skillet, heat the remaining oil and sauté the onion, pepper, and diced eggplant until softened, 5 minutes. Add the garlic and sauté 1 minute more. Add the tomatoes, herbs, and seasonings, and continue cooking over low heat for 15 to 20 minutes, until the eggplant is tender and the mixture is thick.

Meanwhile, cook the orzo according to package directions, undercooking it slightly, and drain. Preheat the oven to 350 degrees F. Stir the orzo into the skillet mixture. Put the eggplant halves into an oiled baking dish and stuff them with the orzo mixture. Sprinkle with the cheese. Bake for 25 to 30 minutes.

Kilocalories 356 Kc • Protein 11 Gm • Fat 14 Gm • Percent of calories from fat 34% • Cholesterol 8 mg • Dietary Fiber 7 Gm • Sodium 510 mg • Calcium 141 mg

Eggplant and Peppers with Rigatoni

4 SERVINGS

1 medium eggplant (1 to
  1¼ pounds)
3 tablespoons olive oil
½ red bell pepper, seeded and
  cut into strips
½ green bell pepper, seeded
  and cut into strips
2 garlic cloves, minced
½ cup vegetable or chicken
  broth, or juice from tomatoes
1 pound fresh plum tomatoes,
  or 5 canned plum tomatoes,
  quartered and seeded

2 tablespoons chopped fresh
  marjoram, or 1 teaspoon
  dried oregano
½ teaspoon salt
¼ teaspoon freshly ground
  pepper
8 ounces (½ pound) rigatoni
½ cup coarsely grated Asiago
  cheese

Peel and slice the eggplant. Salt it and allow it to drain in a colander for a half hour or more. Rinse, drain, and pat the eggplant slices dry in a towel. Cut the slices into ½-inch strips.

In a 12-inch skillet, heat the oil until it's quite hot and stir-fry the bell peppers and eggplant over medium-high heat until they begin to soften. Add the garlic during the last minute. Add the broth or juice and tomatoes and continue cooking until the vegetables are very tender, 20 minutes. Season with the marjoram, salt, and pepper.

Meanwhile, cook the rigatoni according to package directions and drain. Spoon it into a large serving dish. Add the vegetables and cheese and toss to blend.

Kilocalories 424 Kc • Protein 14 Gm • Fat 16 Gm • Percent of calories from fat 34% • Cholesterol 16 mg • Dietary Fiber 6 Gm • Sodium 467 mg • Calcium 177 mg

Garlic-roasted Eggplant and Tomato Sauce with Linguine

---

6 SERVINGS

A really easy dish to prepare for garlic lovers.

1 medium eggplant (1 to 1¼ pounds)
1 large or 2 small garlic cloves, sliced
1 tablespoon olive oil
3 cups tomato sauce (see Marinara Sauce recipe, page 318)

16 ounces (1 pound) linguine
Freshly grated Parmesan cheese

Slice the eggplant in half lengthwise and cut the flesh in a crisscross pattern without cutting through the skin. Salt the eggplant, pressing the salt into the slits, and turn the halves upside down to drain for a half hour. Rinse the salt out and gently squeeze out any accumulated juices.

Preheat the oven to 400 degrees F. Place the halves, cut side up, in an oiled baking dish and insert the garlic slices into the slits. Drizzle the halves with the oil. Roast the eggplant halves on the middle shelf until tender, about 45 minutes.

When cool enough to be handled, remove the garlic slices and mince them. Scoop out the eggplant flesh as much as possible in a large piece or pieces and dice it. Discard the skins. Put the garlic and eggplant into a skillet, add the tomato sauce, and simmer for 10 minutes.

Cook the linguine according to package directions, drain, and spoon it into a large serving dish. Toss it with the eggplant mixture. Pass the grated cheese at the table.

Kilocalories 391 Kc • Protein 11 Gm • Fat 9 Gm • Percent of calories from fat 20% • Cholesterol 0 mg • Dietary Fiber 5 Gm • Sodium 407 mg • Calcium 40 mg

Eggplant and Parsley in Angel Hair Nests

---■---

4 SERVINGS

The angel hair pasta called for in this recipe is coiled into "nests." Regular angel hair pasta can be substituted.

Lots of fresh parsley adds a zesty flavor plus a generous supply of vitamin C to the dish.

1 small eggplant (about ¾ pound)
About 3 tablespoons olive oil
1 red bell pepper, seeded and diced
1 garlic clove, minced
1½ cups chopped, seeded fresh ripe tomatoes (see Note)

½ teaspoon salt
¼ teaspoon cayenne pepper
¼ teaspoon dried oregano
¼ teaspoon sugar
½ cup chopped fresh flat-leaf parsley
8 ounces (½ pound) dried angel hair pasta—in nests

Peel and slice the eggplant. Salt it and allow it to drain in a colander for a half hour or more. Rinse, drain, and pat the eggplant slices dry in a towel. Dice the slices.

Heat 1 tablespoon of the oil in a large skillet and stir-fry the eggplant over medium-high heat, adding more oil as needed. The brisker you stir, the less oil you'll need.

When the eggplant is beginning to brown, add the red bell pepper and garlic. Stir-fry 3 minutes. Add the tomatoes, salt, cayenne, oregano, and sugar. Simmer the mixture over very low heat until the eggplant is tender, 15 to 20 minutes. Remove from the heat and stir in the parsley.

Carefully add the angel hair pasta to a large pot of salted simmering water. Cook without stirring for 5 minutes. The nests usually will stay in shape. Lift the pasta nests out with a slotted spoon and arrange them in a large serving dish. Add any drained loose noodles to the dish.

Spoon the eggplant mixture over the pasta, filling the nests.

NOTE: Juicy summer tomatoes are a must in this dish. Otherwise, there won't be enough moisture in the skillet.

Kilocalories 347 Kc • Protein 9 Gm • Fat 12 Gm • Percent of calories from fat 29% • Cholesterol 0 mg • Dietary Fiber 5 Gm • Sodium 308 mg • Calcium 34 mg

Eggplant Torta

■

6 WEDGES

A great luncheon dish—macaroni pie with an eggplant "crust."

1 garlic clove, pressed through
   a garlic press
1/4 cup olive oil
2 small eggplants (1 1/2 to
   2 pounds altogether)
Salt and freshly ground pepper
1 pound part-skim ricotta
1 egg, beaten
1 tablespoon minced fresh
   flat-leaf parsley

1/2 teaspoon salt
1/4 teaspoon white pepper
1 cup ditali or very small
   elbows
1 cup tomato sauce (see Light
   Tomato Sauce, page 317)
3 tablespoons grated Parmesan
   cheese

Mix the garlic with the olive oil; marinate the mixture while salting and draining the eggplants. Peel and slice the eggplants. Salt them and allow to drain in a colander for a half hour or more. Rinse, drain, and pat the eggplant slices dry in a towel. Preheat the broiler. Brush the eggplant slices on both sides with the garlic oil. (Any leftover oil will be delicious in a vinaigrette.) Lay the slices on an oiled baking sheet and broil them 6 inches below the heat source until they are browned and tender but not mushy, about 7 minutes on each side. Salt and pepper them to your taste. Cut them in half-rounds.

Mix the ricotta with the egg, parsley, salt, and white pepper. Cook the pasta according to package directions and drain.

Line the bottom and sides of a well-oiled 10-inch pie pan with half of the eggplant slices. Spread about half the ricotta mixture over the eggplant. Layer all the pasta over the cheese. Spread the remaining ricotta over the pasta. Arrange the remaining eggplant slices on top. Spread with the tomato sauce and sprinkle with the Parmesan cheese.

When ready to cook, preheat the oven to 375 degrees F. Bake the *torta* on the middle shelf until set, about 30 minutes. Let stand for 10 minutes before cutting into wedges.

Kilocalories 329 Kc • Protein 14 Gm • Fat 19 Gm • Percent of calories from fat 51% • Cholesterol 61 mg • Dietary Fiber 4 Gm • Sodium 483 mg • Calcium 263 mg

Broiled Eggplant with Olive Tapenade and Shells

4 SERVINGS

1 medium eggplant (1 to
1 1/4 pounds)
10 Greek olives, pitted
10 stuffed green olives
Several sprigs of fresh flat-leaf
parsley
1 garlic clove
3 tablespoons olive oil

1 tablespoon drained capers
2 teaspoons minced fresh basil,
or 1/2 teaspoon dried
1/4 teaspoon freshly ground
black pepper
8 ounces (1/2 pound) large
shells

Peel and slice the eggplant. Salt it and allow it to drain in a colander for a half hour or more.

To make the tapenade, finely chop the olives, parsley, and garlic. Mix them with 2 tablespoons of the oil, the capers, basil, and pepper. This can all be done in a food processor if you use an extremely light touch with on/off turns of the motor to achieve a coarse texture.

Rinse, drain, and pat the eggplant slices dry in a towel. Preheat the broiler. Brush the eggplant slices on both sides with the remaining tablespoon of olive oil, or more if you need it. Lay the slices on an oiled baking sheet, and broil them 6 inches below the heat source until they are browned and tender but not mushy, about 7 minutes on each side. Put the slices into a large serving dish and cut them into quarters. Stir in the tapenade. Cook the pasta according to package directions and drain, and toss with the eggplant mixture. Serve warm or at room temperature.

Kilocalories 382 Kc • Protein 8 Gm • Fat 16 Gm • Percent of calories from fat 36% • Cholesterol 0 mg • Dietary Fiber 4 Gm • Sodium 558 mg • Calcium 12 mg

Eggplant Parmesan with Rotelle

■

6 SERVINGS

It's no longer a fattening dish when you broil instead of fry the eggplant. Enjoy without guilt!

1 large eggplant (1¼ to 1½ pounds)
6 ounces (about ⅓ pound) rotelle or any screw-shaped pasta
2 tablespoons olive oil, approximately

3 cups tomato sauce (see Marinara Sauce, page 318)
1 cup freshly grated Parmesan cheese
8 ounces part-skim mozzarella, shredded

Peel and slice the eggplant. Salt it and allow it to drain in a colander for a half hour or more. Rinse, drain, and pat the eggplant slices dry in a towel. Preheat the broiler. Brush the eggplant slices on both sides with about a tablespoon of the olive oil. Lay them on an oiled baking sheet, and broil them 6 inches below the heat source until they are browned and tender but not mushy, about 7 minutes on each side.

Cook the rotelle according to package directions, undercooking it slightly, and drain. Mix it with 1 tablespoon of the olive oil. Preheat the oven to 350 degrees F.

Spread a little of the tomato sauce in a large gratin pan. Layer with half the eggplant, 1 cup of the tomato sauce, and half the Parmesan. Add all the rotelle in one layer. Top with 1 cup sauce and half of the mozzarella. Finish with the remaining eggplant, tomato sauce, Parmesan, and mozzarella. Bake on the middle shelf for 30 minutes. Let rest 10 minutes before cutting into squares to serve.

Kilocalories 377 Kc • Protein 20 Gm • Fat 18 Gm • Percent of calories from fat 43% • Cholesterol 32 mg • Dietary Fiber 4 Gm • Sodium 828 mg • Calcium 459 mg

Eggplant and Orzo Salad

6 SERVINGS

This dish is based on a Greek appetizer, with orzo replacing the traditional semolina.

1 large eggplant (1¼ to 1½ pounds)
3 tablespoons olive oil
1 red bell pepper, seeded and diced
1 green bell pepper, seeded and diced
1 small red onion, chopped
2 celery stalks, diced
½ cup water
Salt

¼ cup extra-virgin olive oil
3 tablespoons fresh lemon juice
1 tablespoon minced fresh flat-leaf parsley
1 teaspoon dried oregano
½ teaspoon salt
¼ teaspoon freshly ground black pepper
1 cup orzo
1 cup diced feta cheese

Peel and slice the eggplant. Salt it and allow it to drain in a colander for a half hour or more. Rinse, drain, and pat the eggplant slices dry in a towel. Dice the eggplant slices.

Heat the olive oil in a large skillet and fry the eggplant, bell peppers, onion, and celery until the vegetables begin to soften. Add the water and continue cooking, uncovered, stirring often, until the mixture is thick and the vegetables are tender but not mushy, 20 minutes. Salt them to your taste and allow them to cool slightly.

In a large salad bowl, whisk together the extra-virgin oil, lemon juice, parsley, oregano, salt, and pepper. Meanwhile, cook the orzo according to package directions and drain; rinse in cold water. Stir the vegetables, orzo, and cheese into the dressing. Let the mixture marinate at room temperature for a half hour before serving. (For longer storage, refrigerate, then bring back to room temperature.)

Kilocalories 430 Kc • Protein 12 Gm • Fat 26 Gm • Percent of calories from fat 53% • Cholesterol 38 mg • Dietary Fiber 5 Gm • Sodium 683 mg • Calcium 232 mg

Pasta Salad with Spicy Eggplant Purée

6 SERVINGS

1 whole medium eggplant
  (about 1 pound), unpeeled
1 clove garlic, peeled
$1/2$ teaspoon ground cumin
$1/2$ teaspoon ground coriander
$1/4$ teaspoon ground cardamom
$3/4$ teaspoon salt
$1/4$ teaspoon freshly ground
  black pepper

2 tablespoons white wine
  vinegar, or more
About $1/4$ cup extra-virgin
  olive oil
2 tablespoons chopped fresh
  flat-leaf parsley
12 ounces ($3/4$ pound) mezzani
1 cup toasted walnut halves

Preheat the oven to 375 degrees F. Prick the eggplant with a fork in several places, place it on a baking sheet, and bake for 45 minutes or until it collapses when lightly pressed with the back of a spoon. Scoop the eggplant pulp out of the skin.

Mince the garlic in a food processor. Add the eggplant pulp and purée it. Blend in the spices, salt, pepper, and vinegar. With the motor running, add the oil in a slow stream until the purée has the consistency of mayonnaise. Taste to correct the seasoning, adding more vinegar or seasonings as needed. Remove the mixture from the processor and stir in the parsley.

Cook the pasta according to package directions, drain, and rinse in cold water to cool it. Spoon it into a bowl, add the purée, and toss to blend well. Sprinkle with the walnuts.

Kilocalories 440 Kc • Protein 13 Gm • Fat 22 Gm • Percent of calories from fat 43% • Cholesterol 0 mg • Dietary Fiber 5 Gm • Sodium 298 mg • Calcium 33 mg

The Infinite Variety of Greens

With a veritable bonanza of beta-carotene, greens help to stave off the effects of aging and to ward off degenerative diseases like cancer. Color is the key; the darker the green, the more beta-carotene. Kale, mustard greens, and watercress are doubly protective, because they're also members of the tumor-fighting cruciferous family.

As if that weren't enough, greens are also a rich source of calcium, which lowers blood pressure and keeps bones strong. All this, plus plenty of vitamin C and iron, makes ample incentive to toss some cooked greens with your hot pasta or chop some raw greens into a pasta salad.

Greens can be classified by their strength, or "bite." Young beet greens, chard, collards, escarole, and lettuce (any kind) are the mildest. Kale and arugula are assertive but not bitter—they need to be teamed up with equally strong flavors. Watercress and parsley are delightfully peppery. Chicory, turnip greens, mustard greens, and dandelions are the sharpest, with a slightly bitter aftertaste—pleasing to aficionados. (See also broccoli de rabe and spinach in separate chapters.)

Greens are so varied that their peak seasons range from early spring for delicate dandelions to late fall for lusty kale. Buy unbagged bunches with no sign of yellowing (too dry) or rot (too wet). My favorite storage method: Wrap greens in clean old dish towels and refrigerate them in a plastic bag. The towel sops up unwanted extra moisture, but the plastic keeps the leaves from drying out completely.

For the freshest taste, use greens as soon as possible after purchase—and don't overcook them. Most greens cook in 3 to 15 minutes, depending how tender they are. Strong-flavored greens taste milder when simmered briefly in broth or bouillon.

Seven-Greens Soup with Egg Noodles

6 SERVINGS

Choose among escarole, collards, chard, beet greens, turnip greens, watercress, romaine lettuce, chicory, and parsley for this soup based on a traditional German dish.

2 tablespoons butter
1 large onion, chopped
1½ pounds assorted fresh greens, cut into strips
6 cups vegetable or chicken stock, or canned broth
¼ cup superfine flour, such as Wondra
¼ cup nonfat dry milk
½ teaspoon salt
⅛ to ¼ teaspoon white pepper

2 cups milk (can be low-fat)
4 ounces (¼ pound) fine egg noodles
1 tablespoon chopped fresh dill
Hard-boiled eggs, peeled and quartered, for garnishing (optional—1 egg for every 2 servings)

Heat the butter in a large pot and slowly sauté the onion until it's golden, 5 to 8 minutes. Add the greens and stock. Bring to a boil, reduce the heat, and simmer, covered, until the greens are tender, about 10 minutes.

Whisk the flour, dry milk, and seasonings into the liquid milk. Pour all at once into the simmering soup and stir constantly until it bubbles and thickens slightly. Taste to correct the seasoning, adding more salt and pepper if needed.

Meanwhile, cook the noodles separately according to package directions and drain. Stir them into the soup and serve. Garnish each soup bowl with dill and 2 egg quarters, if you wish. Dark rye bread makes a good accompaniment.

Kilocalories 241 Kc • Protein 9 Gm • Fat 7 Gm • Percent of calories from fat 24% • Cholesterol 35 mg • Dietary Fiber 5 Gm • Sodium 403 mg • Calcium 191 mg

Asian Soup with Greens and Noodles

■

4 SERVINGS

4 cups chicken stock or
  canned broth
2 cups water
3 tablespoons naturally brewed
  soy sauce
3 cups chopped romaine
  lettuce
1 cup chopped strong-flavored
  greens: mustard greens,
  chicory, or watercress

4 ounces whole wheat angel
  hair pasta or regular angel
  hair pasta
4 scallions, each green top cut
  lengthwise into "brushes"

Combine the stock, water, soy sauce, and greens in a large saucepan. Bring the mixture to a boil, reduce the heat, and simmer, covered, for 7 to 8 minutes.

Meanwhile, cook the wheat noodles separately. If there are no package directions in English, boil the noodles in a large pot of salted water, taste-testing for tenderness. They should be ready in 3 to 4 minutes (keep in mind that they will cook a little more in the soup). Remove the noodles with a slotted spoon and add them to the soup.

Garnish each serving with a scallion "brush."

Kilocalories 174 Kc • Protein 12 Gm • Fat 3 Gm • Percent of calories from fat 13% • Cholesterol 6 mg • Dietary Fiber 2 Gm • Sodium 795 mg • Calcium 114 mg

Escarole Soup with Tortellini

6 SERVINGS

1 bunch escarole (1 to
  1½ pounds)
1 tablespoon olive oil
1 clove garlic, minced
6 cups chicken stock or
  canned broth

1 large carrot, diced small
8 ounces (½ pound) tortellini
Freshly grated Romano cheese

Wash the escarole leaves in several changes of water and chop them coarsely.

Heat the oil in a large pot and sauté the garlic until it's soft and fragrant. Add the stock, escarole, and carrot, and bring the soup to a boil, pushing down the escarole leaves to immerse them. Reduce the heat, cover, and simmer the soup for 10 minutes, or until the escarole is tender.

Meanwhile, cook the tortellini separately according to package directions. Add it to the soup, simmer about 3 minutes to combine the flavors, and serve. Pass the cheese at the table.

Kilocalories 194 Kc • Protein 12 Gm • Fat 6 Gm • Percent of calories from fat 30% • Cholesterol 20 mg • Dietary Fiber 4 Gm • Sodium 594 mg • Calcium 120 mg

Italian Wedding Soup

8 SERVINGS

Follow the preceding recipe, increasing the stock to 8 cups. Add ½ batch of Mini-Meatballs (see basic recipe, page 15) at the same time as the escarole. Simmer about 15 minutes, testing one meatball for doneness by splitting it in half.

Substitute 8 ounces small elbows, cooked separately, for the tortellini.

Kilocalories 301 Kc • Protein 20 Gm • Fat 9 Gm • Percent of calories from fat 27% • Cholesterol 48 mg • Dietary Fiber 4 Gm • Sodium 725 mg • Calcium 87 mg

Portuguese Kale Soup with Shells

6 SERVINGS

This is a vegetable version, although traditionally cooked sausage slices add a spicy, smoky flavor to this soup. If you use sausage, choose the new lighter turkey sausage which has less fat.

1 tablespoon vegetable oil
1 medium onion, chopped
6 cups chicken or vegetable stock, or canned broth
4 cups chopped kale, well packed (³/₄- to 1-pound bunch)

1 yellow potato, such as Yukon Gold, diced
1 carrot, sliced
4 ounces (¹/₄ pound) medium shells

In a large pot, heat the oil and sauté the onion until it's soft and fragrant. Add the stock and vegetables. Bring to a boil, reduce the heat, and simmer for 15 minutes, with cover ajar. Cook the shells according to package directions, drain, and add them to the soup before serving.

Kilocalories 183 Kc • Protein 9 Gm • Fat 4 Gm • Percent of calories from fat 21% • Cholesterol 0 mg • Dietary Fiber 3 Gm • Sodium 445 mg • Calcium 59 mg

Kale and Olive Stew with Ruote

1 bunch kale ($^3/_4$ to 1 pound)
1 tablespoon olive oil
3 garlic cloves, minced
1 red bell pepper, seeded and diced
3 cups vegetable or chicken stock, or canned broth
2 tablespoons tomato paste
1 large red potato, peeled or unpeeled, sliced into half rounds

8 kalamata olives, pitted and halved
4 to 5 fresh sage leaves, chopped, or $^1/_4$ teaspoon ground sage
$^1/_4$ teaspoon salt
Freshly ground black pepper to your taste
1 bay leaf
6 ounces (about $^1/_3$ pound) ruote (wagon wheels)

Wash the kale well and trim off the tough stems. Hold the bunch together and cut it crosswise into fourths.

Heat the oil in a large pot and sauté the garlic and red pepper until they begin to soften. Add the kale and all the remaining ingredients except the pasta, bring to a boil, and simmer, covered, until the vegetables are quite tender, about 15 minutes. Remove the bay leaf.

Meanwhile, cook the ruote separately according to package directions. Drain and stir into the stew. Serve in bowls, with crusty Italian bread as an accompaniment.

Kilocalories 292 Kc • Protein 9 Gm • Fat 6 Gm • Percent of calories from fat 19% • Cholesterol 0 mg • Dietary Fiber 6 Gm • Sodium 317 mg • Calcium 101 mg

Kale with Tomato Sauce and Fusilli Lungi

---

4 SERVINGS

1 bunch kale (³/₄ to 1 pound)
³/₄ cup chicken stock or canned
  broth
1 cup tomato sauce, warmed
  (from a jar or see Light
  Tomato Sauce, page 317)

¹/₄ teaspoon hot red pepper
  flakes
8 ounces (¹/₂ pound) fusilli
  lungi (long corkscrews) or
  rotini

Wash the kale well and trim off the tough stems. Hold the bunch together and cut it crosswise into fourths. Put the kale in a large pot with the stock and bring it to a boil. Reduce the heat and simmer, covered, until tender, 10 to 12 minutes. Stir in the tomato sauce and hot pepper flakes.

Meanwhile, cook the fusilli lungi according to package directions; drain. Toss the kale and pasta together in a large serving dish.

Kilocalories 269 Kc • Protein 11 Gm • Fat 2 Gm • Percent of calories from fat 6% • Cholesterol 0 mg • Dietary Fiber 6 Gm • Sodium 329 mg • Calcium 97 mg

Collards with Walnuts and Cavatelli

■

Collards, the mildest of the mild greens, make a pleasing background for strong-flavored or spicy foods, such as the cherry peppers in this dish or the Gorgonzola in the following recipe.

½ cup walnut halves or broken
  pieces
1 tablespoon olive oil
2 garlic cloves, minced
1 bunch collards (½ to ¾
  pound), washed, stemmed,
  and coarsely chopped
¾ cup chicken stock or
  canned broth

1 to 2 hot cherry peppers,
  seeded and finely diced
Salt and freshly ground black
  pepper
8 ounces (½ pound) cavatelli

Put the walnuts into a small saucepan with water to cover. Bring to a boil, then drain the walnuts. Toast the walnuts in a toaster oven or broiler until lightly colored.

Heat the oil in a large saucepan and sauté the garlic until softened and fragrant, 3 minutes. Add the collards and stock. Cover and simmer until the vegetable is tender, 10 minutes. Add the hot cherry peppers. Season with salt and pepper to your taste.

Meanwhile, cook the cavatelli according to package directions and drain. In a large serving dish, toss the cavatelli with the collard mixture. Top with the walnuts.

Kilocalories 358 Kc • Protein 13 Gm • Fat 13 Gm • Percent of calories from fat 33% • Cholesterol 0 mg • Dietary Fiber 2 Gm • Sodium 152 mg • Calcium 35 mg

Collards, Red Bell Pepper, and Gorgonzola with Ziti

4 SERVINGS

1 bunch collards ($^1/_2$ to
 $^3/_4$ pound)
2 tablespoons olive oil
1 red bell pepper, seeded and
 cut into strips
1 garlic clove, minced
$^3/_4$ cup chicken or vegetable
 stock, or canned broth

Salt and freshly ground pepper
8 ounces ($^1/_2$ pound) ziti
$^2/_3$ cup loosely packed,
 crumbled Gorgonzola cheese
 or any blue cheese

Wash the collards well and remove any tough stems. Chop the greens coarsely (about 1-inch pieces).

Heat the oil in a large saucepan and sauté the red pepper and garlic for 3 minutes. Add the collards and stock. Cover and simmer until the vegetable is tender, 10 to 15 minutes. Season with salt and pepper to your taste. (The cheese adds salt.)

Meanwhile, cook the ziti according to package directions and drain. Spoon it into a large serving dish and toss with half the cheese. Add the collard mixture and toss again. Sprinkle the remaining cheese on top before serving.

Kilocalories 375 Kc • Protein 14 Gm • Fat 15 Gm • Percent of calories from fat 35% • Cholesterol 17 mg • Dietary Fiber 2 Gm • Sodium 408 mg • Calcium 146 mg

Escarole with Feta and Linguine

—■—

4 SERVINGS

1 bunch escarole (about
  1 pound)
2 tablespoons olive oil
2 garlic cloves, minced
1^1/$_2$ cups chopped canned
  tomatoes, drained
^{1}/$_4$ teaspoon salt

Several grindings of black
  pepper
8 ounces (^{1}/$_2$ pound) thin
  linguine
1 cup loosely packed,
  crumbled feta cheese

Wash the escarole well. Hold the bunch together and cut it into thirds crosswise.

Heat the oil in a large skillet and sauté the garlic until softened and fragrant. Add the tomatoes, salt, and pepper, and sauté uncovered for 5 minutes. Add the escarole, cover, and continue to cook until it is tender, about 10 minutes.

Meanwhile, cook the linguine according to package directions. Drain and spoon the pasta into a large serving dish. Toss with the escarole and feta cheese.

Kilocalories 472 Kc • Protein 18 Gm • Fat 22 Gm • Percent of calories from fat 41% • Cholesterol 57 mg • Dietary Fiber 6 Gm • Sodium 890 mg • Calcium 389 mg

Braised Escarole with Orzo

A mild-flavored green cooked in a comforting way—a nice dish for soothing the tummy.

2 tablespoons butter
¼ cup chopped shallots
1 bunch escarole (about
  1 pound)

¾ cup chicken or vegetable
  stock, or canned broth
Salt and pepper
1½ cups orzo

Carefully wash the escarole and chop it into 1-inch pieces.

Heat the butter in a large pot and sauté the shallots over low heat until they are softened, 3 minutes. Add the escarole and sauté, stirring, until wilted. Add the stock and simmer until the escarole is tender, about 10 minutes. Season with salt and pepper to your taste.

Meanwhile, cook the orzo according to package directions and drain. Combine the orzo with the greens in a serving dish.

Kilocalories 381 Kc • Protein 13 Gm • Fat 8 Gm • Percent of calories from fat 19% • Cholesterol 16 mg • Dietary Fiber 7 Gm • Sodium 167 mg • Calcium 63 mg

Escarole Napoli

■

Mild greens in the spicy, savory style of Naples! This combination of flavors shows the influence of Arab traders.

1 bunch escarole (about ³/₄ to
  1 pound)
2 tablespoons olive oil
4 anchovy fillets, chopped
2 garlic cloves, minced
³/₄ cup chicken or vegetable
  stock, or canned broth

3 tablespoons dried currants
Freshly ground pepper
3 tablespoons pine nuts, lightly
  toasted
¹/₂ cup pitted, halved kalamata
  olives
8 ounces (¹/₂ pound) spaghetti

Wash the escarole well. Hold the bunch together and cut it into thirds crosswise.

Heat the oil in a large skillet and sauté the anchovies and garlic over very low heat for 3 minutes. Add the escarole, stock, and currants. Cover and continue to cook until the greens are tender, about 10 minutes. Season with pepper to your taste. (The anchovies add enough salt.) Sprinkle with the pine nuts and olives.

Meanwhile, cook the spaghetti according to package directions and drain. Spoon the pasta into a large serving dish and toss with the greens.

Kilocalories 417 Kc • Protein 13 Gm • Fat 17 Gm • Percent of calories from fat 35% • Cholesterol 3 mg • Dietary Fiber 5 Gm • Sodium 390 mg • Calcium 76 mg

Lettuce Lasagne

8 SERVINGS

1 pound romaine and escarole (about ½ head each; use outside leaves, saving inner leaves for salads)
1 tablespoon olive oil
1 garlic clove, minced
Freshly ground black pepper
12 lasagna noodles (plus a few extras, in case of breakage)
32 ounces part-skim ricotta cheese
2 eggs, beaten
¼ cup loosely packed, freshly grated Romano cheese
¼ teaspoon white pepper
3 cups tomato sauce (see A Fragrant Marinara Sauce or Tomato-Meat Sauce recipe, pages 318 and 322)
8 ounces part-skim mozzarella, shredded

Wash and coarsely chop the greens, leaving them slightly wet. Heat the oil in a large pot and sauté the garlic until it sizzles. Add the greens and cook, stirring, until they have wilted, 3 minutes. Drain well and season the greens to your taste with black pepper.

Cook the noodles according to package directions and drain. Lay the pieces out on foil or plastic wrap. Mix the ricotta with the eggs, Romano cheese, and white pepper.

Preheat the oven to 350 degrees F.

Use a stainless steel or glass baking pan, 3 inches deep with a 3½-quart capacity. Spoon 1 cup of the tomato sauce over the bottom of the pan. Lay 3 noodles over it and spread them with half the ricotta. Make another layer of noodles, followed by a layer of all the greens. Add 1 cup of the tomato sauce over the greens, 3 noodles, and the rest of the ricotta. Top with the remaining 3 noodles and remaining 1 cup tomato sauce, and sprinkle the mozzarella on top.

Bake uncovered for 45 minutes or until the ricotta is set and no longer runny. Let stand 10 minutes before cutting into squares.

Kilocalories 414 Kc • Protein 26 Gm • Fat 21 Gm • Percent of calories from fat 47% • Cholesterol 107 mg • Dietary Fiber 3 Gm • Sodium 631 mg • Calcium 570 mg

Red Swiss Chard with Hazelnuts and Fusilli

4 SERVINGS

1 bunch red Swiss chard (¹/₂ to ³/₄ pound)
1 tablespoon olive oil
2 leeks, white part only, chopped
³/₄ cup chicken stock or canned broth

2 tablespoons balsamic vinegar
Salt and freshly ground black pepper
8 ounces (¹/₂ pound) fusilli
¹/₂ cup hazelnuts, toasted, very coarsely chopped

Wash the chard well. Hold the bunch together and cut it crosswise into quarters.

Heat the oil in a large saucepan and sauté the leeks, very slowly, until they are softened and beginning to brown, 5 to 7 minutes. Add the chard and stock. Cover and simmer until the chard is tender, 10 minutes. Add the vinegar and season with salt and pepper to your taste.

Meanwhile, cook the fusilli according to package directions; drain. In a large serving dish, toss the pasta with the chard and stock. Top with the hazelnuts.

Kilocalories 443 Kc • Protein 16 Gm • Fat 15 Gm • Percent of calories from fat 29% • Cholesterol 0 mg • Dietary Fiber 9 Gm • Sodium 457 mg • Calcium 193 mg

Mustard Greens and
Black Olives with Spaghetti

———◼———

4 SERVINGS

The strong-flavored greens like mustard greens are especially high in calcium.

**1 bunch mustard greens (about
1 pound)**
2 tablespoons olive oil
2 garlic cloves, minced
**1 cup chicken or vegetable
stock, or canned broth**

1 cup pitted black olives
**¼ teaspoon hot red pepper
flakes**
8 ounces (½ pound) spaghetti

Wash the greens well and chop them coarsely into 2-inch pieces.

Heat the oil in a large skillet and sauté the garlic until it's sizzling. Add the greens, stock, and olives; cover and simmer until tender, 7 to 8 minutes. Season with hot red pepper flakes.

Meanwhile, cook the spaghetti according to package directions and drain. Spoon the pasta into a large serving dish, add the `greens, and toss them together.

Kilocalories 183 Kc • Protein 4 Gm • Fat 17 Gm • Percent of calories from fat 74% • Cholesterol 0 mg • Dietary Fiber 2 Gm • Sodium 625 mg • Calcium 89 mg

Mustard Greens and Onions with Yogurt and Couscous

---

4 SERVINGS

1 bunch mustard greens (about
  1 pound), well washed, cut
  into 2-inch pieces
1 cup couscous, raw
2 tablespoons olive oil
1 cup chopped onions

1 garlic clove, minced
$\frac{1}{2}$ cup (or more) chicken
  or vegetable stock, or
  canned broth
1 cup plain nonfat yogurt, at
  room temperature

Prepare the couscous (see page 12 for basic recipe or follow package directions); fluff and separate the grains.

Heat the oil in a large skillet and sauté the onions and garlic until they are softened, 3 minutes. Add the greens and stock, cover, and simmer until tender, 7 to 8 minutes, adding more stock if needed. Transfer the greens to a bowl and cool slightly. Stir in the yogurt.

Spoon the couscous onto a platter and arrange the greens on top. Serve at room temperature.

Kilocalories 317 Kc • Protein 14 Gm • Fat 8 Gm • Percent of calories from fat 23% • Cholesterol 1 mg • Dietary Fiber 5 Gm • Sodium 572 mg • Calcium 248 mg

Szechuan Beet Greens with Asian Noodles

4 SERVINGS

2 tablespoons vegetable oil
4 ounces fresh shiitake
  mushroom caps, cleaned and
  sliced
1 garlic clove, finely chopped
3 slices fresh ginger, peeled
  and finely chopped
1/2 to 1 teaspoon hot red
  pepper flakes, to your taste
1 bunch beet greens (1/2 to
  3/4 pound), well washed, cut
  into 2-inch pieces

1 teaspoon cornstarch
1/2 cup chicken stock or canned
  broth
1 tablespoon rice vinegar
1 teaspoon sesame oil
1/2 teaspoon sugar
6 ounces (about 1/3 pound)
  Asian thin flat noodles or
  American thin linguine

Wash the beet greens well and chop them coarsely into 2-inch pieces.

Heat the oil in a large wok or skillet and stir-fry the mushrooms, garlic, ginger, and hot pepper flakes for 2 minutes. Add the beet greens and stir-fry until they are wilted.

Stir the cornstarch into the stock. Add the stock mixture, vinegar, sesame oil, and sugar, and cook, stirring constantly, until the beet greens and mushrooms are just tender, about 3 minutes.

Meanwhile, cook the noodles according to package directions and drain. Spoon them into a serving dish and arrange the vegetables on top.

Kilocalories 286 Kc • Protein 5 Gm • Fat 9 Gm • Percent of calories from fat 26% • Cholesterol 0 mg • Dietary Fiber 5 Gm • Sodium 375 mg • Calcium 164 mg

Beet Greens with Ricotta and Shells

4 SERVINGS

Ricotta and freshly grated Romano cheese make an easy and delectable topping to complement a dish of greens and pasta.

1 cup part-skim ricotta cheese
1/2 cup freshly ground Romano cheese
2 tablespoons olive oil
1 clove garlic, minced
1 bunch beet greens (1/2 to 3/4 pound), well washed, cut into 2-inch pieces
3/4 cup chicken or vegetable stock, or canned broth

1/4 teaspoon salt
1/8 teaspoon freshly ground black pepper
1/8 teaspoon hot red pepper flakes
8 ounces (1/2 pound) medium shells

Mix the ricotta and Romano cheese and set them aside.

Heat the oil in a large skillet and sauté the garlic until it's sizzling and fragrant, 2 minutes. Add the beet greens and stock. Cover and simmer until tender, 10 minutes. Season with salt and black pepper and red pepper flakes.

Meanwhile, cook and drain the shells according to package directions. Combine the shells with the beet greens and toss to blend.

Divide the pasta among 4 serving dishes. Top with spoonfuls of the ricotta mixture.

Kilocalories 440 Kc • Protein 22 Gm • Fat 16 Gm • Percent of calories from fat 32% • Cholesterol 29 mg • Dietary Fiber 5 Gm • Sodium 737 mg • Calcium 426 mg

Lemony Wilted Beet Greens with Angel Hair

4 SERVINGS

2 tablespoons butter
1/4 cup chopped shallots
1 bunch beet greens (1/2 to
  3/4 pound), well washed and
  cut into 2-inch pieces
3 tablespoons fresh
  lemon juice

Salt and freshly ground pepper
8 ounces (1/2 pound) angel hair
  pasta
1 tablespoon olive oil
2 tablespoons chopped fresh
  flat-leaf parsley

Heat the butter in a large skillet and sauté the shallots until they are sizzling. Add the beet greens with the water that clings to the leaves after washing and the lemon juice. Cook, stirring, until the greens are wilted and tender, 5 to 7 minutes. If the pan seems too dry, add a tablespoon or two of water. Season with salt and pepper to your taste.

Meanwhile, cook the angel hair pasta according to package directions and drain. Spoon it into a serving dish and toss with the oil and parsley. Spoon the beet greens on top.

Kilocalories 333 Kc • Protein 11 Gm • Fat 11 Gm • Percent of calories from fat 28% • Cholesterol 16 mg • Dietary Fiber 5 Gm • Sodium 382 mg • Calcium 165 mg

Arugula with Prosciutto and Fettuccine

---

4 SERVINGS

1 tablespoon butter
1 tablespoon olive oil
2 ounces ($^1/_8$ pound) prosciutto, cut into slivers
3 tablespoons nonfat dry milk
3 tablespoons superfine flour, such as Wondra
$^1/_4$ teaspoon salt
Freshly ground black pepper to your taste

$1^1/_2$ cups milk (whole or low-fat)
1 bunch cleaned, spun-dry, chopped arugula or watercress
8 to 9 ounces (about $^1/_2$ pound) fresh fettuccine
Freshly ground Parmesan cheese

Heat the butter and oil in a large skillet and sauté the prosciutto for 2 minutes.

Whisk the dry milk, flour, salt, and pepper into the liquid milk. Pour all at once into the skillet and cook, stirring constantly, until the sauce bubbles and thickens. Simmer, stirring often, for 3 minutes. Stir in the arugula or watercress and remove from the heat.

Meanwhile, cook the fettuccine according to package directions and drain. Spoon the pasta into a large serving dish and toss with the sauce. Pass the Parmesan cheese at the table.

Kilocalories 314 Kc • Protein 13 Gm • Fat 11 Gm • Percent of calories from fat 32% • Cholesterol 81 mg • Dietary Fiber 2 Gm • Sodium 375 mg • Calcium 157 mg

Watercress and Scrambled Eggs
with Capellini

4 SERVINGS

A beautiful late supper or brunch dish. Serve a platter of sliced tomatoes drizzled with extra-virgin olive oil on the side.

6 eggs
3 tablespoons milk
1/2 teaspoon salt
1/4 teaspoon white pepper
3 tablespoons butter

2 scallions, chopped
1 1/2 cups stemmed and
  chopped watercress
8 ounces (1/2 pound) capellini
1/2 cup crumbled goat cheese

Beat the eggs with the milk, salt, and pepper. Heat 2 tablespoons of the butter in a large heavy skillet and stir-fry the scallions for 3 minutes. Add the eggs and cook them over very low heat, stirring constantly. When they are almost cooked, stir in the watercress.

Meanwhile, cook the capellini according to package directions and drain. Toss it with the remaining tablespoon of butter and the goat cheese. Spoon it onto a platter and top with the scrambled eggs.

Kilocalories 475 Kc • Protein 21 Gm • Fat 23 Gm • Percent of calories from fat 44% • Cholesterol 371 mg • Dietary Fiber 2 Gm • Sodium 593 mg • Calcium 112 mg

Middle Eastern Salad of Swiss Chard with Couscous

---

4 SERVINGS

1 cup couscous, raw
1 bunch Swiss chard (1 to
  1½ pounds)
1 cup vegetable or chicken
  stock, or canned broth

¼ cup olive oil
Salt and freshly ground black
  pepper
4 to 6 scallions, chopped
1 lemon, cut into 4 wedges

Prepare the couscous (see page 12 for basic recipe or follow package directions); fluff and separate the grains.

Wash the chard well. Separate the stems and leaves. Cut the stems into ½-inch pieces. Coarsely chop the leaves. Heat the stock in a large skillet and add the stems. Simmer 3 minutes. Add the leaves and continue cooking for 3 minutes, or until just tender. Drain, pressing out excess water.

Toss the greens with the oil. Salt and pepper them to your taste. Spoon the couscous onto a platter and arrange the greens on top. Sprinkle with the scallions. Serve slightly warm or at room temperature, garnished with lemon wedges to squeeze over the salad.

Kilocalories 403 Kc • Protein 14 Gm • Fat 14 Gm • Percent of calories from fat 30% • Cholesterol 0 mg • Dietary Fiber 11 Gm • Sodium 788 mg • Calcium 250 mg

Chicory and Spinach Fusilli Salad

◼

4 SERVINGS

A green-on-green salad with the "bite" of blue cheese.

3¹/₂ tablespoons extra-virgin olive oil

2 tablespoons red wine vinegar

¹/₄ teaspoon salt

Several grinds of black pepper

¹/₄ cup crumbled Gorgonzola cheese

2 scallions, chopped

4 ounces (¹/₄ pound) spinach fusilli

1 large tomato, chopped

¹/₂ cucumber, chopped

3 to 4 cups chopped chicory, washed, spun dry (about 8 ounces)

In a salad bowl, whisk together the oil, vinegar, salt, and pepper. Stir in the cheese and scallions.

Cook the fusilli according to package directions and drain. Rinse it under cold water until cool.

Combine the tomato, cucumber, chicory, and fusilli with the dressing and toss well.

Kilocalories 281 Kc • Protein 9 Gm • Fat 16 Gm • Percent of calories from fat 48% • Cholesterol 32 mg • Dietary Fiber 8 Gm • Sodium 326 mg • Calcium 198 mg

Caesar Salad with Pasta

---

4 SERVINGS

In this Caesar salad, the traditional raw egg dressing has been replaced with a safer mustard-based vinaigrette, and the salad is topped with homemade, low-fat croutons.

2 slices Italian bread, diced
1/2 teaspoon Italian herbs (or a mixture of dried oregano and dried basil)
1/2 cup Mustard Vinaigrette (see page 11 for basic recipe)
1 garlic clove, pressed through a garlic press
4 anchovy fillets, chopped (optional)

6 ounces (about 1/3 pound) mezzani
8 large outer leaves of romaine lettuce
1 bunch arugula or watercress, tough stems removed, chopped
1/4 cup freshly coarse-grated Parmesan cheese

Preheat the oven to 250 degrees F. Make a single layer of the diced bread in an oiled baking pan. Bake until lightly colored and crisp, 20 to 30 minutes. Remove, sprinkle with the herbs, and cool.

In a large salad bowl, blend the vinaigrette, garlic, and anchovies, if using. Cook the mezzani according to package directions and drain. Rinse under cold water until cool. Stir the pasta into the dressing. Tear the romaine into bite-size pieces and lay it on top of the pasta. Add the arugula or watercress to the salad. Chill, without tossing, until ready to serve. Just before serving, toss the greens with the pasta. Sprinkle the cheese and croutons on top.

Kilocalories 425 Kc • Protein 10 Gm • Fat 25 Gm • Percent of calories from fat 52% • Cholesterol 4 mg • Dietary Fiber 2 Gm • Sodium 327 mg • Calcium 128 mg

Watercress, Cherry Tomato, and Tortellini Salad

4 SERVINGS

Watercress will keep longer if you treat it like a bunch of flowers. Stand the stems in an inch of water, cover the top loosely with a plastic bag, and refrigerate on the lowest shelf.

⅓ to ½ cup **Herb Vinaigrette** (see page 10 for basic recipe)
¼ **cup chopped red onion**
8 cherry tomatoes, halved

8 ounces (½ pound) cheese tortellini
1 bunch watercress, stemmed, chopped

Pour the vinaigrette into a salad bowl. Add the onion and tomatoes and allow them to marinate at room temperature.

Meanwhile, cook the tortellini according to package directions. Drain the pasta and rinse in cold water. Stir the tortellini into the salad. Top with the watercress and refrigerate until ready to serve. Just before serving, toss the greens with the tortellini. Taste to correct the seasonings, adding more dressing if needed.

Kilocalories 307 Kc • Protein 10 Gm • Fat 18 Gm • Percent of calories from fat 51% • Cholesterol 30 mg • Dietary Fiber 3 Gm • Sodium 341 mg • Calcium 126 mg

Flavorsome Onions, Leeks, and Garlic

‾‾‾‾‾‾‾‾‾‾‾‾‾‾‾‾■‾‾‾‾‾‾‾‾‾‾‾‾‾‾‾‾

From the most ancient times, these pungent flavorers of soups and stews have been valued for their medicinal properties, and modern science has proved the truth of this time-honored prescription. Rich in plant chemicals that are antibacterial, antiviral, and antifungal, this important vegetable family is tops in preventive medicine: It also boosts the immune system. A heart-healthy choice, too, garlic and onions have been identified as agents in lowering cholesterol and in reducing the tendency of blood to clot, thus helping to prevent strokes. All this and great taste, too!

When shopping for onions and garlic, avoid those showing incipient green sprouts. Store them in a dark, cool, airy place, never the refrigerator. In buying leeks, look for green tops in good condition, perky rather than limp and yellowing. Refrigerate leeks in a perforated plastic bag and use them within three days or so.

There is scarcely a pasta dish that will not be improved by one or another of these zesty bulbs. Besides the dishes that follow in this chapter, you'll find onions, leeks, and garlic working their magic throughout the book.

French Onion Soup with Farfallini

6 SERVINGS

For a new twist, replace the bread crouton with a tomato slice.

2 tablespoons olive oil
1 tablespoon butter
5 cups thinly sliced yellow
   onions (about 1$\frac{1}{2}$ pounds)
$\frac{1}{4}$ teaspoon freshly ground
   black pepper
2 tablespoons flour
7 cups hot beef or chicken
   stock, or canned broth

1 tablespoon chopped fresh
   basil, or 1 teaspoon dried
Salt (optional)
1 cup farfallini (small egg bows)
6 slices of a large firm tomato
1 cup grated Gruyère or Swiss
   cheese

Heat the oil and butter in a large pot. Add the onions and pepper, and sauté until the onions are light golden-brown, 15 minutes. Sprinkle the onions with the flour and cook, stirring, for 3 minutes. Add the hot stock all at once and stir until the mixture boils. Reduce the heat and simmer the soup for 30 minutes. Stir in the basil. Taste to see if you need salt.

When ready to serve, cook the farfallini according to package directions, drain, and stir into the soup.

Preheat the broiler. Lay the tomato slices on an oiled baking sheet and spoon the cheese on top. Broil just until the cheese melts. Use a spatula carefully to transfer a tomato slice to float on top of each bowl of soup.

Kilocalories 253 Kc • Protein 18 Gm • Fat 13 Gm • Percent of calories from fat 46% • Cholesterol 32 mg • Dietary Fiber 3 Gm • Sodium 230 mg • Calcium 219 mg

Good-for-What-Ails-You Garlic and Pastina Soup

---

2 SERVINGS

Feel as if you're "coming down with something"? Here's some comforting, easy-to-make first aid.

1 tablespoon olive oil	1 carrot, coarsely grated
1 to 2 garlic cloves, minced	1/2 cup pastina
4 cups chicken stock or canned broth	2 tablespoons chopped fresh flat-leaf parsley

Heat the oil in a large saucepan and sauté the garlic until it's soft and fragrant. Add the stock and carrot, bring to a simmer, and cook 5 minutes. Raise the heat to medium-high, add the pastina in a slow stream, and cook until the pastina is tender to your taste, about 5 minutes. Sprinkle with the parsley and serve.

Kilocalories 357 Kc • Protein 17 Gm • Fat 11 Gm • Percent of calories from fat 27% • Cholesterol 0 mg • Dietary Fiber 3 Gm • Sodium 867 mg • Calcium 37 mg

Nutmeg-scented Baby Onions with Shells

1 pound small (the size of walnuts) boiling onions, or a 16-ounce bag frozen peeled baby onions
1 cup chicken stock or canned broth
1 tablespoon butter
1/4 cup superfine flour, such as Wondra

1/4 cup nonfat dry milk
1/2 teaspoon salt
1/4 teaspoon white pepper
1/4 teaspoon nutmeg, plus more for garnishing
2 cups milk (whole or low-fat)
6 ounces (about 1/3 pound) medium shells

If using fresh onions, parboil them in boiling water to cover to loosen the skins, about 5 minutes. Cool enough to handle; peel the onions. If using frozen onions, simply proceed as follows.

Combine the onions, stock, and butter in a saucepan and bring to a boil. Reduce the heat, cover, and simmer until the onions are quite tender, about 10 minutes. Remove the onions with a slotted spoon.

Whisk the flour, dry milk, salt, pepper, and nutmeg into the liquid milk and pour the mixture into the broth remaining in the saucepan. Cook over medium-high heat, stirring constantly, until bubbling and thickened. Return the onions to the pan. Reduce the heat and simmer over very low heat, stirring often, for 5 minutes.

Meanwhile, cook the shells according to package directions and drain. Combine the shells with the onion mixture in a serving dish and sprinkle with a dash or two of additional nutmeg.

Kilocalories 231 Kc • Protein 9 Gm • Fat 6 Gm • Percent of calories from fat 22% • Cholesterol 17 mg • Dietary Fiber 2 Gm • Sodium 333 mg • Calcium 128 mg

Onion, Pepper, and Mushroom Sauté with Egg Noodles

4 SERVINGS

3 tablespoons olive oil
2 large yellow onions, sliced
2 bell peppers (green or red), seeded and cut into strips
8 ounces fresh mushrooms, cleaned and sliced
1/2 tablespoon chopped fresh tarragon, or 1/2 teaspoon dried

1/2 tablespoon chopped fresh cilantro, or 1/2 teaspoon dried
Salt and freshly ground pepper
8 ounces (1/2 pound) broad egg noodles

Heat the oil in a 12-inch skillet and slowly sauté the vegetables until they are quite tender and lightly colored. Season them with the tarragon and cilantro, and salt and pepper to your taste.

Meanwhile, cook the egg noodles according to package directions and drain. Toss them with the vegetables.

Kilocalories 361 Kc • Protein 10 Gm • Fat 13 Gm • Percent of calories from fat 32% • Cholesterol 54 mg • Dietary Fiber 4 Gm • Sodium 18 mg • Calcium 41 mg

Szechuan Stir-fried Leeks with Asian Noodles

■

4 SERVINGS WITH VEGETABLES AS A SIDE DISH
4 SERVINGS WITH CHICKEN AND
EXTRA NOODLES AS AN ENTRÉE

For a more substantial main dish, 2 cups cooked chicken, cut into strips, can be added to the vegetables when the stock is added.

3 to 4 leeks (1 bunch)
2 tablespoons vegetable oil
1 red bell pepper, seeded and
   cut into strips
About 4 ounces fresh
   mushrooms, cleaned and
   sliced
1 garlic clove, finely chopped
3 slices fresh ginger, peeled
   and finely chopped
$^1/_2$ to 1 teaspoon hot red
   pepper flakes, to your taste

1 teaspoon cornstarch
$^1/_2$ cup chicken stock or
   canned broth
1 tablespoon rice vinegar
1 teaspoon sesame oil
$^1/_2$ teaspoon sugar
6 to 8 ounces ($^1/_3$ to $^1/_2$ pound)
   Asian thin flat noodles or
   American thin linguine

Trim off and discard the tough green part of the leeks. Cut the leeks in half lengthwise. Soak and rinse well under cold running water to remove all grit. Cut them into quarters lengthwise and into $^1/_2$-inch slices crosswise. Shake them dry in a towel.

Heat the oil in a large wok or skillet and stir-fry the leeks, bell pepper, mushrooms, garlic, ginger, and hot pepper flakes for 2 minutes. Blend the cornstarch into the stock. Add the stock mixture, vinegar, sesame oil, and sugar, and cook, stirring constantly, until the vegetables are just tender, 2 to 3 minutes.

Meanwhile, cook 6 ounces of noodles (8 ounces if using as an entrée meal with chicken) according to package directions; drain. Spoon them into a serving dish and arrange the vegetables on top.

Kilocalories 297 Kc • Protein 8 Gm • Fat 9 Gm • Percent of calories from fat 27% • Cholesterol 0 mg • Dietary Fiber 3 Gm • Sodium 336 mg • Calcium 84 mg

with chicken:
Kilocalories 418 Kc • Protein 29 Gm • Fat 12 Gm • Percent of calories from fat 26% • Cholesterol 60 mg • Dietary Fiber 3 Gm • Sodium 390 mg • Calcium 94 mg

Leeks with Anchovies and Orecchiette

◼

4 SERVINGS

2 large leeks (1 pound untrimmed)
2 tablespoons olive oil
4 anchovy fillets, or more, chopped

1 cup tomato sauce (from a jar or see Light Tomato Sauce, page 317)
8 ounces ($^1/_2$ pound) orecchiette or small shells

Trim off and discard the tough green part of the leeks. Cut the leeks in half lengthwise. Soak and rinse well under cold running water to remove all grit. Cut them into quarters lengthwise and into $^1/_2$-inch slices crosswise. Shake them dry in a towel.

Heat the oil in a skillet and slowly sauté the leeks until they begin to brown, about 10 minutes. Add the anchovies and tomato sauce, cover, and simmer until the leeks are tender, 15 to 20 minutes, stirring often.

Meanwhile, cook the orecchiette according to package directions; drain. Toss the leeks with the pasta in a serving dish.

Kilocalories 341 Kc • Protein 10 Gm • Fat 8 Gm • Percent of calories from fat 22% • Cholesterol 3 mg • Dietary Fiber 3 Gm • Sodium 176 mg • Calcium 54 mg

Creole Leeks with Peas and Fettuccine

■

4 SERVINGS

6 leeks (about 2 bunches)
3 tablespoons olive oil
1 green bell pepper, seeded
  and cut into strips
1 cup chicken stock or
  canned broth
1 cup fresh shelled or frozen
  peas, thawed just enough to
  separate
2 teaspoons chopped fresh
  marjoram, or ½ teaspoon
  dried oregano

½ teaspoon paprika
½ teaspoon salt
¼ teaspoon cumin
¼ teaspoon cayenne pepper
¼ teaspoon black pepper
8 to 9 ounces (about ½ pound)
  fresh or dried fettuccine

Trim off and discard the tough green part of the leeks. Cut the leeks in half lengthwise. Soak and rinse well under cold running water to remove all grit. Cut them into quarters lengthwise. Shake them dry in a towel.

Heat the oil in a large skillet and sauté the leeks and bell pepper very slowly, with cover ajar, until tender and lightly colored, 10 to 15 minutes. Add the stock, peas, marjoram, paprika, salt, cumin, cayenne and black peppers; simmer 2 to 5 minutes.

Meanwhile, cook the fettuccine according to package directions and drain. Arrange the pasta on a platter with the leeks in a row on top. Pour the peas and pan juices over all.

Kilocalories 420 Kc • Protein 13 Gm • Fat 14 Gm • Percent of calories from fat 29% • Cholesterol 58 mg • Dietary Fiber 7 Gm • Sodium 458 mg • Calcium 142 mg

Ravioli all'Olio
(Ravioli with Olive Oil and Garlic)

■

2 SERVINGS

Simply delicious. Keep the ingredients on hand and you'll always be able to dazzle unexpected company.

¼ cup extra-virgin olive oil
½ cup finely diced red bell pepper
2 cloves garlic, finely minced
¼ cup chopped fresh flat-leaf parsley
¼ cup chopped pitted black olives

¼ teaspoon hot red pepper flakes
8 ounces (½ pound) frozen small, round cheese ravioli
¼ cup chicken stock or canned broth
2 tablespoons freshly grated Parmesan cheese

Heat the olive oil in a medium skillet and sauté the bell pepper until tender, 5 minutes. Add the garlic and continue sautéing until it's fragrant but not brown, 2 minutes. Remove from the heat and add the parsley, olives, and red pepper flakes. Let the mixture marinate while cooking the ravioli.

Cook the ravioli according to package directions and drain. Stir the stock into the garlic sauce. Spoon the ravioli onto a platter and pour the sauce over all. Stir gently. Sprinkle with the cheese.

Kilocalories 613 Kc • Protein 20 Gm • Fat 38 Gm • Percent of calories from fat 55% • Cholesterol 81 mg • Dietary Fiber 3 Gm • Sodium 701 mg • Calcium 217 mg

Vermicelli all'Olio
(Vermicelli with Olive Oil and Garlic)

2 SERVINGS

A departure from the traditional dish, this one uses the milder, sweeter flavor of roasted garlic—and plenty of it!

1 whole bulb of garlic
1 cup chicken stock or canned broth
1 tablespoon olive oil
2 tablespoons extra-virgin olive oil
1/4 cup chopped fresh flat-leaf parsley
1/4 teaspoon freshly ground black pepper
12 ounces (3/4 pound) fresh or dried vermicelli
1/2 cup lightly toasted pine nuts
Freshly grated Romano cheese (optional)

Preheat the oven to 350 degrees F. Slice the tops off the garlic bulb to expose the tips of each clove and stand them in a small casserole. Pour in 1/2 cup of the stock and drizzle the tips with 1 tablespoon olive oil. Cover and bake until soft when pressed, 35 to 40 minutes.

Press the garlic purée out of the papery shells, clove by clove, into a small bowl. Stir in the extra-virgin oil, parsley, and black pepper. Stir in the remaining 1/2 cup stock.

Cook the vermicelli according to package directions and drain. Toss the pasta with the garlic sauce in a warm serving dish. Sprinkle with the pine nuts and serve immediately. Pass Romano cheese at the table, if desired.

Kilocalories 964 Kc • Protein 35 Gm • Fat 49 Gm • Percent of calories from fat 43% • Cholesterol 174 mg • Dietary Fiber 7 Gm • Sodium 286 mg • Calcium 122 mg

Red Onion Salad with Penne

4 SERVINGS

2 cups loosely packed, thinly sliced red onion rings (1 large onion)
$1/4$ cup extra-virgin olive oil
2 tablespoons red wine vinegar
$1/2$ teaspoon caraway seeds
$1/2$ teaspoon sugar

$1/2$ teaspoon salt
$1/4$ teaspoon freshly ground pepper
4 ounces ($1/4$ pound) penne
2 cups chopped fresh young spinach leaves, washed and spun dry

Soak the sliced onions in ice water for a half hour or more. Drain well.

In a salad bowl, mix together the oil, vinegar, caraway seeds, sugar, salt, and pepper. Stir in the onion rings.

Cook the penne according to package directions and drain. Rinse under cold water until cool. Stir the penne and spinach into the onion mixture.

Kilocalories 264 Kc • Protein 5 Gm • Fat 14 Gm • Percent of calories from fat 48% • Cholesterol 0 mg • Dietary Fiber 3 Gm • Sodium 317 mg • Calcium 51 mg

Pleasing Peas

"Good things come in small packages," particularly nature's little seed packets. Perhaps the most common of American vegetable side dishes, and definitely lacking in avant-garde fanfare, peas are a surprisingly nutritious vegetable. A cup of peas contains more protein than a large egg, with less than half a gram of fat. Peas are rich in vitamin C, vitamin A, iron, and fiber, too—a kind of vegetable multivitamin! Take a cup of peas to ward off heart disease, built up energy, defend against cancer, and generally fight off the effects of aging.

Delectable fresh peas are a bit of work to shell, but well worth the effort during their short season. To make easy work of it, snap off the top of a pod, pull the string down the side, and press open the side seam. The peas will fall right out into a bowl or strainer.

Fresh peas are an early summer vegetable. The rest of the year we must make do with frozen peas, an acceptable substitute—but never use canned peas! Snow peas and sugar snap peas are meant to be eaten "pods and all." With snow peas, just trim both ends. With sugar snaps, you must remove the stem and then pull the strings off both sides. Dried peas make a substantial, nourishing winter soup.

Refrigerate fresh peas of any variety in a perforated plastic bag and cook them soon—the same day, if possible. If necessary, however, they may be kept three to four days.

Snow peas add a nice crunch to stir-fries. Sugar snaps, lightly cooked, are great in salads. Raw sugar snaps can be served with dips. Any way you serve them, peas are pleasingly plump with good food value!

Sweet Pea Soup with Stellini

---

4 SERVINGS

2 tablespoons olive oil
1 cup chopped yellow onion
1 cup chopped celery with
  leaves
3 cups fresh shelled or frozen
  sweet peas, thawed just
  enough to separate (if frozen,
  pour from a 20-ounce bag)

4 cups chicken or vegetable
  stock, or canned broth
2 teaspoons chopped
  fresh tarragon, or
  ½ teaspoon dried
½ teaspoon salt
¼ teaspoon white pepper
1 cup stellini (little stars)

In a large pot, heat the oil and sauté the onion and celery very slowly until golden, 10 minutes. Add the peas, stock, tarragon, salt, and pepper. Simmer the soup until the peas are very tender, 10 minutes.

Purée the soup in a food processor, in batches, since hot foods tend to bubble up. Return the soup to the pot and reheat. Meanwhile, cook the stellini according to package directions. Drain the pasta and stir it into the soup.

Kilocalories 304 Kc • Protein 15 Gm • Fat 9 Gm • Percent of calories from fat 26% • Cholesterol 0 mg • Dietary Fiber 7 Gm • Sodium 751 mg • Calcium 64 mg

Split Pea Soup with Quadrettini

Slowly sautéed vegetables give this vegetarian soup its rich flavor.

¼ cup olive oil

1 medium yellow onion, chopped

2 celery stalks, diced

1 large carrot, diced

2 garlic cloves, minced

1 cup dried split peas, sorted, washed, and drained

7 cups water

1 cup chopped canned tomatoes

2 tablespoons chopped fresh flat-leaf parsley

½ teaspoon salt

¼ teaspoon pepper

1 cup quadrettini (small flat squares; very small elbows can be substituted)

About 2 tablespoons Herb Medley Pesto or Basil Pesto (optional, but flavorful—see pages 10 and 11 for basic recipes)

In a large heavy pot, heat the oil and sauté the onion, celery, carrot, and garlic until they are golden but not brown, 10 minutes. Add the peas, water, tomatoes, parsley, salt, and pepper. Bring the soup to a boil and simmer it over low heat, covered, for 1 hour, stirring frequently, especially toward the end of the cooking time. If the soup becomes too thick, add a little more water.

Cook the quadrettini according to package directions and drain. Stir the pasta into the soup before serving. If you wish, swirl a scant teaspoon of pesto in each bowl.

Kilocalories 237 Kc • Protein 8 Gm • Fat 10 Gm • Percent of calories from fat 36% • Cholesterol 0 mg • Dietary Fiber 4 Gm • Sodium 287 mg • Calcium 44 mg

Peas Paprika with Egg Noodles

---

4 SERVINGS

Prepared in a classic Hungarian manner, but with a lighter touch.

2 tablespoons olive oil
1 large onion, diced
1 celery stalk, diced
2 teaspoons cornstarch
2 tablespoons sweet paprika
1 cup chicken stock or
  canned broth
1½ cups fresh shelled peas, or
  a 10-ounce package frozen,
  thawed just enough to
  separate

½ cup plain nonfat yogurt, at
  room temperature
8 ounces (½ pound) medium
  egg noodles

Heat the oil in a skillet and sauté the onion and celery over very low heat until they are soft and golden, 8 to 10 minutes. Whisk the cornstarch and paprika into the stock. Add the peas and stock to the skillet and simmer, stirring constantly, until the mixture is thick and bubbling. Continue to cook over very low heat, stirring occasionally, for 5 minutes. Remove from the heat and whisk in the yogurt.

Meanwhile, cook the egg noodles according to package directions. Drain and spoon into a serving dish. Spoon the peas on top.

Kilocalories 378 Kc • Protein 15 Gm • Fat 10 Gm • Percent of calories from fat 24% • Cholesterol 55 mg • Dietary Fiber 6 Gm • Sodium 154 mg • Calcium 108 mg

Peas, Tomatoes, and Pesto with Small Shells

4 SERVINGS

2 tablespoons olive oil
1/4 cup finely chopped shallots
1 cup peeled, seeded, diced
  fresh tomatoes
1 1/2 cups fresh shelled peas, or
  a 10-ounce package frozen,
  thawed just enough to
  separate

2 tablespoons basil pesto (from
  a jar or see page 9 for basic
  recipe)
8 ounces (1/2 pound) small
  shells

Heat the oil in a large skillet and sauté the shallots until they are soft and fragrant. Add the tomatoes and continue cooking, uncovered, stirring often, for 5 minutes.

Add the peas and cook over low heat, stirring occasionally, until tender, about 5 minutes. Remove from the heat and stir in the pesto.

Meanwhile, cook the shells according to package directions and drain. Toss with the peas.

Kilocalories 373 Kc • Protein 11 Gm • Fat 13 Gm • Percent of calories from fat 31% • Cholesterol 0 mg • Dietary Fiber 4 Gm • Sodium 55 mg • Calcium 30 mg

Peas and Prosciutto with Fettuccine

---

4 SERVINGS

A slimmed-down version of a Northern Italian spring dish.

3 tablespoons nonfat dry milk

3 tablespoons superfine flour, such as Wondra

1 teaspoon chopped fresh thyme, or ¼ teaspoon dried

½ teaspoon salt

¼ teaspoon white pepper

2 cups milk (whole or low-fat)

1 tablespoon olive oil

¼ cup finely chopped shallots

4 ounces (¼ pound) prosciutto, cut into slivers

1½ cups fresh shelled peas, or a 10-ounce package frozen, thawed just enough to separate

12 ounces (¾ pound) fettuccine

2 tablespoons grated Parmesan cheese

1 tablespoon minced fresh flat-leaf parsley

Whisk the dry milk, flour, thyme, salt, and pepper into the liquid milk.

Heat the oil in a large skillet and sauté the shallots and prosciutto for 2 to 3 minutes. Pour the milk mixture into the skillet and cook over medium-high heat, stirring constantly, until the mixture bubbles and thickens. Add the peas and simmer until they are just tender, about 5 minutes.

Meanwhile, cook the fettuccine according to package directions and drain. Spoon it into a large serving dish and toss with the pea mixture, the cheese, and the parsley.

Kilocalories 545 Kc • Protein 27 Gm • Fat 11 Gm • Percent of calories from fat 19% • Cholesterol 34 mg • Dietary Fiber 5 Gm • Sodium 789 mg • Calcium 232 mg

Peas, Onion, and Bell Pepper with Orzo Risotto

4 SERVINGS

2 tablespoons olive oil
1/2 cup chopped onion
1/2 cup chopped red bell pepper
1 garlic clove, minced
1 1/2 cups fresh shelled peas, or a 10-ounce package frozen, thawed just enough to separate

1 cup chicken stock or canned broth
1/4 teaspoon salt
1/4 teaspoon freshly ground black pepper
8 ounces (1/2 pound) orzo
1/2 cup loosely packed, freshly grated Parmesan cheese

In a medium-size skillet, heat the oil and sauté the onion, red pepper, and garlic for 3 minutes. Add the peas, stock, salt, and pepper, cover, and cook until the peas are tender, about 5 minutes.

Meanwhile, preheat the oven to 350 degrees F. Cook the orzo according to package directions and drain. (Slightly undercook the orzo—it will get softer when the dish is baked.) Combine the peas, orzo, and half of the cheese in a 2-quart casserole. Sprinkle the remaining cheese on top and bake for 15 to 20 minutes.

Kilocalories 370 Kc • Protein 16 Gm • Fat 11 Gm • Percent of calories from fat 27% • Cholesterol 8 mg • Dietary Fiber 5 Gm • Sodium 442 mg • Calcium 161 mg

Peas and Porcini Mushrooms with Orzo Risotto

---

4 SERVINGS

Dried porcini mushrooms are an imported treat but inclined to be gritty with sand. The method of cleaning them given in this recipe is well worth the trouble for a grit-free finished dish.

¹/₂ cup dried porcini
  mushrooms
1¹/₄ cups very hot water
2 tablespoons olive oil
2 garlic cloves, minced
1¹/₂ cups fresh shelled peas, or
  a 10-ounce package frozen,
  thawed just enough to
  separate

¹/₄ teaspoon salt
¹/₄ teaspoon freshly ground
  black pepper
8 ounces (¹/₂ pound) orzo
¹/₂ cup loosely packed, freshly
  grated Parmesan cheese

Soak the mushrooms in the water for 30 minutes. Drain, reserving the liquid. Rinse each mushroom under running water to remove all grit. Drain and chop the reconstituted mushrooms. Put a paper coffee filter in a medium-size strainer and strain the reserved mushroom liquid.

In a medium-size skillet, heat the oil and sauté the garlic until softened and fragrant. Add the peas, mushrooms, reserved mushroom liquid, salt, and pepper, and cook, uncovered, until the peas are tender, about 5 minutes.

Meanwhile, preheat the oven to 350 degrees F. Cook the orzo al dente according to package directions and drain. Combine the peas, orzo, and half of the cheese in a 2-quart casserole. Sprinkle the remaining cheese on top and bake for 15 to 20 minutes.

Kilocalories 394 Kc • Protein 16 Gm • Fat 11 Gm • Percent of calories from fat 25% • Cholesterol 8 mg • Dietary Fiber 6 Gm • Sodium 339 mg • Calcium 158 mg

Sautéed Peas and
Lettuce à la Français with Capellini

2 LUNCHEON ENTRÉE SERVINGS

Peas taste even sweeter when they are braised with lettuce. This makes a very nice (and very quick!) luncheon dish for two.

2 tablespoons butter
¼ cup chopped shallots
1½ cups fresh shelled peas, or
  a 10-ounce package frozen,
  thawed just enough to
  separate
2 cups shredded lettuce
  (iceberg or romaine)
½ cup chicken stock or canned
  broth

1 teaspoon chopped fresh
  thyme, or ¼ teaspoon dried
1 teaspoon chopped
  fresh tarragon, or
  ¼ teaspoon dried
Salt and freshly ground pepper
4 ounces (¼ pound) capellini
2 slices smoked salmon,
  slivered, for garnish
  (optional)

Heat the butter in a large skillet and sauté the shallots until softened, 3 minutes. Add the peas, lettuce, stock, herbs, and salt and pepper to your taste. Cover and simmer until the peas are tender, 5 minutes.

Meanwhile, cook the capellini according to package directions and drain. Divide it between two wide pasta dishes or soup plates. Divide the pea mixture between the two dishes. If desired, top with smoked salmon slivers.

Kilocalories 424 Kc • Protein 15 Gm • Fat 14 Gm • Percent of calories from fat 30% • Cholesterol 33 mg • Dietary Fiber 8 Gm • Sodium 245 mg • Calcium 62 mg

Sautéed Peas and Walnuts with Shell Pasta

4 SERVINGS

1 cup walnut halves
1 tablespoon butter
1 tablespoon olive oil
1 bunch scallions, cut into
  1-inch pieces
1½ cups fresh shelled peas, or
  a 10-ounce package frozen,
  thawed just enough to
  separate

½ cup chicken stock or canned
  broth
¼ teaspoon salt
⅛ teaspoon cayenne pepper
8 ounces (½ pound) medium
  shells

In a small saucepan, cover the walnuts with water and bring to a boil. Drain and rinse the walnuts.

Heat the butter and oil in a large skillet and toast the walnuts lightly. Remove them with a slotted spoon. Add the scallions to the butter and sauté for 3 minutes. Add the peas and stock, and cook uncovered, stirring often, until the broth has evaporated and the peas are tender, 5 minutes. Season with the salt and cayenne pepper, distributing the latter evenly. Stir in the walnuts.

Meanwhile, cook the shells according to package directions and drain. In a large serving dish, toss the pasta with the peas.

Kilocalories 511 Kc • Protein 18 Gm • Fat 26 Gm • Percent of calories from fat 44% • Cholesterol 8 mg • Dietary Fiber 6 Gm • Sodium 234 mg • Calcium 40 mg

Curried Peas and Mushrooms with Orzo

4 SERVINGS

Based on a spicy Indian vegetable curry, with pasta replacing the traditional rice.

2 tablespoons vegetable oil
1 large yellow onion, sliced
1 slice fresh ginger, peeled and minced
10 ounces button mushrooms, cleaned and halved
2 cups peeled chopped fresh or canned tomatoes

1½ cups fresh shelled peas, or a 10-ounce package frozen, thawed just enough to separate
1 teaspoon curry powder
⅛ teaspoon cayenne pepper
Pinch of ground cinnamon
8 ounces (½ pound) orzo

Heat the oil in a large skillet and sauté the onion and ginger for 3 minutes. Add the mushrooms and continue to sauté until the mushrooms are beginning to brown. Add the tomatoes, peas, curry, cayenne, and cinnamon. Braise over low heat until the peas are tender, 5 to 7 minutes. Taste to correct the seasonings; you may want more curry or cayenne.

Meanwhile, cook the orzo according to package directions and drain. Spoon into a large serving dish. Toss with half the vegetable mixture. Top with the remaining vegetables and serve.

Kilocalories 345 Kc • Protein 13 Gm • Fat 10 Gm • Percent of calories from fat 25% • Cholesterol 58 mg • Dietary Fiber 8 Gm • Sodium 37 mg • Calcium 54 mg

Peas and Bell Peppers with Spinach Fettuccine

4 SERVINGS

A colorful dish that's chock-full of vitamin C.

2 tablespoons olive oil
1 yellow bell pepper, seeded and cut into strips
1 green bell pepper, seeded and cut into strips
1 red bell pepper, seeded and cut into strips
2 garlic cloves, minced
1½ cups fresh shelled peas, or a 10-ounce package frozen, thawed just enough to separate

½ cup chicken or vegetable stock, or canned broth
½ teaspoon salt
Freshly ground black pepper
2 tablespoons chopped fresh flat-leaf parsley
8 ounces (½ pound) spinach fettuccine
½ cup loosely packed, freshly grated Romano cheese

Heat the oil in a large skillet and sauté the bell peppers until they begin to soften slightly, 2 minutes. Add the garlic and continue cooking for 1 minute. Add the peas and stock; cover and simmer over low heat until the peas are tender, 5 minutes. Season with the salt and pepper to your taste. Sprinkle with parsley.

Meanwhile, cook the fettuccine according to package directions and drain. Spoon it into a large serving dish and toss with the vegetables and cheese.

Kilocalories 381 Kc • Protein 16 Gm • Fat 13 Gm • Percent of calories from fat 29% • Cholesterol 64 mg • Dietary Fiber 8 Gm • Sodium 510 mg • Calcium 164 mg

Stir-fried Snow Peas and Bean Sprouts with Asian Noodles

4 SERVINGS

1/2 cup chicken stock or canned broth
1 teaspoon cornstarch
1 tablespoon soy sauce
1 teaspoon sesame oil
1 teaspoon sugar
1/2 teaspoon salt
1 tablespoon vegetable oil
About 1 1/2 cups fresh snow peas, ends trimmed

1 red bell pepper, seeded and cut into strips
4 scallions, cut into 2-inch lengths
1/2 pound fresh bean sprouts
8 ounces (1/2 pound) dried thin Asian noodles or American vermicelli
1/2 cup cashews or peanuts (optional)

Whisk together the stock, cornstarch, soy sauce, sesame oil, sugar, and salt.

Heat the oil in a large wok or skillet and add the snow peas, bell pepper, and scallions; stir-fry for 2 minutes. Add the bean sprouts and stir-fry 1 to 2 minutes longer. Pour in the stock mixture and stir until the vegetables are coated with the thickened sauce. Continue cooking over very low heat for 2 to 3 minutes.

Meanwhile, cook the noodles according to package directions and drain. Spoon them into a large serving dish and toss with the vegetables. If you wish, sprinkle with cashews or peanuts.

Kilocalories 278 Kc • Protein 9 Gm • Fat 5 Gm • Percent of calories from fat 16% • Cholesterol 0 mg • Dietary Fiber 2 Gm • Sodium 862 mg • Calcium 57 mg

Sugar Snap Peas and Tomatoes with Rotelle

2 tablespoons olive oil
2 teaspoons minced garlic
1 cup peeled, seeded, diced
   ripe tomatoes
1 tablespoon minced fresh
   basil, or 1 teaspoon dried
1/2 pound fresh sugar snap
   peas, strings removed, or a
   10-ounce package frozen

Salt and freshly ground pepper
8 ounces (1/2 pound) rotelle
2 tablespoons freshly grated
   Parmesan cheese, plus more
   to pass

Heat the oil in a large skillet and sauté the garlic until it's soft but not brown. Add the tomatoes and basil; simmer until slightly thickened, 5 minutes.

Add the sugar snap peas and stir until they separate, if frozen. Cover and cook until they are almost tender, 2 to 3 minutes, allowing the heat of the sauce to finish the cooking. Season them with salt and pepper to your taste.

Cook the rotelle according to package directions; drain. In a large serving dish, toss the pasta with the vegetables. Stir in the cheese and pass more cheese at the table.

Kilocalories 316 Kc • Protein 10 Gm • Fat 9 Gm • Percent of calories from fat 25% • Cholesterol 2 mg • Dietary Fiber 3 Gm • Sodium 57 mg • Calcium 75 mg

Peas and Pastina Salad

4 SERVINGS

¼ cup olive oil
Juice of 1 large lemon (about ¼ cup)
1 tablespoon chopped fresh mint, or 1 teaspoon dried
½ teaspoon salt
⅛ to ¼ teaspoon pepper

1 10-ounce package frozen petit peas
8 radishes, sliced
2 celery stalks, chopped
4 scallions with green tops, chopped
1 cup pastina

In a salad dish, whisk together the oil, lemon juice, mint, salt, and pepper.

Cook the peas according to package directions, but just until barely tender; do not overcook. Rinse in cold water and drain. Toss the peas, radishes, celery, and scallions with the dressing.

Cook the pastina for 3 minutes only. Drain in a close-meshed strainer and rinse in cold water until cool. Stir the pastina into the salad. Allow the salad to marinate at room temperature for a half hour or so.

Kilocalories 385 Kc • Protein 11 Gm • Fat 15 Gm • Percent of calories from fat 33% • Cholesterol 0 mg • Dietary Fiber 6 Gm • Sodium 485 mg • Calcium 34 mg

Snow Peas and Turnip Pasta Salad

---

4 SERVINGS

$^1/_2$ **pound fresh snow peas, ends trimmed**
$^1/_3$ **cup olive oil**
2 to 3 tablespoons lemon juice, to your taste
2 tablespoons snipped chives (or $^1/_4$ cup chopped scallion tops)
$^1/_2$ **teaspoon salt**

Freshly ground black pepper
6 ounces (about $^1/_3$ pound) mezzani
6 radishes, thinly sliced
1 cucumber, peeled and thinly sliced
1 small young purple-topped turnip, peeled and thinly sliced

Cook the snow peas in boiling salted water for 1 minute. Drain and rinse in cold water.

Whisk together the oil, lemon juice, chives, salt, and pepper to your taste. Cook the mezzani according to package directions and drain. Rinse in cold water until cool to the touch and spoon the pasta into a large serving dish. Toss with the dressing. Add all the remaining ingredients, including the snow peas, and chill.

Just before serving, toss the salad again and taste to correct the seasonings, adding more oil, lemon juice, salt, or pepper as desired.

Kilocalories 365 Kc • Protein 8 Gm • Fat 19 Gm • Percent of calories from fat 47% • Cholesterol 0 mg • Dietary Fiber 3 Gm • Sodium 317 mg • Calcium 54 mg

Snow Peas and Scallops Pasta Salad

4 SERVINGS

Follow the preceding recipe, omitting the turnip and radishes. Poach $^1/_2$ pound small bay scallops in 1 cup vegetable broth or bouillon until they are cooked through, 3 minutes. Drain and cool slightly. Add the scallops with the pasta

Kilocalories 430 Kc • Protein 20 Gm • Fat 19 Gm • Percent of calories from fat 42% • Cholesterol 30 mg • Dietary Fiber 3 Gm • Sodium 558 mg • Calcium 112 mg

Peppers to Add Zing

Not only do peppers offer a wide range of pungent flavors, from mild to fiery, they also add a generous supply of nutrients and healing power to the dishes they enliven. Surprisingly, sweet bell peppers contain twice as much vitamin C as citrus fruits do, and hot peppers even more. Red bell peppers are rich in carotene, a champion cancer-fighter. Hot peppers contain capsaicin—the hotter the pepper, the more of this important food chemical it contains. Capsaicin alleviates respiratory problems as well as functioning as an antioxidant, like vitamin C, to sponge up the free radicals that cause cell mutation in the body.

Choices! Choices! Enjoy the endless variety that peppers offer. Bell peppers come in green, red, yellow, and purple (which turns green when cooked). Green bells have the sharpest flavor of the "sweet" peppers. Red bells are the sweetest. Yellow bells are the mildest and therefore most digestible, so I prefer them for stuffing. Italian frying peppers also have a mild flavor, and their very thin skins make them perfect for quick sautés and salads.

Among the hot peppers or chilies, the Anaheim (sometimes called the "California pepper") has a mild zing that's easily tolerated by most palates. For more assertive "hot stuff," jalapeños are generally available fresh or canned.

Buy peppers that are unwrinkled, glossy, and free of cracks, with healthy stems. Peppers stored in a perforated plastic bag in the refrigerator will keep three to four days. Red bells spoil fastest of all the peppers.

The hottest parts of hot chilies are the white pith and seeds. Some people's skins are allergic to capsaisin, so as a precaution, wear rubber gloves when cleaning and seeding hot chilies.

Philadelphia Pepper-Pot Soup with Egg Noodles

■

6 SERVINGS

Originally a Dutch soup that relied on cayenne pepper for its "heat," this translated version uses chilies instead. Just the dish to relieve those cold weather woes!

2 tablespoons olive oil
2 red bell peppers, seeded
   and diced
2 Anaheim chilies, seeded
   and diced
1 jalapeño chili, seeded and
   minced (wear rubber gloves)
1 large yellow onion, chopped
2 celery stalks, diced
1 large carrot, diced

1 large white potato, peeled,
   whole
6 cups chicken stock or
   canned broth
Several sprigs of fresh flat-leaf
   parsley, chopped
$1/2$ teaspoon salt
$1/4$ teaspoon freshly ground
   pepper
4 ounces ($1/4$ pound) medium
   egg noodles

Heat the oil in a large pot and slowly sauté the peppers, chilies, onion, celery, and carrot over low heat until soft, 10 minutes. Add the potato, stock, parsley, and seasonings and simmer the soup for 20 to 25 minutes. Remove the potato, mash it, and return it to the soup.

Meanwhile, cook the noodles separately according to package directions and drain. Stir them into the soup.

Kilocalories 205 Kc • Protein 9 Gm • Fat 7 Gm • Percent of calories from fat 30% • Cholesterol 18 mg • Dietary Fiber 3 Gm • Sodium 655 mg • Calcium 41 mg

Chili Chowder with Sweet Potatoes and Shells

6 SERVINGS

2 tablespoons olive oil
2 Anaheim chilies, seeded and diced
1 to 2 jalapeño chilies, seeded and minced (wear rubber gloves)
1 large yellow onion, chopped
1 pound sweet potatoes, peeled, diced
2 cups chicken stock or canned broth

3 cups milk (whole or low-fat)
1/4 cup nonfat dry milk
3 tablespoons superfine flour, such as Wondra
1/2 teaspoon ground cumin
1/2 teaspoon salt
1/4 teaspoon white pepper
4 ounces (1/4 pound) medium shells
Several sprigs of fresh flat-leaf parsley, chopped

Heat the oil in a large pot and sauté the chilies and onion until softened, 5 minutes. Add the potatoes and stock and simmer, covered, until the vegetables are tender, 10 minutes. Add 2 cups of the milk and heat, but do not boil yet.

Whisk the dry milk, flour, cumin, salt, and pepper into the remaining cup of liquid milk and pour the mixture all at once into the soup. Cook over medium heat, stirring, until the mixture bubbles and thickens slightly. Reduce the heat to very low and simmer the chowder for 5 minutes.

Meanwhile, cook the shells according to package directions and drain. Stir the pasta and parsley into the soup. Taste to correct the seasoning, adding more salt if needed.

Kilocalories 306 Kc • Protein 10 Gm • Fat 10 Gm • Percent of calories from fat 28% • Cholesterol 17 mg • Dietary Fiber 3 Gm • Sodium 449 mg • Calcium 192 mg

Stir-fry Peppers with Rice Stick Noodles

4 SERVINGS

Stir-frying in a wok requires less oil than any other method.

1 tablespoon vegetable oil
4 bell peppers, seeded and cut
  into large triangles—if
  possible, use different colors
1 large sweet onion, such as
  Vidalia, thinly sliced
6 large radishes, thinly sliced
2 tablespoons naturally brewed
  soy sauce, plus more to pass

1 teaspoon oyster sauce
  (available in the Asian
  food section of most
  supermarkets)
6 ounces (about $1/3$ pound) rice
  stick noodles (see Note)

Heat the oil in a large wok or skillet and stir-fry the vegetables until they are tender-crisp, 3 to 5 minutes. (You may need a little more oil if you use a skillet.) Blend the soy sauce and oyster sauce, and stir the mixture into the vegetables.

Heat a pot of water to the boiling point, remove from the heat, and soak the noodles in it until they are tender, 5 to 7 minutes. Drain. Gently toss the vegetables with the noodles. Pass more soy sauce at the table.

NOTE: If you substitute American capellini for the Asian noodles, cook according to the package directions.

Kilocalories 221 Kc • Protein 2 Gm • Fat 4 Gm • Percent of calories from fat 15% • Cholesterol 0 mg • Dietary Fiber 2 Gm • Sodium 550 mg • Calcium 28 mg

Sautéed Bell Peppers, Provolone, and Rigatoni

4 SERVINGS

3 tablespoons olive oil
1 large onion, chopped
6 large bell peppers (mixed colors, if possible), seeded and cut into strips
1 to 2 garlic cloves, chopped
$1/2$ cup vegetable or chicken stock, or canned broth, or juice from tomatoes
1 pound fresh plum tomatoes, or 5 canned plum tomatoes, quartered and seeded

2 tablespoons chopped fresh basil, or 1 teaspoon dried
$1/2$ teaspoon salt
$1/4$ teaspoon freshly ground pepper
12 ounces ($3/4$ pound) rigatoni
About 4 ounces provolone cheese, diced

Heat the oil in a large skillet and slowly sauté the onion and bell peppers until softened but not brown, 5 to 8 minutes. Add the garlic during the last minute. Add the stock or juice and tomatoes and continue cooking until the vegetables are very tender, 10 minutes. Season with the basil, salt, and pepper.

Meanwhile, cook the rigatoni according to package directions and drain. Spoon it into a large serving dish. Add the cheese and bell pepper mixture and toss to blend.

Kilocalories 576 Kc • Protein 21 Gm • Fat 19 Gm • Percent of calories from fat 30% • Cholesterol 20 mg • Dietary Fiber 6 Gm • Sodium 865 mg • Calcium 271 mg

Roasted Peppers with Spaghetti

■

Plan on preparing the peppers at least an hour before cooking the pasta, or roast them the night before.

3 large red bell peppers—or
  2 red and 1 yellow
2¹⁄₂ tablespoons olive oil
1 garlic clove, halved
Salt and freshly ground black
  pepper
1 cup fresh bread crumbs,
  made in a food processor
  from 1 slice Italian bread

¹⁄₄ cup pine nuts
2 tablespoons golden raisins
12 ounces (³⁄₄ pound) spaghetti
2 tablespoons freshly ground
  Parmesan cheese
2 tablespoons chopped fresh
  flat-leaf parsley

Lay the bell peppers on a broiling pan and broil them 3 to 4 inches from the heat source. Turn them with tongs as they cook, until most sides are slightly charred and the peppers are tender, 6 to 10 minutes; they will collapse when pressed with a fork.

Put the peppers in a covered casserole to cool; the steam will loosen their skins. When they are cool enough to handle, peel off the skins, cut the peppers in half, and scrape out the seeds. Cut the peppers into strips.

Rinse and dry the casserole; put the pepper strips back into it. Add 2 tablespoons of the oil, the garlic, salt, and black pepper to your taste. Allow the roasted peppers to marinate, stirring once or twice, for at least 1 hour or overnight, refrigerated. Remove the garlic before proceeding with the recipe.

Heat the remaining ¹⁄₂ tablespoon oil in a large skillet. Add the bread crumbs and nuts, and lightly toast, stirring constantly, until they are barely golden. Add the peppers and the marinating oil and the raisins, and warm the mixture over low heat.

Meanwhile, cook the spaghetti according to package directions. Drain and toss the spaghetti with the bell pepper mixture and the grated cheese.

Divide the pasta among 4 serving dishes, and sprinkle with chopped parsley.

Kilocalories 456 Kc • Protein 13 Gm • Fat 11 Gm • Percent of calories from fat 22% • Cholesterol 2 mg • Dietary Fiber 4 Gm • Sodium 99 mg • Calcium 67 mg

Roasted Peppers, Anchovies, and Spaghettini

4 SERVINGS

Follow the preceding recipe. Substitute 6 to 8 flat anchovy fillets, chopped, for the nuts, raisins, and Parmesan, as follows: Heat the remaining $1/2$ tablespoon oil in a skillet and slowly warm the anchovies until they begin to dissolve. Add the bread crumbs and lightly toast them, stirring. Add the peppers and continue with the recipe as above, substituting spaghettini for spaghetti. Coarsely grated Asiago cheese can be used as a topping with the parsley.

Kilocalories 439 Kc • Protein 14 Gm • Fat 11 Gm • Percent of calories from fat 22% • Cholesterol 5 mg • Dietary Fiber 3 Gm • Sodium 273 mg • Calcium 44 mg

Red Bell Peppers Stuffed with Orzo

4 SERVINGS

2 large red bell peppers (box-shaped rather than long)
$2/3$ cup orzo
3 tablespoons chopped sun-dried tomatoes (use oil-packed tomatoes)
1 tablespoon oil from the tomatoes

3 tablespoons toasted pine nuts
2 tablespoons raisins
1 tablespoon chopped fresh flat-leaf parsley
Salt and freshly ground black pepper

Cut the bell peppers in half lengthwise and seed them. Bring a medium-large pot of water to a boil, add the salt you would add for pasta, and parboil the peppers until soft, 5 to 7 minutes. Remove them with a slotted spoon and drain them upside down. Add the orzo to the same water, cook according to package directions (undercooking it slightly), and drain.

Preheat the oven to 350 degrees F.

Mix the orzo with the sun-dried tomatoes, oil, pine nuts, raisins, parsley, and salt and pepper to your taste. Stuff the peppers with this mixture and arrange them in an oiled baking dish. Bake 20 to 25 minutes, until hot throughout.

Kilocalories 204 Kc • Protein 7 Gm • Fat 5 Gm • Percent of calories from fat 19% • Cholesterol 0 mg • Dietary Fiber 3 Gm • Sodium 55 mg • Calcium 12 mg

Yellow Bell Peppers Florentine with Pastina

— ■ —

4 SERVINGS

2 large yellow bell peppers
  (box-shaped rather than long)
$1/2$ cup pastina
1 tablespoon olive oil
1 cup cooked drained spinach
$1/4$ cup chopped sweet onion,
  such as Vidalia

2 tablespoons freshly grated
  Parmesan cheese
1 slice crisply cooked bacon,
  crumbled (optional)
Salt and freshly ground black
  pepper

Cut the bell peppers in half lengthwise and seed them. Bring a medium-large pot of water to a boil, add the salt you would add for pasta, and par-boil the peppers until soft, 5 to 7 minutes. Remove them with a slotted spoon and drain them upside down. Add the pastina to the same water, cook according to package directions (undercooking it slightly), and drain.

Preheat the oven to 350 degrees F.

Mix the cooked pastina with all the remaining ingredients and salt and pepper to your taste. Stuff the peppers and arrange the halves in an oiled baking dish. Bake 25 to 30 minutes, until hot and fragrant.

Kilocalories 168 Kc • Protein 6 Gm • Fat 5 Gm • Percent of calories from fat 25% • Cholesterol 2 mg • Dietary Fiber 3 Gm • Sodium 88 mg • Calcium 109 mg

Melting Pot Peppers, Shrimp, and Pineapple with Couscous

4 SERVINGS

This is truly a dish of mixed cultures, which makes it uniquely American.

1 cup couscous, raw
2 tablespoons olive oil
3 green bell peppers, seeded and cut into chunks
1 bunch scallions, cut into 2-inch lengths
1 garlic clove, minced
2 tablespoons chopped fresh flat-leaf parsley
$1/8$ to $1/4$ teaspoon cayenne pepper, to your taste

12 ounces cooked, shelled, deveined shrimp (see page 14 for basic recipe)
$2/3$ cup canned unsugared pineapple chunks, drained (reserve juice)
1 tablespoon naturally brewed soy sauce
2 teaspoons cornstarch
$1/2$ cup juice from the pineapple

Prepare the couscous (see page 12 for basic recipe or follow package directions); fluff and separate the grains.

In a large skillet, heat the oil and sauté the bell peppers and scallions until they are soft, 5 minutes, adding the garlic during the last minute. Add the parsley and cayenne pepper; stir to blend. Add the shrimp and pineapple. Stir the soy sauce and cornstarch into the juice until blended. Add the juice mixture all at once and cook, stirring, until the sauce thickens and coats the peppers and shrimp. Keep warm for a few minutes to blend the flavors.

To serve, spoon the warm couscous onto a large platter and top with the pepper-shrimp mixture.

Kilocalories 392 Kc • Protein 25 Gm • Fat 8 Gm • Percent of calories from fat 19% • Cholesterol 166 mg • Dietary Fiber 4 Gm • Sodium 498 mg • Calcium 72 mg

Fettuccine with Red Bell Pepper Sauce

4 SERVINGS

A puréed sauce with the zing of cayenne.

2 red bell peppers
2 tablespoons olive oil
2 celery stalks, diced
1 yellow onion, chopped
2 garlic cloves, minced
2 cups chicken stock or
  canned broth

1/2 teaspoon salt
1 teaspoon minced fresh
  thyme, or 1/4 teaspoon dried
1/4 teaspoon cayenne pepper
1/4 teaspoon black pepper
12 ounces (3/4 pound)
  fettuccine

Lay the bell peppers on a broiling pan and broil them 3 to 4 inches from the heat source. Turn them with tongs as they cook, until most sides are slightly charred and the peppers are tender, 6 to 10 minutes; they will collapse when pressed with a fork.

Put the peppers in a covered dish to cool; the steam will loosen their skins. When they are cool enough to handle, peel off the skins, cut the peppers in half, and scrape out the seeds.

In a medium skillet, heat the oil and sauté the celery, onion, and garlic until they are softened, 3 to 5 minutes. Add the stock and boil until the mixture is reduced to about 1 1/2 cups.

In a food processor, purée the roasted peppers, gradually adding the stock and sautéed vegetables. Return the purée to the skillet. Add the salt, thyme, cayenne, and black pepper, and continue to cook over low heat, stirring often, until the sauce is as thick as salsa.

Meanwhile, cook the fettuccine according to package directions and drain. In a large serving dish, toss the pasta with the bell pepper sauce.

Kilocalories 425 Kc • Protein 14 Gm • Fat 9 Gm • Percent of calories from fat 19% • Cholesterol 0 mg • Dietary Fiber 4 Gm • Sodium 529 mg • Calcium 43 mg

Pepper and Olive Salad with Couscous

4 SERVINGS

3 tablespoons olive oil

2 red bell peppers, seeded and cut into triangles

2 green bell peppers, seeded and cut into triangles

1 large onion, chopped

2 garlic cloves, minced

$\frac{1}{2}$ cup sliced pitted Sicilian green olives (see Note)

$\frac{1}{4}$ cup slivered sun-dried tomatoes

2 tablespoons drained capers

$\frac{1}{4}$ cup chopped fresh flat-leaf parsley

3 tablespoons red wine vinegar

$\frac{1}{2}$ teaspoon salt

$\frac{1}{8}$ to $\frac{1}{4}$ teaspoon black pepper

1 cup couscous, raw

Heat the oil in a large skillet and sauté the bell peppers, onion, and garlic until the vegetables are partly softened, 3 to 5 minutes. Remove from the heat and stir in the olives, sun-dried tomatoes, capers, parsley, vinegar, salt, and black pepper. Allow this mixture to marinate for a half hour or so.

Prepare the couscous (see page 12 for basic recipe or follow package directions); fluff and separate the grains. Spoon the prepared couscous into a salad bowl and blend with the bell pepper mixture. Serve at room temperature.

NOTE: To pit the olives, whack each one with a wooden mallet or the side of a heavy knife to loosen the flesh from the stone.

Kilocalories 380 Kc • Protein 8 Gm • Fat 16 Gm • Percent of calories from fat 38% • Cholesterol 0 mg • Dietary Fiber 5 Gm • Sodium 692 mg • Calcium 38 mg

Lemon Pepper Salad with Couscous

—■—

Even though you peel off the charred skin, the lovely roasted flavor remains in peppers cooked under a broiler.

4 yellow bell peppers	**Pinch of cayenne pepper**
1/4 cup olive oil	**1 teaspoon chopped fresh mint**
1/4 cup fresh lemon juice	**leaves, or 1/4 teaspoon dried**
1/4 teaspoon salt	**1 garlic clove, halved**
Several grinds of black pepper	**1 cup couscous, raw**

Lay the bell peppers on a broiling pan and broil them 3 to 4 inches from the heat source. Turn them with tongs as they cook, until most sides are slightly charred and the peppers are tender, 6 to 8 minutes; they will collapse when pressed with a fork.

Put the peppers in a covered casserole to cool; the steam will loosen their skins. When they are cool enough to handle, peel off the skins, cut the peppers in half, and scrape out the seeds. Cut the peppers into strips.

Rinse and dry the casserole; put the pepper strips into it. Add all the remaining ingredients except the couscous. Allow the peppers to marinate, stirring once or twice, for at least 1 hour, or overnight, refrigerated. Remove the garlic before proceeding with the recipe.

Prepare the couscous (see page 12 for basic recipe or follow package directions); fluff and separate the grains. Spoon the prepared couscous into a salad bowl and top with the lemon-pepper mixture. Serve at room temperature.

Kilocalories 327 Kc • Protein 8 Gm • Fat 14 Gm • Percent of calories from fat 39% • Cholesterol 0 mg • Dietary Fiber 4 Gm • Sodium 593 mg • Calcium 21 mg

Norwegian Roasted Pepper Salad with Pasta

■

4 SERVINGS

2 large red bell peppers
2 large green bell peppers
4 anchovy fillets, rinsed in
  vinegar and chopped
1 tablespoon drained capers
1/4 cup chopped fresh flat-leaf
  parsley

1/4 cup chopped scallions
1/2 cup or more Mustard
  Vinaigrette (see page 11 for
  basic recipe)
6 ounces (about 1/3 pound)
  mostaccioli or penne

Lay the bell peppers on a broiling pan and broil them 3 to 4 inches from the heat source. Turn them with tongs as they cook, until most sides are slightly charred and the peppers are tender, 6 to 10 minutes; they will collapse when pressed with a fork.

Put the peppers in a covered casserole to cool; the steam will loosen their skins. When they are cool enough to handle, peel off the skins, cut the peppers in half, and scrape out the seeds. Cut the peppers into strips.

Rinse and dry the casserole; put the pepper strips back into it. Toss them with the anchovies, capers, parsley, and scallions. Blend in the vinaigrette.

Meanwhile, cook the mostaccioli al dente according to package directions; rinse in cold water, drain well, and stir into the bell pepper mixture. Serve immediately or chill until needed. When ready to serve, toss again and taste to see if the salad needs more vinaigrette.

Kilocalories 387 Kc • Protein 8 Gm • Fat 23 Gm • Percent of calories from fat 53% • Cholesterol 3 mg • Dietary Fiber 3 Gm • Sodium 368 mg • Calcium 42 mg

Roasted Yellow Pepper and Dandelion Salad with Goat Cheese and Rotelle

2 large yellow bell peppers
Salt and freshly ground
  black pepper
4 tablespoons olive oil, or
  more as needed
1 garlic clove, halved
¼ cup chopped scallions
2 tablespoons white wine
  vinegar, or more as needed

4 ounces (¼ pound) rotelle
4 cups loosely packed
  dandelion greens (escarole
  can be substituted), chopped
8 slices goat cheese (from a
  cheese log) for garnishing

Lay the bell peppers on a broiling pan and broil them 3 to 4 inches from the heat source. Turn them with tongs as they cook, until most sides are slightly charred and the peppers are tender, 6 to 10 minutes; they will collapse when pressed with a fork.

Put the peppers in a covered dish to cool; the steam will loosen their skins. When they are cool enough to handle, peel off the skins, cut the peppers in half, and scrape out the seeds. Cut the peppers into strips.

Combine the peppers, salt and black pepper to your taste, olive oil, and garlic in a large serving dish and allow the mixture to marinate at room temperature for 30 minutes or so. Remove the garlic and stir in the scallions and vinegar.

Cook the rotelle according to package directions and drain. Rinse the pasta in cold water and toss it with the salad. Put the dandelion greens on top and chill the salad until ready to serve. Toss again, incorporating the greens. Taste the salad and add more oil or vinegar if desired.

Divide the salad among 4 plates and garnish with goat cheese slices.

Kilocalories 303 Kc • Protein 8 Gm • Fat 18 Gm • Percent of calories from fat 50% • Cholesterol 6 mg • Dietary Fiber 5 Gm • Sodium 92 mg • Calcium 151 mg

Green Bell Pepper and Mushroom Salad with Shells

4 SERVINGS

2 tablespoons olive oil
2 green bell peppers, seeded
  and cut into triangles
10 ounces mushrooms, cleaned
  and sliced
1 garlic clove, minced
1 teaspoon minced fresh
  tarragon, or
  ¼ teaspoon dried

Salt and freshly ground
  black pepper
¼ cup olive oil
3 tablespoons white wine
  vinegar
6 cherry tomatoes, halved
6 ounces (about ⅓ pound)
  medium shells

Heat the oil in a large skillet and sauté the bell peppers and mushrooms until they are lightly cooked; the peppers should still be tender-crisp. Add the garlic during the last minute of cooking. Season the peppers and mushrooms with the tarragon, and salt and black pepper to your taste.

Combine the pepper-mushroom mixture with all the remaining ingredients except the pasta in a large salad bowl and toss the mixture to blend. Allow the salad to marinate while cooking the pasta according to package directions. Drain and rinse the shells in cold water and stir them into the salad. Chill until ready to serve.

Kilocalories 372 Kc • Protein 7 Gm • Fat 21 Gm • Percent of calories from fat 51% • Cholesterol 0 mg • Dietary Fiber 3 Gm • Sodium 6 mg • Calcium 10 mg

Bell Pepper, Pecan, and Pasta Salad

———— ■ ————

4 SERVINGS

Nuts are good sources of vitamin E and many B vitamins.

3 bell peppers (different colors, if possible)
3 tablespoons olive oil
1 cup pecan halves or pieces

8 ounces (¹/₂ pound) mezzani
¹/₃ to ¹/₂ cup Herb Vinaigrette, to your taste (see page 10 for basic recipe)

Seed the bell peppers and cut them into small triangles. Heat the oil in a large skillet and sauté the peppers until they are barely tender-crisp, 3 minutes. Stir in the pecans. Transfer the peppers to a large salad bowl.

Meanwhile, cook the mezzani according to package directions and drain. Rinse in cold water and add to the peppers. Toss with the dressing.

Kilocalories 594 Kc • Protein 10 Gm • Fat 41 Gm • Percent of calories from fat 60% • Cholesterol 0 mg • Dietary Fiber 4 Gm • Sodium 97 mg • Calcium 26 mg

Italian Frying Pepper and Chickpea Pasta Salad

---

4 SERVINGS

Add some warm rolls or garlic bread and you'll have a quick summer luncheon or supper.

2 tablespoons olive oil
4 Italian frying peppers, seeded and cut into chunks
1 garlic clove, minced
1 16-ounce can chickpeas, drained and rinsed
1 tablespoon chopped fresh marjoram, or ¹/₂ teaspoon dried oregano
Salt and freshly ground black pepper

4 ounces (¹/₄ pound) medium shells
¹/₃ cup Herb Vinaigrette, or more to taste (see page 10 for basic recipe)
3 cups chopped escarole, inner leaves of 1 medium head
1 large ripe tomato, cut into wedges
4 hard-boiled eggs, quartered, as garnish (optional)

Heat the oil in a skillet and stir-fry the frying peppers until they are tender-crisp, 3 minutes. Add the garlic during the last minute. Stir in the chickpeas. Season the mixture with marjoram and salt and black pepper to your taste.

Meanwhile, cook the shells according to package directions and drain. Rinse them in cold water. Combine the vegetables, shells, and vinaigrette in a large salad bowl and toss.

Just before serving, add the escarole and tomato and toss. Taste to correct the seasoning, adding more vinaigrette if needed. Garnish with egg quarters, if using.

Kilocalories 446 Kc • Protein 11 Gm • Fat 21 Gm • Percent of calories from fat 42% • Cholesterol 0 mg • Dietary Fiber 9 Gm • Sodium 451 mg • Calcium 71 mg

Bell Pepper and Tuna Pasta Salad

—◼—

4 SERVINGS

2 tablespoons olive oil
1 red bell pepper, seeded and
 cut into strips
1 green bell pepper, seeded
 and cut into strips
1 yellow bell pepper, seeded
 and cut into strips
1 garlic clove, minced
1 6- or 7-ounce can imported
 Italian tuna, packed in oil,
 well drained, flaked

1 4-ounce can chickpeas,
 drained and rinsed
1/4 cup sliced pitted black
 olives
2 tablespoons red wine vinegar
2 tablespoons chopped fresh
 flat-leaf parsley
Freshly ground black pepper
6 ounces (about 1/3 pound)
 medium elbows

In a large skillet, heat the oil and sauté the bell peppers with the garlic until they are barely tender-crisp, 3 minutes. Transfer the peppers to a large salad bowl. Mix in the tuna, chickpeas, olives, vinegar, parsley, and black pepper to your taste.

Cook the elbows according to package directions and drain. Rinse them in cold water. Toss them with the pepper-tuna mixture. Taste to correct the seasonings; you may want to add salt or more vinegar.

Kilcalories 368 Kc • Protein 20 Gm • Fat 13 Gm • Percent of calories from fat 31% • Cholesterol 8 mg • Dietary Fiber 3 Gm • Sodium 315 mg • Calcium 31 mg

Splendid Spinach

So special in its nutritional profile and so versatile in cooking, spinach simply cannot be tossed in with other greens; it rates a chapter of its own! Although low in calories, spinach is amazingly high in beta-carotene (vitamin A), which defends against cancer and the degenerative effects of aging. It's also a powerhouse of potassium for heart health. And spinach is a good source of folic acid, for protecting against birth defects, and vitamin B_6, for keeping the immune system strong.

Unlike stronger-flavored greens, spinach tastes as good raw as it does cooked. In fact, youngsters who are turned off by plain boiled spinach may be turned on to this healthy vegetable in a perky salad.

Good spinach is available all year, even when other vegetables may be wan and limp. If possible, buy loose rather than packaged spinach so that you can see what you're getting. Choose small, springy leaves with thin stems.

To store, wrap unwashed spinach in a cloth or paper towel, place it in a plastic bag, and refrigerate; it will keep three to four days. Crinkly spinach holds on to grit, so when you're ready to cook, wash it well in several changes of water, starting with lukewarm and progressing to cold.

Frozen spinach is an acceptable substitute for fresh spinach in some recipes. For better quality, choose whole-leaf rather than chopped frozen spinach.

Spinach and Mushroom Soup with Tubettini

2 tablespoons olive oil
10 ounces mushrooms, cleaned
  and sliced
$1/4$ cup chopped shallots
5 cups chicken or vegetable
  stock, or canned broth
10 ounces spinach, well
  washed, tough stems
  removed, chopped

$1/2$ teaspoon salt
Freshly ground black pepper
1 cup tubettini
1 tablespoon snipped fresh
  chives

Heat the oil in a large pot and sauté the mushrooms over high heat, stirring very often, until their juice evaporates and they begin to brown. Lower the heat and add the shallots and continue cooking and stirring for 3 minutes. Add the stock, spinach, salt, and pepper to your taste; simmer the soup for 15 minutes.

Meanwhile, cook the tubettini separately according to package directions and drain. Stir the tubettini and chives into the soup and remove it from the heat.

Kilocalories 160 Kc • Protein 9 Gm • Fat 6 Gm • Percent of calories from fat 35% • Cholesterol 0 mg • Dietary Fiber 2 Gm • Sodium 589 mg • Calcium 61 mg

Greek-style Spinach with Yogurt and Macaroni

4 SERVINGS

The Greeks have a special affinity for spinach, using it in many of their traditional dishes and savory pastries.

²/₃ cup nonfat plain yogurt
10 ounces fresh spinach, well washed, tough stems removed
Salt and freshly ground pepper
3 tablespoons olive oil
1 large yellow onion, chopped
¹/₄ cup pine nuts

Several dashes of cayenne pepper
8 kalamata olives, pitted and halved
8 ounces (¹/₂ pound) penne, ziti, or mezzani
3 tablespoons freshly grated Romano cheese

Put the yogurt into a paper coffee filter set into a strainer and allow it to drain for 30 minutes. Discard the liquid.

Steam the wet spinach in a large pot, in just the water that clings to the leaves, until it has wilted, 3 to 5 minutes. Remove the spinach from the heat and drain it. Add salt and pepper to your taste.

In a small skillet, heat the oil and sauté the onion with the pine nuts and cayenne until the onion is soft and fragrant. Remove from the heat and add the olives.

Cook the pasta according to package directions and drain. In a large serving dish, toss the pasta with the onion mixture, Romano cheese, and drained yogurt. Spoon the spinach on top and serve.

Kilocalories 434 Kc • Protein 15 Gm • Fat 19 Gm • Percent of calories from fat 38% • Cholesterol 5 mg • Dietary Fiber 4 Gm • Sodium 209 mg • Calcium 207 mg

Spinach Casserole with a Crusty Tomato Topping

4 SERVINGS

10 ounces fresh spinach, well washed, tough stems removed
2 tablespoons olive oil
2 garlic cloves, chopped
Salt and freshly ground pepper
8 ounces (1/2 pound) medium elbows

1 cup diced mozzarella cheese
1 to 1 1/2 cups tomato sauce (Marinara or Summer Fresh Sauce, pages 318 and 321)
3/4 cup herb stuffing mix (not an instant stuffing mix)
3 tablespoons grated Parmesan cheese

Preheat the oven to 350 degrees F.

While the spinach is still wet from washing, put it into a large pot with the oil and garlic. Steam the spinach in just the water that clings to the leaves until it's wilted and tender, 3 to 5 minutes. Chop the spinach and season it with salt and pepper to your taste. Reserve the pan juices.

Meanwhile, cook the elbows according to package directions and drain. Spoon them into a 2-quart gratin dish or casserole and toss with the spinach, 1/2 cup of the reserved pan juices, and the mozzarella cheese. Spread the top with the tomato sauce, cover with the stuffing mix, and sprinkle with the Parmesan. Bake until bubbly throughout and crusty on top, about 30 minutes. Let rest a few minutes and cut into squares to serve.

Kilocalories 454 Kc • Protein 20 Gm • Fat 16 Gm • Percent of calories from fat 33% • Cholesterol 19 mg • Dietary Fiber 5 Gm • Sodium 611 mg • Calcium 338 mg

New Spinach with Couscous

---

4 SERVINGS

Although spinach is available all year, springtime brings bunches of tender, sweet young spinach that need little cooking and seasoning to be wonderful.

1 cup whole wheat
  couscous, raw
2 tablespoons olive oil
¼ cup chopped shallots
1 cinnamon stick or a pinch of
  ground cinnamon

1 pound tender young spinach,
  well washed, tough stems
  removed
2 tablespoons stock, canned
  broth, or water
Freshly ground black pepper

Prepare the couscous (see page 12 for basic recipe or follow package directions); fluff and separate the grains.

Heat the oil in a large skillet and sauté the shallots with the cinnamon stick (or ground cinnamon) until softened. Add the spinach and stock, cover, and simmer over low heat just until the leaves are wilted, 3 to 5 minutes. Add pepper to your taste.

Spread hot couscous on a medium-size platter; remove the cinnamon stick and spoon the spinach on top.

NOTE: Servings can be garnished with a dollop of plain yogurt or yogurt mixed with snipped chives.

Kilocalories 292 Kc • Protein 9 Gm • Fat 8 Gm • Percent of calories from fat 22% • Cholesterol 0 mg • Dietary Fiber 8 Gm • Sodium 189 mg • Calcium 113 mg

Spinach with Raisins, Pine Nuts, and Couscous

Follow the preceding recipe, adding 2 tablespoons plumped raisins and 2 tablespoons lightly toasted pine nuts to the spinach.

Kilocalories 334 Kc • Protein 10 Gm • Fat 11 Gm • Percent of calories from fat 62% • Cholesterol 0 mg • Dietary Fiber 8 Gm • Sodium 190 mg • Calcium 117 mg

Spinach with Gorgonzola and Fettuccine

---

10 ounces fresh spinach well
  washed, tough stems
  removed
Salt and freshly ground pepper
9- to 10-ounce package fresh
  fettuccine

2 tablespoons butter, in
  4 pieces
3 ounces crumbled Gorgonzola
  cheese or other blue cheese

Steam the wet spinach in a large pot, in just the water that clings to the leaves, until it has wilted, 3 to 5 minutes. Remove the spinach from the heat and drain it. Add salt and pepper to your taste.

Meanwhile, cook the fettuccine according to package directions. Drain and spoon into a large serving dish; toss with the butter and Gorgonzola. Add the spinach and toss again.

Kilocalories 358 Kc • Protein 15 Gm • Fat 15 Gm • Percent of calories from fat 38% • Cholesterol 105 mg • Dietary Fiber 4 Gm • Sodium 440 mg • Calcium 201 mg

Spinach with Spanish Sauce and Fusilli

---

4 SERVINGS

Fusilli lungi are spaghetti-length twists. Regular spaghetti can be substituted.

10 ounces fresh spinach, well washed, tough stems removed
Salt and freshly ground pepper
8 ounces (¹/₂ pound) fusilli lungi (long corkscrews)

1 tablespoon extra-virgin olive oil
1¹/₂ cups Spanish Sauce, heated (see page 13 for basic recipe)

Steam the wet spinach in a large pot, in just the water that clings to the leaves, until it has wilted. Remove the spinach from the heat and drain, leaving it slightly moist. Add salt and pepper to your taste.

Meanwhile, cook the fusilli according to package directions. Drain the pasta and spoon it into a large serving dish. Toss with the oil and the spinach. Top with the Spanish Sauce.

Kilocalories 337 Kc • Protein 11 Gm • Fat 9 Gm • Percent of calories from fat 23% • Cholesterol 0 mg • Dietary Fiber 6 Gm • Sodium 543 mg • Calcium 132 mg

Torta di Spinaci
(Spinach Tart)

MAKES 1 TART, 6 SLICES

This is a great way to use leftover spaghetti, with or without sauce.

6 ounces (about ¹/₃ pound)
   spaghettini
2 tablespoons olive oil
Freshly ground black pepper
Dried oregano
1 cup chopped onion
10 ounces fresh spinach, well
   washed, tough stems
   removed

2 cups (1 pound) part-skim
   ricotta cheese
2 tablespoons Parmesan
   cheese, plus more for
   sprinkling
2 whole eggs plus 1 egg white
¹/₄ teaspoon salt
Few dashes of nutmeg

Cook the spaghettini according to package directions and drain. Toss it with 1 tablespoon of the oil; sprinkle with pepper and oregano to your taste. Press the spaghettini onto the bottom and sides of an oiled 10-inch pie pan.

Heat the remaining tablespoon of oil in a large skillet and sauté the onion until translucent, 5 to 7 minutes. Add the spinach and steam it, covered, in just the water that clings to the leaves from washing, until it's wilted. Gently drain the spinach, without pressing it dry, and chop it.

When ready to assemble the tart, preheat the oven to 350 degrees F.

Blend together the ricotta, 2 tablespoons Parmesan, eggs, egg white, salt, ¹/₈ teaspoon pepper, and nutmeg. Fold in the spinach. Spoon the mixture into the prepared pan and sprinkle the top with additional Parmesan cheese. Bake the tart on the middle shelf until the ricotta is set, about 45 minutes. Cool 15 minutes. Cut into wedges to serve.

Kilocalories 314 Kc • Protein 18 Gm • Fat 14 Gm • Percent of calories from fat 39% • Cholesterol 97 mg • Dietary Fiber 2 Gm • Sodium 301 mg • Calcium 312 mg

Braised Spinach with Linguine

4 SERVINGS

This typical Tuscan preparation makes an easy, tasty after-work dish.

3 tablespoons olive oil
1 large yellow onion, chopped
2 garlic cloves, minced
10 ounces fresh spinach, well washed, tough stems removed
Salt and freshly ground black pepper

A few dashes of hot red pepper flakes
8 ounces (¹/₂ pound) thin linguine
Freshly grated Romano cheese

In a large pot, heat the oil and sauté the onion and garlic until they are softened. Add the spinach, still wet from washing. Cover the pan and steam the spinach over low heat until it's wilted, about 3 minutes. Add salt, black pepper, and hot red pepper flakes to your taste.

Meanwhile, cook the linguine according to package directions and drain. Combine the linguine with the spinach in a large serving dish and toss well. Pass the cheese at the table.

Kilocalories 332 Kc • Protein 10 Gm • Fat 11 Gm • Percent of calories from fat 30% • Cholesterol 0 mg • Dietary Fiber 4 Gm • Sodium 61 mg • Calcium 91 mg

Creamed Spinach with Cavatelli

———————————◾———————————

4 SERVINGS

Creamy dishes are real comfort food—and this one is rich in B vitamins to defend the nerves against stress.

10 ounces fresh spinach, well washed, tough stems removed	**1½ cups heated milk**
½ cup chicken stock or canned broth	**½ teaspoon salt**
	⅛ teaspoon freshly ground black pepper
3 tablespoons butter	**A few dashes of cayenne pepper**
¼ cup chopped shallots	**A few dashes of nutmeg**
3 tablepoons superfine flour such as Wondra	**6 ounces (about ⅓ pound) cavatelli**

In a large pot, steam the spinach in the stock until it has wilted, 3 minutes. Remove the spinach from the heat and drain it, reserving ½ cup of the liquid.

Heat the butter in a saucepan and slowly sauté the shallots until they are golden. Add the flour and cook over low heat for 3 minutes, stirring often. Add the hot milk all at once and cook over medium-high heat, stirring constantly, until the sauce is bubbling and thickened. Whisk in the reserved spinach liquid, salt, black pepper, cayenne, and nutmeg, and cook over very low heat, stirring often, for 5 minutes.

Meanwhile, cook the cavatelli according to package directions and drain. Combine the spinach, cavatelli, and sauce in a large serving dish.

Kilocalories 335 Kc • Protein 12 Gm • Fat 13 Gm • Percent of calories from fat 35% • Cholesterol 37 mg • Dietary Fiber 3 Gm • Sodium 541 mg • Calcium 192 mg

Spinach and Mushrooms with Mezzani

4 SERVINGS

2 tablespoons olive oil
6 ounces mushrooms, cleaned
  and sliced
1 small yellow onion, chopped
10 ounces fresh spinach, well
  washed, tough stems
  removed, and coarsely
  chopped

1 tablespoon dry sherry or
  lemon juice
2 teaspoons minced
  fresh tarragon, or
  $1/2$ teaspoon dried
$1/2$ teaspoon salt
Several grinds of black pepper
8 ounces ($1/2$ pound) mezzani

Heat the oil in a large skillet and stir-fry the mushrooms over high heat until their juices evaporate and they begin to brown, about 5 minutes. Reduce the heat; add the onion and continue cooking until it's translucent. Add the spinach and cook, stirring often, until it has wilted. Season with sherry or lemon juice, tarragon, salt, and pepper.

Meanwhile, cook the mezzani according to package directions and drain. Toss the mezzani with the spinach mixture in a large serving dish.

Kilocalories 312 Kc • Protein 11 Gm • Fat 8 Gm • Percent of calories from fat 23% • Cholesterol 0 mg • Dietary Fiber 4 Gm • Sodium 353 mg • Calcium 89 mg

Spinach with Cheddar and Elbows

---

10 ounces fresh spinach
2 tablespoons olive oil
1 small yellow onion, chopped
1 celery stalk, diced
1 small green bell
  pepper, seeded and diced

1 teaspoon ground cumin
1/4 teaspoon salt
Several grinds of black pepper
2 cups small elbows
4 ounces Cheddar cheese,
  diced small

Wash the spinach well; break off and discard any tough stems. Chop the spinach into large 2- to 3-inch pieces.

Heat the oil in a large skillet and sauté the onion, celery, and bell pepper until they are softened, 3 to 5 minutes. Add the spinach and cook, stirring often, until it has wilted. Season with the cumin, salt, and pepper.

Meanwhile, cook the elbows according to package directions and drain. In a serving bowl, toss the elbows with the Cheddar, and when it begins to melt, blend in the spinach mixture.

Kilocalories 407 Kc • Protein 17 Gm • Fat 17 Gm • Percent of calories from fat 38% • Cholesterol 30 mg • Dietary Fiber 5 Gm • Sodium 393 mg • Calcium 302 mg

Stir-fried Spinach with Water Chestnuts and Asian Noodles

4 SERVINGS

1 tablespoon vegetable oil
1 bunch scallions, cut into 2-inch pieces
1 large red bell pepper, seeded and cut into strips
2 garlic cloves, minced
1 4-ounce can water chestnuts, drained
5 ounces fresh spinach, well washed, tough stems removed, and finely chopped

2 tablespoons naturally brewed soy sauce
$\frac{1}{2}$ teaspoon sugar
Several dashes of cayenne pepper
8 ounces ($\frac{1}{2}$ pound) Asian noodles or American thin linguine
$\frac{1}{2}$ cup hot chicken stock or canned broth

Heat the oil in a large wok or skillet and stir-fry the scallions, red bell pepper, and garlic until tender-crisp, about 2 minutes. Add the water chestnuts and spinach and cook 1 minute, until the greens have wilted. Season the vegetables with 1 tablespoon of the soy sauce, sugar, and cayenne. Toss to blend.

Meanwhile, cook the noodles according to package directions and drain. Spoon them into a large serving dish. Mix the hot stock with the remaining tablespoon of soy sauce, pour over the noodles, and toss. Top with the vegetables.

Kilocalories 271 Kc • Protein 3 Gm • Fat 4 Gm • Percent of calories from fat 12% • Cholesterol 0 mg • Dietary Fiber 2 Gm • Sodium 600 mg • Calcium 57 mg

Spinach and Ricotta with Rotelle

---

10 ounces fresh spinach, well washed, tough stems removed
Salt and freshly ground black pepper
2 tablespoons olive oil
$^{1}/_{4}$ cup chopped shallots
$^{1}/_{2}$ cup chicken stock or canned broth

8 ounces ($^{1}/_{2}$ pound) rotelle
1 cup (8 ounces) part-skim ricotta cheese, at room temperature
$^{1}/_{2}$ cup loosely packed, grated Romano cheese

Steam the spinach in a large pot, in just the water that clings to the leaves from washing, until it has wilted. Remove the spinach from the heat and drain it. Add salt and pepper to your taste.

Heat the oil in a large skillet and sauté the shallots until softened. Add the spinach and heat through. Stir in the stock and keep warm.

Meanwhile, cook the rotelle according to package directions and drain. Spoon it into a large serving dish. Mix the ricotta with the spinach. Toss the rotelle with the spinach-ricotta mixture and the Romano cheese.

Kilocalories 414 Kc • Protein 20 Gm • Fat 16 Gm • Percent of calories from fat 34% • Cholesterol 29 mg • Dietary Fiber 3 Gm • Sodium 310 mg • Calcium 356 mg

Asian Spinach Salad with Walnuts and Noodles

4 SERVINGS

Serve at room temperature or chilled for a summer luncheon dish. An omelet goes well alongside.

3 tablespoons walnut oil
3 tablespoons seasoned rice vinegar
1 tablespoon naturally brewed soy sauce
1/4 teaspoon ground ginger
4 ounces (1/4 pound) Asian noodles or American thin linguine

5 to 6 ounces fresh young spinach, well washed, tough stems removed, spun dry
4 scallions, chopped
4 to 6 radishes, sliced
1/2 cup walnut halves or pieces

Combine the oil, vinegar, soy sauce, and ginger in a salad bowl. Cook the noodles according to package directions. Drain and rinse until they are cool. Toss them with the dressing.

Tear the spinach into bite-size pieces. Add the spinach, scallions, radishes, and walnuts to the noodles. Toss again. Taste to correct the seasonings, adding more vinegar or soy sauce if desired.

Kilocalories 303 Kc • Protein 5 Gm • Fat 19 Gm • Percent of calories from fat 56% • Cholesterol 0 mg • Dietary Fiber 2 Gm • Sodium 291 mg • Calcium 57 mg

Spinach and Pasta Salad with Balsamic Dressing

4 SERVINGS

If possible, use tender, young smooth-leaf spinach, sold loose in bunches, for this salad.

¹/₄ cup extra-virgin olive oil
3 tablespoons balsamic vinegar
1 garlic clove, pressed through a garlic press
¹/₄ teaspoon salt
¹/₈ teaspoon freshly ground pepper

4 ounces (¹/₄ pound) medium elbows
1 red bell pepper, seeded and cut into small triangles
About 6 ounces fresh spinach, well washed, spun dry

In a salad bowl, whisk together the olive oil, vinegar, garlic, salt, and pepper.

Cook the elbows according to package directions. Drain and rinse until they are cool. Toss them with the dressing and bell pepper. Tear the spinach into bite-size pieces and add them to the salad, tossing again.

Kilocalories 255 Kc • Protein 5 Gm • Fat 14 Gm • Percent of calories from fat 49% • Cholesterol 0 mg • Dietary Fiber 2 Gm • Sodium 184 mg • Calcium 52 mg

The Rugged Winter Squashes, Pumpkin, and Sweet Potatoes

The orange-fleshed winter vegetables—squashes, pumpkin, and I'm including sweet potatoes, too, because they're one of the richest sources—are plump with antioxidant beta-carotene and fiber, two first-rate defenders against the formation of tumors. A single serving of butternut squash contains enough beta-carotene to meet the RDA for vitamin A. These vegetables are also good sources of vitamin C, an important healer, and potassium, which helps keep hearts healthy.

Although squash and pumpkin all belong to the same family of "edible gourds," there's a great deal of diversity in their appearance. This chapter features major varieties only, those that are easily purchased during the fall and winter months. *Acorn squash* are acorn-shaped, oval, with pointed ends, dark green rinds, and golden flesh. A small amount of orange appears when they mature, but don't buy all-orange acorns; they may be stringy. *Butternut squash* have tan skins, thick necks, bulbous ends, and orange flesh. Avoid those with greenish skins. *Hubbard squash* are the largest; their hard shells are pebbled and may be yellow, green, or grayish-blue; their flesh is deep orange. *Spaghetti squash* are submarine-shaped, with yellow skins and pale cream flesh that separates into spaghettilike strands after cooking.

The larger the squash (within a variety), the sweeter the flesh—but the same cannot be said for *pumpkins*. Look for relatively small (2- to 3-pound) "sugar pumpkins," especially cultivated for cooking rather than carving, and available briefly from just before Halloween to just after Thanksgiving. The rest of the year, unflavored solid-pack canned pumpkin can be used for pumpkin soup as well as pumpkin pie.

Moist sweet potatoes are characterized by tan-brown skins and deep orange flesh that is very soft when cooked. They are often called yams, but this is a misnomer. True yams belong to a different botanical genus found only in Africa. *Dry sweet potatoes* have light tan skins and light yellow to orange flesh that is firmer when cooked. I find that they can be used interchangeably. Although the dry keep their shapes better in a soup or stew, I'm partial to moist sweet potatoes with their very orange, carotene-rich flesh, and I use them almost exclusively.

Unlike summer squashes, the winter varieties, harvested at a mature stage, are protected by inedible shells that aid in their storage. Squashes should be evenly colored, dull not shiny, with no soft spots. Check the tips of sweet potatoes, where decay sometimes begins. Squashes, pumpkins, and sweet potatoes should be stored in a cool, dry place—50 degrees is ideal. Squashes and pumpkins will keep for weeks, but plan to use sweet potatoes within a few days of purchase.

Butternut Soup with Stars

■

If you happen to have 1¹/₂ cups of leftover mashed squash, this is a great way to use it—in which case, simmer the soup for 10 minutes only and skip the puréeing step.

2 cups diced butternut squash (about ¹/₂ pound trimmed)
3 cups chicken stock or canned broth
2 teaspoons minced fresh basil, or ¹/₂ teaspoon dried

2 teaspoons minced fresh chervil, or ¹/₂ teaspoon dried
¹/₄ teaspoon salt
¹/₈ teaspoon pepper
1 cup stellini (little stars)

Combine the squash and stock in a saucepan and bring it to a boil. Lower the heat and simmer the soup until the squash is very tender, 10 to 15 minutes.

Remove the squash with a slotted spoon and purée it in a food processor or mash it by hand. Gradually add the broth. Return the soup to the pan. Add the herbs, salt, and pepper. Keep warm for 5 minutes or so to develop the flavor.

Meanwhile, cook the stars separately according to package directions. Drain and stir them into the soup.

Kilocalories 168 Kc • Protein 8 Gm • Fat 2 Gm • Percent of calories from fat 8% • Cholesterol 0 mg • Dietary Fiber 2 Gm • Sodium 471 mg • Calcium 56 mg

Hubbard Soup with Shells

■

4 cups chicken stock or
canned broth
$\frac{1}{2}$ cup tomato purée, or 2
tablespoons tomato paste
plus $\frac{1}{3}$ cup water
3 cups peeled diced Hubbard
squash (about $\frac{3}{4}$ pound
trimmed)

$\frac{1}{4}$ teaspoon salt
$\frac{1}{8}$ teaspoon cayenne pepper
2 tablespoons snipped fresh
chives
1 cup small shells
$\frac{1}{2}$ cup light sour cream, as a
garnish (optional)

Combine the stock, tomato purée, squash, and salt in a saucepan. Bring to a boil, reduce the heat, cover, and simmer until the squash is quite tender, 10 to 15 minutes.

Remove the squash with a slotted spoon and purée it in a food processor or mash it by hand. Gradually add the stock. Return the soup to the pan. Add the cayenne pepper and chives. Keep warm for 5 minutes or so to develop the flavor.

Meanwhile, cook the shells separately according to package directions, drain, and stir the pasta into the soup. Garnish each portion with sour cream, if desired.

Kilocalories 202 Kc • Protein 11 Gm • Fat 3 Gm • Percent of calories from fat 11% • Cholesterol 0 mg • Dietary Fiber 7 Gm • Sodium 588 mg • Calcium 38 mg

Curried Sweet Potato and Barley Soup with Ditali

6 SERVINGS

2 tablespoons olive oil
1 large yellow onion, chopped
1 green bell pepper, seeded
  and diced
1 garlic clove, minced
1 teaspoon curry powder
6 cups vegetable or chicken
  stock, or canned broth

2 sweet potatoes (about
  1 pound), peeled and diced
$^1/_2$ cup barley, rinsed
1 tablespoon sherry vinegar or
  cider vinegar
$^1/_2$ teaspoon salt
$^1/_8$ teaspoon cayenne pepper
1 cup ditali

Heat the oil in a large pot and sauté the onion and green pepper until soft, 5 minutes. Add the garlic and curry powder during the last minute.

Add the stock, potatoes, barley, vinegar, and salt, and bring the soup to a boil. Reduce the heat and simmer the soup, covered, stirring often, for 45 to 50 minutes. Stir in the cayenne during the last few minutes.

Meanwhile, cook the ditali according to package directions and drain. Stir the pasta into the soup before serving.

Kilocalories 340 Kc • Protein 10 Gm • Fat 7 Gm • Percent of calories from fat 17% • Cholesterol 0 mg • Dietary Fiber 7 Gm • Sodium 1086 mg • Calcium 35 mg

Creamy Pumpkin Soup with Orecchiette

———— ■ ————

6 SERVINGS

2 tablespoons olive oil
2 leeks, white part only, well washed and chopped
4 cups chicken stock or canned broth
3 cups cubed pared pumpkin (see Note)
1/2 cup nonfat dry milk
3 tablespoons superfine flour, such as Wondra

1/2 teaspoon salt
1/4 teaspoon dried thyme
1/8 teaspoon pepper
Dash or two of ground nutmeg
2 cups milk (whole or low-fat)
1 cup orecchiette or small elbows
2 tablespoons chopped fresh flat-leaf parsley

Heat the oil in a large pot and sauté the leeks until they're soft and translucent, 10 minutes. Add the stock and pumpkin. Bring to a boil, reduce the heat, cover, and simmer until the pumpkin is very tender, about 20 minutes.

Remove the pumpkin with a slotted spoon and purée it in a food processor or mash it by hand. Gradually add the stock. Return the soup to the pan.

Whisk the dry milk, flour, and seasonings into the liquid milk and pour it into the simmering soup, stirring constantly, until the soup bubbles and thickens. Simmer 3 minutes or more, stirring often. Taste to correct the seasonings, adding more salt and pepper to your taste.

Meanwhile, cook the pasta according to package directions and drain. Stir it into the finished soup. Stir in the parsley.

NOTE: A 15-ounce can of unflavored solid-pack pumpkin can be substituted, in which case it won't be necessary to purée. Cook until the leeks are quite tender.

Kilocalories 241 Kc • Protein 10 Gm • Fat 9 Gm • Percent of calories from fat 32% • Cholesterol 11 mg • Dietary Fiber 2 Gm • Sodium 539 mg • Calcium 172 mg

Butternut Squash and Olives with Shells

■

4 SERVINGS

Combining butternut with tomatoes and garlic gives a whole new dimension to squash.

2 tablespoons olive oil
1 to 2 garlic cloves, minced
2 large plum tomatoes, seeded and diced (1 cup or more)
3 cups diced butternut squash (about 3/4 pound trimmed)
Salt and freshly ground pepper

Water, as needed
8 kalamata olives, pitted and halved
1/4 cup coarsely chopped fresh flat-leaf parsley
8 ounces (1/2 pound) medium shells

Heat the olive oil in a medium-size skillet and sauté the garlic and tomatoes, uncovered, until slightly softened. Add the squash and salt and pepper to your taste. Cover and braise over low heat, stirring often, until the squash is tender, 10 to 15 minutes. (Braising, like steaming, takes longer than boiling.) There should be sufficient moisture from the tomatoes to keep the squash from browning; if the mixture seems too dry, add tablespoons of water as needed. Stir in the olives and parsley and cook, uncovered, 2 to 3 minutes more.

Meanwhile, cook the shells according to package directions and drain. In a large serving dish, toss the pasta with the butternut mixture.

Kilocalories 329 Kc • Protein 9 Gm • Fat 9 Gm • Percent of calories from fat 25% • Cholesterol 0 mg • Dietary Fiber 3 Gm • Sodium 167 mg • Calcium 42 mg

Four Corners Butternut Stew with Chilies and Elbows

◼

4 SERVINGS

This hearty Southwestern stew is a meal in itself. Just add a cool tossed green salad and hot corn bread.

2 tablespoons olive oil
1 Anaheim chili, seeded and cut into strips
1 jalapeño chili, seeded and minced (wear rubber gloves)
1 red bell pepper, seeded and cut into strips
1 large yellow onion, chopped
2 garlic cloves, minced
1 16-ounce can tomatoes with juice
1 cup vegetable or chicken stock, or canned broth
2 cups butternut squash chunks (about 1/2 pound trimmed)

1 tablespoon chopped fresh cilantro, or 1 teaspoon dried
1/2 teaspoon ground cumin
1/2 teaspoon salt
1/4 teaspoon freshly ground black pepper
1 small zucchini, diced
1 cup frozen corn, thawed to separate
1 cup small elbows
2 teaspoons chopped fresh mint leaves, or 1/2 teaspoon dried

Heat the oil in a large pot and gently sauté the chilies, bell pepper, and onion until softened, 5 to 7 minutes. Add the garlic during the last minute.

Add the tomatoes, stock, butternut, cilantro, cumin, salt, and pepper, and simmer for 15 minutes. Add the zucchini and corn, and continue cooking for 5 minutes, or until all the vegetables are tender.

Meanwhile, cook the elbows according to package directions and drain. Stir the elbows and mint into the stew and serve.

Kilocalories 284 Kc • Protein 9 Gm • Fat 8 Gm • Percent of calories from fat 24% • Cholesterol 0 mg • Dietary Fiber 6 Gm • Sodium 709 mg • Calcium 84 mg

Stir-fried Sesame Butternut with Asian Noodles

---

4 SERVINGS

1 tablespoon vegetable oil
1 teaspoon sesame oil
1 bunch scallions, cut into
  1-inch lengths
1 green bell pepper, seeded
  and cut into strips
2 slices fresh ginger, minced
4 cups peeled and diced
  butternut squash (about
  1 pound trimmed)
1 cup chicken or vegetable
  stock, or canned broth

$1^{1}/_{2}$ teaspoons cornstarch
$^{1}/_{4}$ teaspoon salt
$^{1}/_{8}$ teaspoon cayenne pepper
6 ounces (about $^{1}/_{3}$ pound)
  Asian flat noodles or
  American linguine
1 tablespoon toasted
  sesame seeds (see Note
  page 128)

In a large wok or skillet, heat the oils and stir-fry the scallions, bell pepper, and ginger until the vegetables are tender-crisp, 3 minutes. Remove them with a slotted spoon.

Put the butternut into the wok with $^{1}/_{2}$ cup of the stock, cover, and simmer until just tender, 5 to 8 minutes. Blend the cornstarch, salt, and cayenne into the remaining $^{1}/_{2}$ cup of stock and stir into the hot squash. Cook, stirring, 1 minute. Return the scallions and bell pepper to the wok and reheat.

Meanwhile, cook the noodles according to package directions. If none are given, fresh noodles take 2 to 3 minutes, dried 5 to 8. Taste-test for desired tenderness. Drain. Spoon them into a large serving dish and toss gently with the squash. Sprinkle with the sesame seeds before serving.

Kilocalories 754 Kc • Protein 4 Gm • Fat 57 Gm • Percent of calories from fat 66% • Cholesterol 0 mg • Dietary Fiber 4 Gm • Sodium 267 mg • Calcium 118 mg

Butternut Squash Gratin with Gremolata and Farfalle

4 TO 6 SERVINGS

A gremolata is a flavorful mixture of parsley, garlic, and lemon.

1 cup stemmed parsley sprigs, loosely packed
1 garlic clove, roughly chopped
2 teaspoons grated lemon zest
1/2 teaspoon kosher salt or table salt
2 cups fresh bread crumbs
4 cups butternut squash cubes (about 1 pound trimmed)

6 ounces (about 1/3 pound) farfalle (egg bows)
1/2 cup warm chicken or vegetable stock, or canned broth
2 tablespoons olive oil
2 tablespoons grated Parmesan cheese

Mince together the parsley, garlic, lemon zest, and salt. Blend well with the bread crumbs.

Put 1 inch of water in a steamer. Put the squash in the steamer basket, cover, and steam over simmering water until tender, about 15 minutes.

Cook the farfalle according to package directions and drain. Toss it with the stock and 1 tablespoon of the olive oil.

Preheat the oven to 350 degrees F. In a 2-quart gratin pan or ceramic baking dish, make a layer of half the squash and half the parslied bread crumbs. Spread the farfalle on top. Cover with the remaining squash. Top with the remaining parslied bread crumbs. Sprinkle with the cheese. Drizzle with the remaining tablespoon of oil.

Bake the gratin until lightly colored on top and heated through, 20 to 25 minutes if the ingredients are still warm.

Kilocalories 329 Kc • Protein 11 Gm • Fat 10 Gm • Percent of calories from fat 28% • Cholesterol 42 mg • Dietary Fiber 4 Gm • Sodium 500 mg • Calcium 120 mg

Butternut Succotash with Shell Beans and Shells

4 SERVINGS

2 tablespoons olive oil
$^1/_4$ cup chopped shallots
3 cups diced butternut squash
   (about $^3/_4$ pound trimmed)
$1^1/_2$ cups shelled fresh shell
   beans (about 1 pound
   unshelled—see Note)
1 cup vegetable or chicken
   stock, or canned broth
$^1/_2$ cup tomato purée

8 leaves fresh sage, chopped,
   or a pinch of ground sage
$^1/_2$ teaspoon ground coriander
$^1/_2$ teaspoon salt
$^1/_4$ teaspoon hot red pepper
   flakes
6 ounces (about $^1/_3$ pound)
   medium shells
$^1/_4$ cup chopped scallion tops

Heat the oil in a large pot and sauté the shallots until they are sizzling. Add the butternut, shell beans, stock, tomato purée, herbs, and seasonings. Bring to a boil, reduce the heat, and simmer, covered, until the butternut and beans are tender, about 20 minutes.

Meanwhile, cook the shells according to package directions and drain. Stir the pasta and chopped scallion tops into the succotash.

NOTE: A 16-ounce can of pinto beans, drained and rinsed, can be substituted. Add canned beans when the butternut is nearly tender.

Kilocalories 502 Kc • Protein 22 Gm • Fat 9 Gm • Percent of calories from fat 15% • Cholesterol 0 mg • Dietary Fiber 16 Gm • Sodium 536 mg • Calcium 104 mg

Butternut Squash with Walnuts and Rotelle

4 SERVINGS

1 cup walnut halves
2 tablespoons olive oil
1 green bell pepper, diced
2 garlic cloves, minced
4 cups butternut squash cubes
  (about 1 pound trimmed)

1/4 cup water
Salt and freshly ground black
  pepper
8 ounces (1/2 pound) rotelle
2 tablespoons chopped fresh
  cilantro

Put the walnuts in a small saucepan with water to cover and bring it to a boil. Drain and rinse the walnuts. Dry them well and toast them lightly in a toaster oven or under a heated broiler, watching closely that they don't burn.

Heat the oil in a large skillet and sauté the bell pepper until it's soft, 3 minutes. Add the garlic during the last minute. Add the butternut and water, cover, and steam over low heat until the squash is tender but holds its shape, 10 to 15 minutes. Season with salt and pepper to your taste.

Meanwhile, cook the rotelle according to package directions and drain. In a large serving dish, toss the pasta with the squash, walnuts, and cilantro.

Kilocalories 510 Kc • Protein 17 Gm • Fat 26 Gm • Percent of calories from fat 43% • Cholesterol 0 mg • Dietary Fiber 5 Gm • Sodium 11 mg • Calcium 72 mg

Butternut with Mozzarella and Spinach Penne

■

Some recipes instruct the cook to moisten cooked pasta with a little of the cooking water, but the finished dish is more flavorful if stock or broth is used instead, as in the following.

3 cups butternut squash
   chunks (about ³/₄ pound
   trimmed)
1 tablespoon olive oil
1 tablespoon butter
¹/₄ cup chopped shallots
Salt and freshly ground pepper

8 ounces (¹/₂ pound)
   spinach penne
1 cup shredded mozzarella
   cheese
¹/₄ cup hot chicken or
   vegetable stock, or
   canned broth

Put 1 inch of water in a steamer. Put the squash in the steamer basket, cover, and steam over simmering water until tender, about 15 minutes.

In a large skillet, heat the olive oil and butter and sauté the shallots until they are tender but not brown. Add the squash to the shallots. Add salt and pepper to your taste.

Meanwhile, cook the penne according to package directions; drain. Spoon the pasta into a large serving dish and toss with the cheese. Add the butternut mixture and hot stock and toss again.

Kilocalories 388 Kc • Protein 17 Gm • Fat 15 Gm • Percent of calories from fat 34% • Cholesterol 77 mg • Dietary Fiber 5 Gm • Sodium 252 mg • Calcium 261 mg

Butternut Squash with Parsley Pesto and Ziti

4 SERVINGS

3 cups butternut squash
  chunks (about ¾ pound
  trimmed)
8 ounces (½ pound) ziti

3 to 4 tablespoons Herb
  Medley Pesto (see page 10 for
  basic recipe), or substitute
  basil pesto, homemade (page
  9) or from a jar

Put 1 inch of water in a steamer. Put the squash in the steamer basket, cover, and steam over simmering water until tender, about 15 minutes.

Meanwhile, cook the ziti according to package directions and drain. In a large serving dish, toss the ziti with the pesto, varying the amount according to your taste. Add the butternut and toss again, gently.

Kilocalories 313 Kc • Protein 10 Gm • Fat 8 Gm • Percent of calories from fat 24% • Cholesterol 1 mg • Dietary Fiber 3 Gm • Sodium 83 mg • Calcium 65 mg

Roasted Acorn Squash

Although baked acorn squash cooks in less time when placed cut side down (because it steams), the flavor is much nuttier when the halves are roasted with the cut sides up.

Preheat the oven to 375 degrees F. Cut the squash in half and remove the seeds. Cut off a thin slice from the rounded side of the squash halves so that they will stand upright. Arrange the squash halves, cut sides up, in a baking dish. Add salt and pepper to your taste. A sprinkle of nutmeg is also nice, especially when the squash will be stuffed with couscous or orzo.

Place the pan on the middle shelf of the oven and pour 1 cup hot water around the squash. Bake until tender, about 45 minutes. It's okay if the water evaporates.

Baked Acorn Squash Stuffed with Orzo

4 SERVINGS

1 cup orzo
2 tablespoons butter
1 egg, beaten
4 tablespoons freshly grated
   Parmesan cheese
1 tablespoon minced fresh
   flat-leaf parsley

Freshly ground black pepper
2 medium acorn squash
   (2 pounds total), halved and
   roasted (see preceding
   recipe)

Cook the orzo according to package directions and drain. Stir in the butter until melted. Cool slightly, then stir in the egg until blended. Stir in 3 tablespoons of the cheese, the parsley, and freshly ground black pepper to your taste. Stuff the roasted squash with the orzo and place them in a baking dish. Sprinkle the tops with the remaining tablespoon of cheese.

Preheat the oven to 350 degrees F. Bake the squash for 20 to 25 minutes (10 to 15 minutes longer, if refrigerated between preparation and baking) or until hot and golden-brown on top.

Kilocalories 379 Kc • Protein 14 Gm • Fat 10 Gm • Percent of calories from fat 24% • Cholesterol 73 mg • Dietary Fiber 5 Gm • Sodium 180 mg • Calcium 148 mg

Acorn Squash Stuffed with Spiced Couscous

4 SERVINGS

1 cup couscous, raw
3 tablespoons golden raisins
2 tablespoons toasted
  pine nuts
$1/8$ teaspoon ground cinnamon
1 teaspoon chopped fresh
  thyme, or $1/4$ teaspoon dried
Salt and freshly ground black
  pepper

2 medium acorn squash
  (2 pounds total), halved and
  roasted (see page 302 for
  instructions)
About $1/4$ cup chicken stock,
  canned broth, or bouillon

Prepare the couscous (see page 12 for basic recipe or follow package directions), stirring in the raisins, pine nuts, cinnamon, and thyme when you add the broth or water. Season with salt and pepper to your taste.

Preheat the oven to 350 degrees F. Stuff the roasted squash with the couscous mixture, and drizzle about 1 tablespoon stock over each. Cover lightly with foil (not tucked in) and bake until heated through, 20 to 35 minutes, depending on whether the squash and couscous were refrigerated.

Kilocalories 319 Kc • Protein 12 Gm • Fat 4 Gm • Percent of calories from fat 11% • Cholesterol 0 mg • Dietary Fiber 6 Gm • Sodium 483 mg • Calcium 91 mg

Roasted Acorn Squash with Parsley-Walnut Pesto and Spaghetti

4 SERVINGS

2 medium acorn squash
  (2 pounds total), halved and
  roasted (see page 302 for
  instructions)
8 ounces (1/2 pound) spaghetti

1/2 cup Parsley-Walnut Pesto
  (see page 9 for basic recipe)
1/2 cup coarsely chopped
  walnut pieces

Allow the baked squash to cool until you can handle it. Gently peel and cut the squash into chunks. Reheat when ready to serve.

Meanwhile, cook the spaghetti according to package directions and drain. Spoon it into a large serving dish and toss with the Parsley-Walnut Pesto. Add the reheated squash chunks and toss again. Sprinkle with the chopped walnuts.

Kilocalories 562 Kc • Protein 17 Gm • Fat 28 Gm • Percent of calories from fat 43% • Cholesterol 0 mg • Dietary Fiber 6 Gm • Sodium 170 mg • Calcium 119 mg

Roasted Acorn Squash with Fennel, Sage, and Penne

4 SERVINGS

2 medium acorn squash
  (2 pounds total), halved
  and roasted (see page 302
  for instructions)
2 tablespoons olive oil
1 small bulb of fennel, cored
  and diced (reserve leaves)

$^1/_4$ cup chopped shallots
8 to 10 fresh sage leaves,
  minced
$^1/_4$ cup vegetable or chicken
  stock, or canned broth
8 ounces ($^1/_2$ pound) penne

Allow the baked squash to cool until you can handle it. Gently peel and cut the squash into chunks.

Heat the oil in a large skillet and sauté the fennel, shallots, and sage leaves until the fennel is tender-crisp, 10 minutes. Add the squash and stock and heat through.

Meanwhile, cook the penne according to package directions and drain. Spoon the pasta into a large serving dish and toss with the squash mixture.

Kilocalories 363 Kc • Protein 11 Gm • Fat 8 Gm • Percent of calories from fat 20% • Cholesterol 0 mg • Dietary Fiber 5 Gm • Sodium 80 mg • Calcium 99 mg

Hubbard Squash Casserole with Rotelle

4 SERVINGS

A single Hubbard squash can weigh as much as fifteen pounds, but fortunately, many supermarkets split them and sell quarters or halves wrapped in plastic.

2-pound piece of Hubbard squash, unpeeled (weight can vary a bit)
1 tablespoon olive oil
1 tablespoon chopped fresh rosemary, or 1 teaspoon dried
Salt and freshly ground black pepper

3 tablespoons butter
1 shallot, chopped
1/4 cup flour
3 cups heated milk
1/2 teaspoon salt
1/4 teaspoon white pepper
4 tablespoons freshly grated Parmesan cheese
8 ounces (1/2 pound) rotelle

Preheat the oven to 350 degrees F. Remove any seeds or stringy pulp from the squash and brush it with the oil. Bake for 30 minutes. Sprinkle with the rosemary and salt and pepper to your taste, and continue baking until the squash is tender when pierced with the point of a paring knife, 15 to 20 minutes longer. Allow the squash to cool until you can handle it, then cut it into cubes, discarding the shell. You should have 3 to 3 1/2 cups.

In a saucepan, melt and heat the butter; sauté the shallot until sizzling. Remove from the heat and stir in the flour, then cook the roux over low heat for 3 minutes, stirring often. Add the heated milk all at once and cook over medium-high heat, stirring constantly, until bubbling and slightly thickened. Reduce the heat and simmer over very low heat for 5 minutes, stirring often. Blend in the salt, white pepper, and 2 tablespoons of the cheese.

Meanwhile, cook the rotelle according to package directions (undercooking it slightly), and drain. Mix it with half of the sauce. Layer the pasta in an oiled 2 1/2-quart baking dish and top with the squash cubes. Pour the remaining sauce on top and sprinkle with the remaining cheese.

Bake until lightly colored on top and heated through, 20 to 25 minutes if the ingredients are still warm.

Kilocalories 555 Kc • Protein 18 Gm • Fat 21 Gm • Percent of calories from fat 33% • Cholesterol 51 mg • Dietary Fiber 5 Gm • Sodium 533 mg • Calcium 340 mg

Nutmeg-scented Spaghetti Squash with Spaghetti

---

4 SERVINGS

The long strands of squash and spaghetti were made for each other.

1 small spaghetti squash (3 to
  4 pounds)
3 tablespoons melted butter
1/4 teaspoon ground nutmeg
  (freshly ground is best)
1/2 teaspoon salt
1/4 teaspoon white pepper

8 ounces (1/2 pound) spaghetti
1 tablespoon olive oil
1/2 cup loosely packed, freshly
  grated Romano cheese
Several sprigs of fresh flat-leaf
  parsley, chopped

Preheat the oven to 375 degrees F. Pierce the squash in several places, place it in a casserole, and bake until fork-tender, about 50 minutes. Allow the squash to cool until you can handle it comfortably, about 10 minutes. Cut it in half lengthwise and remove the seeds. With a fork, twist out the spaghettilike strands into a serving dish. Toss the strands with 2 tablespoons of the melted butter. Season them with the nutmeg, salt, and pepper; keep warm in the oven.

Meanwhile, cook the spaghetti according to package directions and drain; return it to the pot. Toss the spaghetti with the remaining tablespoon of melted butter, the oil, Romano cheese, and parsley. Combine the spaghetti with the squash and toss well to blend.

Kilocalories 487 Kc • Protein 16 Gm • Fat 17 Gm • Percent of calories from fat 30% • Cholesterol 35 mg • Dietary Fiber 7 Gm • Sodium 523 mg • Calcium 230 mg

Baked Pumpkin Wedges
on a Bed of Spiced Couscous

4 SERVINGS

1 sugar pumpkin (2 to
  2 1/2 pounds)
2 tablespoons melted butter
2 tablespoons brown sugar,
  sifted
Ground nutmeg

1 cup couscous, raw
1/4 cup golden raisins
1/4 teaspoon dried thyme
1/8 teaspoon ground allspice
Salt and freshly ground black
  pepper

Preheat the oven to 350 degrees F.

Wash the pumpkin and cut it into 8 wedges. Scrape out the seeds and stringy pulp. Make several shallow cuts in each wedge. Place them in an oiled baking dish and drizzle the butter over them. Pour about 1/2 cup of water in the baking dish and bake for 30 minutes. Sprinkle the wedges with brown sugar and nutmeg. Continue baking until tender, 15 to 25 more minutes.

Prepare the couscous (see page 12 for basic recipe or follow package directions), stirring in the raisins, thyme, and allspice when you add the broth or water. Season with salt and pepper to your taste. Arrange the couscous on a serving platter with the pumpkin wedges on top.

Kilocalories 353 Kc • Protein 10 Gm • Fat 7 Gm • Percent of calories from fat 17% • Cholesterol 16 mg • Dietary Fiber 7 Gm • Sodium 514 mg • Calcium 74 mg

Gingered Pumpkin and Red Lentil Stew with Elbows

4 SERVINGS

1 tablespoon olive oil
1 tablespoon butter
¼ cup chopped shallots
1 cup red lentils, picked over
 and rinsed
3 cups water
½ teaspoon ground ginger
½ teaspoon ground cumin
¾ teaspoon salt

⅛ teaspoon pepper
3 cups cubed sugar pumpkin
 (or butternut squash)
1 tablespoon fresh lemon juice
4 ounces (¼ pound) medium
 elbows
¼ cup snipped fresh chives or
 scallion tops

Heat the oil and butter in a Dutch oven and sauté the shallots until they are sizzling. Add the lentils, water, spices, and seasonings. Bring to a boil, reduce the heat, cover, and simmer, stirring often, until the lentils are almost tender, 25 to 30 minutes. Add the pumpkin and lemon juice, and continue cooking for 12 to 15 minutes, or until the pumpkin is tender.

Meanwhile, cook the elbows according to package directions and drain. Stir them into the stew with the chives.

Kilocalories 335 Kc • Protein 14 Gm • Fat 7 Gm • Percent of calories from fat 19% • Cholesterol 8 mg • Dietary Fiber 5 Gm • Sodium 490 mg • Calcium 88 mg

West African Stew with Couscous

4 SERVINGS

A hot and spicy vegetarian entrée.

1 cup couscous, raw
2 tablespoons olive oil
1 large onion, sliced
2 celery stalks, cut diagonally
  into 1-inch pieces
1 green bell pepper, seeded
  and cut into chunks
2 garlic cloves, minced
3 slices fresh ginger, peeled
  and chopped (about
  1 tablespoon)
1 16-ounce Italian plum
  tomatoes with juice
1/4 cup peanut butter

1/2 teaspoon salt
1/4 teaspoon cayenne pepper
2 large sweet potatoes
  (1 1/2 pounds), peeled and
  sliced into 1/2-inch half
  rounds
1 medium pattypan squash—
  sometimes called scallop
  squash—(1/2 pound),
  unpeeled, cut into 1/2-inch
  half slices.
About 1/2 cup chicken stock or
  canned broth

Prepare the couscous (see page 12 for basic recipe or follow package directions); fluff and separate the grains.

In a Dutch oven or large heavy pan with a lid, heat the oil and sauté the onion, celery, and bell pepper until softened and lightly colored, 5 minutes. Add the garlic and ginger during the last minute.

Add the tomatoes, peanut butter, salt, and cayenne pepper, and stir until blended, breaking up the tomatoes. Add the sweet potatoes, squash, and enough stock so that the liquid comes nearly to the top of the vegetables. Simmer the stew, covered, stirring often, until the vegetables are very tender, 15 to 20 minutes.

Serve the stew spooned over the couscous.

Kilocalories 582 Kc • Protein 17 Gm • Fat 16 Gm • Percent of calories from fat 24% • Cholesterol 0 mg • Dietary Fiber 10 Gm • Sodium 1191 mg • Calcium 137 mg

Sweet Potatoes with Pesto and Rotelle

———■———

4 SERVINGS

2 large sweet potatoes (1 to 1½ pounds)
½ teaspoon salt
8 ounces (½ pound) rotelle

3 tablespoons basil pesto (from a jar or see page 9 for basic recipe)

Peel and cut the sweet potatoes into 1-inch chunks. Cover with water, add salt, and boil until just tender, not mushy, 15 to 20 minutes. Drain.

Cook the rotelle according to package directions and drain. Toss it with the pesto. Add the sweet potato and toss again.

Kilocalories 396 Kc • Protein 11 Gm • Fat 8 Gm • Percent of calories from fat 18% • Cholesterol 1 mg • Dietary Fiber 5 Gm • Sodium 378 mg • Calcium 63 mg

Saucy Tomatoes

The pairing of tomatoes and pasta was a marriage made in heaven, because this combination is the all-time favorite pasta dish of popular culture. Tomatoes are also a healthy food choice, full of the antioxidant vitamin C and a carotene called lycopene that is different from the carotene found in orange vegetables and fruits. Vitamin C is a great infection fighter and wound healer; lycopene defends against cancers of the prostate, cervix, bladder, and pancreas. In addition, tomatoes are rich in potassium, which protects the heart. So sauce up the pasta with the many varieties of tomato toppings, and enjoy! You're being good to your body as well as to your taste buds.

Botanically speaking, the tomato is a fruit—a berry, to be exact. In colloquial and culinary terms, however, the tomato is a sweet-tart vegetable of amazing versatility. It comes in three basic shapes: the globular slicing tomato, the firm-fleshed plum tomato, and the small round cherry tomato. The best tomatoes of any shape are vine-ripened, locally grown beauties, the glory of summer. Globe tomatoes are all-purpose, for slicing, stewing, or stuffing. Plum tomatoes are tops for sauces because of their mild flavor and dense flesh. Cherry tomatoes are especially nice for salads or garnishes. Available in season, yellow tomatoes have a more mellow flavor than red ones and, obviously, less lycopene.

Never refrigerate fresh tomatoes—it ruins their flavor. Arrange them stem up in one layer on a dish, out of the sunlight, and try to use them up within a few days of purchase. Those pale pink "tennis ball" tomatoes sold in cellophane packages in winter are harvested when green in order to withstand transport—and are worthless for any purpose. If you must have tomatoes in the cold months, buy ones raised in greenhouses; they are picked at a later stage and usually have small stems attached. Sometimes you can find ripe cherry tomatoes for salads in the off-seasons; if not, substitute shredded radicchio or carrot for color. When good fresh ripe red tomatoes are not available for sauces, I recommend substituting imported canned Italian plum tomatoes.

Summer Tomato Soup with Stars

6 SERVINGS

So nice for a rainy summer night!

2 tablespoons butter
1 cup chopped sweet onion, such as Vidalia
2 celery stalks with leaves, diced
1 red bell pepper, seeded and diced
4 cups peeled, seeded, chopped fresh ripe tomatoes
4 cups chicken or vegetable stock, or canned broth
1/2 teaspoon sugar

1/2 teaspoon salt
1/8 to 1/4 teaspoon freshly ground black pepper, to your taste
2 tablespoons superfine flour, such as Wondra
1/2 cup cold water
3/4 cup stellini ("little stars")
2 tablespoons chopped fresh flat-leaf parsley
1 tablespoon chopped fresh basil

Heat the butter in a large pot and sauté the onion, celery, and bell pepper until they are limp, 5 minutes. Add the tomatoes, stock, sugar, salt, and pepper. Bring the soup to a boil, reduce the heat to a low simmer, and cook the soup uncovered, stirring occasionally, for 30 to 40 minutes. At this point you can purée the soup in a food processor in batches (be careful: hot foods bubble up), if you desire.

After puréeing, return the soup to the pot and bring it to a simmer. Mix the flour with the water and stir it into the soup. Stir constantly until the soup bubbles again and thickens slightly. Cook 5 minutes longer, stirring often.

When ready to serve, cook the stellini according to package directions and drain. Stir the pasta and herbs into the soup.

Kilocalories 162 Kc • Protein 7 Gm • Fat 6 Gm • Percent of calories from fat 31% • Cholesterol 11 mg • Dietary Fiber 3 Gm • Sodium 545 mg • Calcium 31 mg

Tomato Soup with Fresh Peas

4 SERVINGS

Follow the preceding recipe. After thickening the soup with flour, add 1 cup freshly shelled peas (1 pound unshelled) and simmer for 5 minutes. Substitute tiny shells for the stellini. Two cooked sliced Italian-flavored turkey sausages make a nice addition.

with fresh peas only:
Kilocalories 184 Kc • Protein 8 Gm • Fat 6 Gm • Percent of calories from fat 27% • Cholesterol 11 mg • Dietary Fiber 4 Gm • Sodium 546 mg • Calcium 39 mg

with turkey sausage:
Kilocalories 238 Kc • Protein 11 Gm • Fat 11 Gm • Percent of calories from fat 41% • Cholesterol 21 mg • Dietary Fiber 4 Gm • Sodium 649 mg • Calcium 45 mg

Tomato Soup with Fresh Corn

4 SERVINGS

Follow the Summer Tomato Soup with Stars recipe. After thickening the soup with flour, add 2 cups fresh corn cut from the cob and simmer for 5 minutes. Substitute ditalini for the stellini.

Kilocalories 216 Kc • Protein 9 Gm • Fat 6 Gm • Percent of calories from fat 24% • Cholesterol 11 mg • Dietary Fiber 4 Gm • Sodium 548 mg • Calcium 34 mg

Winter Tomato Soup with Ditali

6 SERVINGS

You could also choose to cook alphabet pasta for this easy, basic soup—depending, of course, on the age of the diners.

2 tablespoons olive oil
1 cup chopped yellow onion
2 celery stalks with
  leaves, diced
1 large carrot, coarsely grated
1 28-ounce can imported
  Italian plum tomatoes
4 cups chicken or vegetable
  stock, or canned broth
2 teaspoons chopped fresh
  basil, or ¹/₂ teaspoon dried
2 teaspoons chopped fresh
  thyme, or ¹/₂ teaspoon dried

¹/₂ teaspoon sugar
¹/₂ teaspoon salt
¹/₈ to ¹/₄ teaspoon pepper, to
  your taste
2 tablespoons superfine flour,
  such as Wondra
¹/₂ cup cold water
³/₄ cup ditali
2 tablespoons chopped fresh
  flat-leaf parsley

Heat the oil in a large pot and sauté the onion and celery until they are limp and translucent, 5 minutes. Add the carrot, tomatoes, stock, basil, thyme, sugar, salt, and pepper. Bring the soup to a boil, reduce the heat to a low simmer, and cook the soup uncovered, stirring occasionally, for 30 minutes. At this point you can purée the soup in a food processor in batches (since hot foods bubble up) if you prefer a smoother texture. Mix the flour with the water and stir it into the soup. Stir constantly until the soup returns to a simmer and thickens slightly. Cook 5 minutes longer, stirring often.

When ready to serve, cook the ditali according to package directions and drain. Stir the pasta and parsley into the soup.

Kilocalories 171 Kc • Protein 7 Gm • Fat 6 Gm • Percent of calories from fat 31% • Cholesterol 0 mg • Dietary Fiber 3 Gm • Sodium 737 mg • Calcium 52 mg

A PALETTE OF SIX TOMATO SAUCES

For the quintessential vegetable-and-pasta dish, best known and well loved, choose among any of the following tomato sauces to toss with pasta.

A Light Tomato Sauce

■

MAKES ENOUGH TO SAUCE 1 POUND OF SPAGHETTINI
OR THIN LINGUINE

This is the easiest, most basic sauce to use as an ingredient in casseroles.

3 tablespoons olive oil
1 green bell pepper, seeded and diced
1 garlic clove, minced
1 28-ounce can imported Italian plum tomatoes, with juice
1 tablespoon minced fresh basil, or 1 teaspoon dried basil

3/4 teaspoon salt
1/4 teaspoon freshly ground black pepper
2 tablespoons minced fresh flat-leaf parsley

Heat the oil in a large pot and sauté the green pepper until it's softened, 3 to 5 minutes. Add the garlic during the last minute.

Add all the remaining ingredients except the parsley, and simmer, uncovered, for 30 minutes, stirring often and breaking up the tomatoes as they soften. Remove from the heat and stir in the parsley.

Kilocalories 138 Kc • Protein 2 Gm • Fat 10 Gm • Percent of calories from fat 69% • Cholesterol 0 mg • Dietary Fiber 2 Gm • Sodium 798 mg • Calcium 40 mg

SAUCY TOMATOES

A Fragrant Marinara Sauce

This aromatic sauce is the lowest in fat content (proportionally) of the six. Basil pesto gives a pleasing intensity of flavor to a marinara sauce. Second choice: lots of fresh herbs.

¼ cup olive oil
2 garlic cloves, minced
¼ cup tomato paste
2 28-ounce cans imported
   Italian plum tomatoes with
   juice (not purée)
¾ teaspoon salt
¼ teaspoon freshly ground
   black pepper
Several dashes of hot
   red pepper flakes

1 tablespoon basil pesto (from
   a jar or see page 9 for basic
   recipe) or 2 tablespoons
   minced fresh basil, or
   1 teaspoon dried basil
1 tablespoon minced fresh
   oregano, or ½ teaspoon dried
2 tablespoons minced fresh
   flat-leaf parsley

Heat the oil in a large pot and sauté the garlic until it's softened and fragrant. Add the tomato paste and cook over very low heat, stirring often, for 3 to 5 minutes. Add all the remaining ingredients except the herbs and simmer, uncovered, stirring often and breaking up the tomatoes as they soften, until reduced to a sauce consistency, 45 minutes to 1 hour. Add the basil and oregano during the last 10 minutes of cooking. Remove from the heat before stirring in the parsley.

Kilocalories 161 Kc • Protein 3 Gm • Fat 11 Gm • Percent of calories from fat 62% • Cholesterol 0 mg • Dietary Fiber 3 Gm • Sodium 796 mg • Calcium 59 mg

Salsa di Puttana

■

A quick, hot, garlicky sauce named for Neapolitan ladies of the evening.

¹/₄ cup olive oil
1 red bell pepper, seeded
   and diced
1 green Italian frying pepper,
   seeded and diced
3 garlic cloves, minced
8 anchovy fillets, chopped
   (optional, but traditional)
1 35-ounce can imported
   Italian plum tomatoes
   with juice

8 green Sicilian olives, pitted
   and chopped
8 black olives, pitted and sliced
1 teaspoon dried oregano
¹/₄ teaspoon hot red
   pepper flakes
2 tablespoons minced fresh
   flat-leaf parsley
Salt (optional)

Heat the oil in a large pot and sauté the peppers until they are softened, 3 to 5 minutes. Add the garlic and anchovies during the last minute.

Add all the remaining ingredients except the parsley and optional salt and simmer, uncovered, for 30 minutes, stirring often and breaking up the tomatoes as they soften. Remove from the heat and stir in the parsley. Taste to correct the seasoning, adding salt if needed (the anchovies and olives are salty) or additional red pepper flakes.

Kilocalories 225 Kc • Protein 3 Gm • Fat 17 Gm • Percent of calories from fat 69% • Cholesterol 0 mg • Dietary Fiber 3 Gm • Sodium 764 mg • Calcium 59 mg

"Glory of Summer" Sauce with Mozzarella (uncooked)

MAKES ENOUGH TO SAUCE 1 POUND SHELLS OR PENNE

2 to 2½ pounds (4 or 5 large) vine-ripened tomatoes
¼ cup extra-virgin olive oil
1 to 2 garlic cloves, very finely minced
2 tablespoons chopped fresh parsley
1 tablespoon or more chopped fresh basil

¾ teaspoon salt
¼ teaspoon freshly ground black pepper
Dash or two of hot red pepper flakes
½ pound mozzarella cheese, diced
¼ cup sliced pitted black olives (optional)

Remove the stems and cores from the tomatoes. Cut them in half through the stem end and gently squeeze out the seeds, or spoon them out with the point of a grapefruit spoon, retaining as much juice in the tomatoes as possible. Cut the tomatoes into thin wedges or chunks and put them into a large serving dish. Add the oil, garlic, herbs, and seasonings, and toss to blend. Stir in the cheese and olives, if using. Allow the mixture to marinate at room temperature for a half hour or so before mixing with the pasta. Serve at room temperature.

Kilocalories 313 Kc • Protein 16 Gm • Fat 23 Gm • Percent of calories from fat 64% • Cholesterol 33 mg • Dietary Fiber 3 Gm • Sodium 721 mg • Calcium 384 mg

Summer Fresh Tomato Sauce (cooked)

MAKES ENOUGH TO SAUCE 1 POUND SPAGHETTINI
OR VERMICELLI

3 to 4 pounds (6 or 7 large)
  vine-ripened tomatoes
1/4 cup olive oil
1 red bell pepper, seeded
  and diced
2 garlic cloves, minced
1/2 teaspoon salt
1/4 teaspoon freshly ground
  black pepper

2 tablespoons tomato paste
1/4 cup coarsely chopped
  fresh basil
1/4 cup coarsely chopped fresh
  flat-leaf parsley

Put the tomatoes in a large bowl and cover them with boiling water. Drain as soon as the skins loosen. Peel, seed, and chop the tomatoes.

Heat the oil in a large pot and sauté the bell pepper until it's softened, 3 to 5 minutes. Add the garlic during the last minute.

Add the tomatoes, salt, and pepper. Simmer uncovered, stirring often, for 30 minutes, or until reduced to a sauce consistency. Stir the tomato paste in during the last 10 minutes. Blend in the herbs during the last minute.

Kilocalories 202 Kc • Protein 3 Gm • Fat 15 Gm • Percent of calories from fat 60% • Cholesterol 0 mg • Dietary Fiber 4 Gm • Sodium 352 mg • Calcium 32 mg

SAUCY TOMATOES

Tomato-Meat Sauce (also called "Ragu" or "Gravy")

MAKES ENOUGH TO SAUCE 2 POUNDS ZITI OR
ANY MACARONI

This is a lighter version of a traditional Italian "Sunday dinner" sauce. A pinch of fennel seeds gives the illusionary flavor of Italian sausage. The meat is served separately.

1 to 1½ pounds boneless
  chicken breasts, skinned
¼ cup olive oil
1 dried hot red chili
2 garlic cloves, minced
¼ cup tomato paste
2 28-ounce cans imported
  Italian plum tomatoes
  with juice
1½ teaspoons dried basil
½ teaspoon dried oregano
  (optional)

Pinch of fennel seeds
  (6 to 8 seeds)
1 teaspoon salt
¼ teaspoon freshly ground
  black pepper, or more, to
  your taste
1 batch Mini-Meatballs (see
  page 15 for basic recipe)
2 tablespoons minced fresh
  flat-leaf parsley

Cut whole chicken breasts into quarters; pat them dry if they are damp. Heat the oil in a large heavy pot and brown the chicken lightly. Remove from the pan.

Sauté the chili and garlic until the latter is softened and fragrant. Add the tomato paste and cook over low heat, stirring often, for 3 to 5 minutes. Add all the remaining ingredients, except the meatballs and parsley. Simmer, uncovered, for 30 minutes, stirring often and breaking up the tomatoes as they soften.

Add the chicken and meatballs, and bring to a very low simmer. Continue cooking 40 to 45 minutes longer, stirring occasionally. Remove and discard the chili. Remove the meatballs with a slotted spoon and place on a serving dish. Stir the parsley into the sauce.

Kilocalories 309 Kc • Protein 27 Gm • Fat 14 Gm • Percent of calories from fat 41% • Cholesterol 105 mg • Dietary Fiber 4 Gm • Sodium 560 mg • Calcium 120 mg

Greek-style Fresh Tomatoes with Orzo

4 SERVINGS

2 tablespoons olive oil
$^1/_2$ cup chopped onion
2 garlic cloves, minced
2 cups peeled, seeded, chopped fresh tomatoes
12 Greek olives, pitted and halved
2 tablespoons chopped fresh flat-leaf parsley

2 teaspoons minced fresh oregano, or $^1/_2$ teaspoon dried
$^1/_2$ teaspoon salt
$^1/_4$ teaspoon freshly ground black pepper
$^1/_8$ teaspoon crushed red pepper flakes
8 ounces ($^1/_2$ pound) orzo
$^3/_4$ cup crumbled feta cheese

In a large skillet, heat the oil and sauté the onion and garlic until softened, about 3 minutes. Stir in the tomatoes, olives, parsley, oregano, salt, black pepper, and red pepper flakes. Bring to a simmer and cook, uncovered, for 5 to 8 minutes, stirring often.

Cook the orzo according to package directions until tender but still firm; drain.

Preheat the oven to 350 degrees F. Combine the orzo and tomatoes in a 2-quart baking dish. Sprinkle with the feta cheese and bake for 10 minutes (longer if the ingredients are cold) until the feta has melted and the orzo is heated through.

Kilocalories 448 Kc • Protein 15 Gm • Fat 21 Gm • Percent of calories from fat 42% • Cholesterol 42 mg • Dietary Fiber 4 Gm • Sodium 1163 mg • Calcium 253 mg

Greek-style Tomatoes and Yogurt with Shells

■

4 SERVINGS

A double-tomato treat combining sweet fresh and spicy dried tomatoes.

2 cups peeled, seeded,
chopped fresh tomatoes
6 sun-dried tomatoes (oil-
packed), drained and slivered
1/4 cup minced sweet onion,
such as Vidalia
1 tablespoon oil from the sun-
dried tomatoes
1 tablespoon extra-virgin
olive oil
1 tablespoon minced fresh
basil, or 1 teaspoon dried

1 tablespoon minced fresh
flat-leaf parsley
1/2 teaspoon salt
1/4 teaspoon freshly ground
black pepper
1/2 cup plain nonfat yogurt, at
room temperature
12 ounces (3/4 pound) medium
shells.

In a large serving dish, toss together the fresh tomatoes, sun-dried tomatoes, onion, oils, herbs, and seasonings. Allow them to marinate at room
temperature for a half hour or so.

Cook the pasta according to package directions and drain. Toss the
pasta and the yogurt with the tomato mixture.

Kilocalories 399 Kc • Protein 13 Gm • Fat 6 Gm • Percent of calories from fat
13% • Cholesterol 1 mg • Dietary Fiber 3 Gm • Sodium 335 mg • Calcium 69 mg

Roasted Tomatoes and Garlic with Rotelle

■

Here's a no-watching-and-stirring sauce for a lazy day.

3 pounds (12 large) ripe plum
 tomatoes
2 cloves garlic, chopped
Salt
3 tablespoons olive oil
Freshly ground pepper
Dash of hot red pepper flakes

6 leaves fresh basil, cut into
 slivers
Several sprigs of fresh flat-leaf
 parsley, chopped
12 ounces (3/4 pound) rotelle
Freshly grated Romano cheese

Preheat the oven to 450 degrees F.

Cut the tomatoes in half and scoop out the seeds. Lay them, cut sides up, in a baking dish. Scatter the garlic over the top and salt to your taste. Drizzle with the olive oil. Bake for 20 minutes or until softened.

Coarsely chop the tomatoes and season them with freshly ground black pepper and red pepper flakes to your taste. Stir in the herbs.

Meanwhile, cook the rotelle according to package directions and drain. Combine the pasta with the tomatoes in a serving dish and toss to blend.

Pass the grated Romano cheese at the table.

Kilocalories 478 Kc • Protein 14 Gm • Fat 13 Gm • Percent of calories from fat 23% • Cholesterol 0 mg • Dietary Fiber 6 Gm • Sodium 37 mg • Calcium 37 mg

SAUCY TOMATOES

325

Stir-fried Cherry Tomatoes, Cucumber, and Zucchini with Asian Noodles

4 SERVINGS

2 tablespoons vegetable oil
2 teaspoons sesame oil
1 bunch scallions, cut into 2-inch lengths
1 garlic clove, minced
1 large cucumber, peeled, seeded, and cut into 2-inch sticks
1 medium zucchini (about 3/4 pound), cut into 2-inch sticks

1 pint cherry tomatoes, halved
1 tablespoon naturally brewed soy sauce
8 ounces (1/2 pound) fresh Asian noodles or American thin linguine
2 tablespoons toasted sesame seeds (see Note page 128)

Heat the oils in a large wok or skillet and stir-fry the scallions for 1 minute. Add the garlic, cucumber, and zucchini, and continue stir-frying until the zucchini is tender-crisp, 3 minutes. Add the cherry tomatoes and stir-fry until they are sizzling, 2 more minutes. Season with soy sauce.

Meanwhile, cook the noodles according to package directions and drain. Spoon them into a large serving dish and toss with the vegetables. Sprinkle with the sesame seeds and serve.

Kilocalories 341 Kc • Protein 3 Gm • Fat 11 Gm • Percent of calories from fat 28% • Cholesterol 0 mg • Dietary Fiber 4 Gm • Sodium 279 mg • Calcium 69 mg

Cherry Tomatoes with Chive Butter and Shells

4 SERVINGS

The flavor of this simple dish depends on using fresh, not dried, chives. If chives are unavailable, substitute chopped scallion tops.

2 tablespoons butter
3 cups (1½ pints) cherry tomatoes, halved
½ cup snipped fresh chives
Salt and freshly ground black pepper

8 ounces (½ pound) medium shells
1 cup shredded medium-sharp white Cheddar cheese

Heat the butter in a large skillet until it's just sizzling but not browned and gently sauté the tomatoes until they begin to soften, 3 minutes. Remove from the heat and add the chives. Salt and pepper the tomatoes to your taste.

Meanwhile, cook the shells according to package directions and drain. In a large serving dish, quickly toss the shells with the cheese (to distribute it evenly before it melts), then add the tomatoes and toss again.

Kilocalories 422 Kc • Protein 16 Gm • Fat 17 Gm • Percent of calories from fat 36% • Cholesterol 46 mg • Dietary Fiber 4 Gm • Sodium 255 mg • Calcium 221 mg

Spinach-stuffed Tomatoes on a Bed of Couscous

6 SERVINGS

6 very large ripe tomatoes
2 tablespoons olive oil, plus
   more
4 scallions, chopped
10 ounces fresh spinach,
   washed, stemmed, and
   chopped

Salt and freshly ground pepper
2 tablespoons chopped
   fresh dill weed, or
   2 teaspoons dried
1/2 cup crumbled feta cheese
1 cup couscous, raw

Slice 1/2 inch from the top of each tomato. Scoop out the pulp and seeds. Chop and reserve the pulp; discard the seeds and juice. Lightly salt the tomato cavities and let them drain.

In a medium skillet, heat the oil and sauté the scallions until they are softened, 3 minutes. Add the spinach and tomato pulp, cover, and cook on low heat until the greens have wilted. Salt and pepper to your taste and stir in the dill and feta cheese. Cool slightly.

Stuff the tomatoes with the spinach mixture; if the mixture seems too juicy, strain the stuffing using a slotted spoon.

Preheat the oven to 375 degrees F. Stand the tomatoes in an oiled baking dish that will hold them upright and drizzle a little more oil over them. Bake until the tomatoes are cooked through, about 20 minutes.

Meanwhile, prepare the couscous (see page 12 for basic recipe or follow package directions); fluff and separate the grains. Divide the couscous among 6 plates and place a stuffed tomato in the center of each.

Kilocalories 255 Kc • Protein 10 Gm • Fat 10 Gm • Percent of calories from fat 34% • Cholesterol 19 mg • Dietary Fiber 4 Gm • Sodium 583 mg • Calcium 168 mg

Tomatoes, Pesto, Ricotta, and Tagliatelle

4 SERVINGS

A creamy sauce with the bite of fresh basil. Remember that leftover Basil Pesto can be frozen in cubes, and mighty useful it is to have in the freezer!

2 tablespoons olive oil
1 yellow onion, chopped
1 garlic clove, minced
2 cups peeled, seeded, chopped fresh tomatoes
$1/4$ teaspoon salt
Several grinds of black pepper, to your taste

2 tablespoons Basil Pesto (see page 9 for basic recipe)
$1/2$ cup part-skim ricotta cheese
12 ounces ($3/4$ pound) tagliatelle (wide ribbons)
Freshly grated Parmesan cheese

Heat the oil in a large skillet and sauté the onion and garlic until they are limp and fragrant, 3 minutes. Add the tomatoes, salt, and pepper, and cook uncovered, stirring often, 8 to 10 minutes. Remove from the heat and stir in the pesto. Whisk in the ricotta until well blended.

Meanwhile, cook the tagliatelle according to package directions and drain. Spoon it into a large serving dish and toss with the tomato-ricotta mixture. Pass the Parmesan cheese at the table.

Kilocalories 498 Kc • Protein 17 Gm • Fat 16 Gm • Percent of calories from fat 28% • Cholesterol 10 mg • Dietary Fiber 4 Gm • Sodium 247 mg • Calcium 127 mg

Tomato, Parsley, and Couscous Salad

◼

6 SERVINGS

This dish is similar in flavor to tabbouleh, a bulgur salad of the Middle East. Parsley is a great source of the antioxidant vitamins A and C, and mint is thought by herbalists to promote cheerfulness of mind.

1 cup whole wheat or regular
  couscous, raw
4 large ripe plum tomatoes
  (1 pound), finely chopped
2 cups chopped fresh flat-leaf
  parsley (1 bunch, stemmed)
1/4 cup chopped fresh mint
  leaves, or 2 teaspoons dried
1/4 cup finely chopped
  red onion

1/3 cup extra-virgin olive oil
1/4 cup fresh lemon juice
1/4 teaspoon hot pepper sauce,
  such as Tabasco
1/2 teaspoon salt
1/4 teaspoon freshly ground
  black pepper
Inner leaves of a head of
  romaine lettuce

Prepare the couscous (see page 12 for basic recipe or follow package directions); fluff and separate the grains. You should have 2 1/2 cups cooked couscous.

Mix the couscous with all the remaining ingredients except the lettuce. Toss well. Marinate at room temperature for a half hour or so. Taste to correct seasonings; you may want more oil, lemon juice, hot pepper sauce, salt, or pepper. Serve on "cups" of romaine lettuce leaves. Refrigerate leftovers.

Kilocalories 259 Kc • Protein 6 Gm • Fat 13 Gm • Percent of calories from fat 43% • Cholesterol 0 mg • Dietary Fiber 4 Gm • Sodium 367 mg • Calcium 62 mg

Cherry Tomato Salad with Goat Cheese and Penne

4 SERVINGS

Too much raw garlic does not agree with everyone's digestion. Slightly cooking it, as in the following recipe, takes the edge off its pungency. You can do this with many recipes that call for lots of raw garlic.

3 tablespoons extra-virgin olive oil

1 teaspoon minced garlic

1 pound cherry tomatoes, halved

6 large fresh basil leaves, slivered

Salt and freshly ground black pepper

6 ounces (about $1/3$ pound) penne

8 thin slices goat cheese (about 3 ounces)

In a small skillet, heat the oil to warm and add the garlic. Cook 1 minute longer, then remove from the heat. Let stand for 10 minutes.

In a large salad bowl, toss the tomatoes and basil with the garlic mixture. Add salt and pepper to your taste. Let the mixture marinate while cooking the penne according to package directions. Drain and rinse the pasta in cold water. Toss with the tomatoes.

To serve, divide the salad among 4 plates. Garnish with goat cheese slices.

Kilocalories 349 Kc • Protein 11 Gm • Fat 18 Gm • Percent of calories from fat 45% • Cholesterol 17 mg • Dietary Fiber 3 Gm • Sodium 123 mg • Calcium 78 mg

SAUCY TOMATOES

331

Plum Tomato, Haricots Verts, Mozzarella, and Pasta Salad

Haricots verts *are French cultivated green beans, increasingly available in American markets. This substantial salad can be served as a main dish in summer.*

1/4 cup extra-virgin olive oil
2 tablespoons red wine vinegar
1/2 teaspoon salt
Freshly ground pepper to taste
1 tablespoon chopped
 fresh basil
1 small sweet onion, such as
 Vidalia, sliced and separated
 into rings
4 to 6 large plum tomatoes,
 seeded and cut into thin
 wedges

1/2 pound fresh mozzarella,
 diced
1/2 pound fresh *haricots verts*
 (or any fresh green beans),
 cut into 2-inch lengths
6 ounces (about 1/3 pound)
 mezzani
4 sprigs of fresh basil for
 garnish (optional)

In a large salad bowl, blend together the oil, vinegar, seasonings, chopped basil, and onion rings. Toss with the tomatoes and mozzarella, and allow them to marinate while cooking the green beans and pasta.

Cook the green beans in boiling salted water until tender-crisp, 5 to 7 minutes. Drain and rinse in cold water. Cook the mezzani according to package directions and drain; rinse in cold water. Toss the green beans and pasta with the tomato mixture. Garnish with basil sprigs, if desired.

Kilocalories 518 Kc • Protein 24 Gm • Fat 24 Gm • Percent of calories from fat 41% • Cholesterol 33 mg • Dietary Fiber 4 Gm • Sodium 567 mg • Calcium 420 mg

Spicy Plum Tomato and Blue Cheese Pasta Salad

1/4 cup olive oil
2 tablespoons red wine vinegar
1/4 cup pitted, halved kalamata olives
1/4 cup crumbled blue cheese
1 tablespoon drained capers
Freshly ground black pepper

6 large plum tomatoes, sliced into thin wedges
6 ounces (about 1/3 pound) medium elbows
1 bunch watercress, stemmed and chopped

In a large salad bowl, combine the oil, vinegar, olives, cheese, capers, and black pepper to your taste. Stir in the plum tomatoes and allow the salad to marinate while cooking the pasta.

Cook the elbows according to package directions and drain. Rinse them in cold water and stir them into the tomato mixture. Pile the watercress on top. When ready to serve, toss the salad again, incorporating the watercress.

Kilocalories 346 Kc • Protein 9 Gm • Fat 19 Gm • Percent of calories from fat 47% • Cholesterol 6 mg • Dietary Fiber 2 Gm • Sodium 293 mg • Calcium 96 mg

SAUCY TOMATOES

333

Summer Favorites: Zucchini and Summer Squash

Here's a pair of fair-weather friends for dieters! They're low in calories (because they're 90 percent water!) and low in sodium. Unlike eggplant, zucchini can be sautéed in a minimum of oil for a richer taste. Nutritionally, they offer a pleasant portion of potassium and fiber—all-around good medicine for the heart—as well as the antioxidant vitamin A.

If you've ever grown summer squash or zucchini in your garden, you know how prolific they are. One to three plants are plenty for the average family, and the squash are sweetest and best when harvested as soon as they're four inches long. If you buy them in the market, look for unblemished squash with no soft spots. They should be plump, with a good fresh color; the stems ends should be fresh and green. Refrigerate in perforated plastic bags and use them within two or three days of purchase.

A zucchini's surface is somewhat deceptive; it looks smooth and clean, yet it can hold a lot of grit. It requires thorough washing with a vegetable brush. But neither zucchini nor summer squash needs to be peeled.

Zucchini Soup with Angel Hair

———— ■ ————

6 SERVINGS

With the addition of greens, this soup is transformed into a powerhouse of vitamin A.

1 tablespoon olive oil
¼ cup chopped shallots
  or onion
6 cups chicken stock or
  canned broth
½ cup tomato purée (not
  tomato paste)
1 large carrot, sliced diagonally
¼ cup fresh celery leaves, or 1
  tablespoon dried
Pinch of dried basil

Pinch of dried thyme
1 medium zucchini (½ to
  ¾ pound), cut into ½-inch
  chunks
2 cups coarsely chopped
  greens, such as escarole, kale,
  or outer leaves of romaine
  lettuce
Salt and pepper
4 ounces (¼ pound) angel
  hair pasta

Heat the oil in a large pot and sauté the shallots or onion and carrots until soft and fragrant. Add the stock, tomato purée, celery leaves, basil, and thyme. Bring to a boil, reduce the heat, and simmer 5 minutes. Add the zucchini and greens and continue simmering, covered, until the zucchini is tender, 8 to 10 minutes. Taste to correct the seasonings. Add salt and pepper to your taste.

Cook the angel hair separately according to package directions, but for only the minimum amount of time. Drain and stir the pasta into the soup. Serve as soon as possible after adding the pasta.

Kilocalories 159 Kc • Protein 9 Gm • Fat 4 Gm • Percent of calories from fat 24% • Cholesterol 0 mg • Dietary Fiber 3 Gm • Sodium 455 mg • Calcium 51 mg

Paraguayan Zucchini Soup with Orzo

2 tablespoons olive oil
1 medium onion, chopped
2 garlic cloves, minced
6 cups chicken stock or
  canned broth
2 small zucchini (about 1
  pound), coarsely grated
$1/2$ teaspoon salt

$1/4$ teaspoon freshly ground
  black pepper
1 egg, beaten
1 cup orzo
2 tablespoons chopped fresh
  flat-leaf parsley
Grated Parmesan cheese

Heat the oil in a large pot and sauté the onion and garlic until they are sizzling and fragrant. Add the stock, zucchini, salt, and pepper. Bring to a boil, reduce the heat, and simmer the soup until the zucchini is tender, 10 minutes.

Gradually whisk 2 cups of the hot soup into the egg until smoothly blended. Pour the egg mixture into the remaining soup; stir well while simmering, 2 minutes. If a smoother texture is desired, purée the soup in a processor in batches.

Meanwhile, cook the orzo according to package directions and drain. Stir the orzo and parsley into the soup. Pass the grated cheese at the table.

Kilocalories 371 Kc • Protein 18 Gm • Fat 11 Gm • Percent of calories from fat 27% • Cholesterol 53 mg • Dietary Fiber 4 Gm • Sodium 951 mg • Calcium 52 mg

Zucchini with Fettuccine Alfredo

4 SERVINGS

This recipe uses a much lighter version of the traditional cream-and-butter Alfredo sauce.

1 medium zucchini (about
  ¹/₂ pound)
1 tablespoon olive oil
1 large shallot, minced
2 tablespoons superfine flour,
  such as Wondra
2 tablespoons nonfat dry milk
¹/₄ teaspoon salt
¹/₈ teaspoon white pepper

1¹/₂ cups whole milk
2 tablespoons light cream
  cheese (Neufchâtel)
2 tablespoons grated Parmesan
  cheese
8 to 9 ounces (about ¹/₂ pound)
  fresh fettuccine
2 tablespoons chopped fresh
  flat-leaf parsley

Scrub the zucchini well and cut it into quarters lengthwise; cut the quarters into ¹/₄-inch slices.

Heat the oil in a large skillet and slowly sauté the zucchini and shallot, stirring often, until they are tender, about 8 minutes. Remove them from the skillet.

Whisk the flour, dry milk, salt, and pepper into the liquid milk and pour it into the skillet. Cook over medium-high heat, stirring constantly, until thickened and bubbling. Simmer over very low heat for 5 minutes. Combine the sauce with the cream cheese and Parmesan cheese in a food processor or blender and blend until smooth, taking care since hot foods tend to bubble up.

Pour the sauce back into the skillet and add the zucchini. Reheat when ready to serve.

Meanwhile, cook the fettuccine according to package directions; drain. Spoon the pasta into a large serving dish and top with the sauce. Sprinkle with parsley.

Kilocalories 334 Kc • Protein 15 Gm • Fat 11 Gm • Percent of calories from fat 30% • Cholesterol 79 mg • Dietary Fiber 2 Gm • Sodium 326 mg • Calcium 264 mg

Sesame Zucchini with Fresh Asian Noodles

4 SERVINGS

1 tablespoon vegetable oil
1 teaspoon sesame oil
2 small zucchini (about
 ¾ pound), sliced into
 thin half rounds
1 red bell pepper, seeded and
 cut into small triangles
2 celery stalks, thinly sliced
1 onion, thinly sliced
2 tablespoons naturally brewed
 soy sauce

1 teaspoon oyster sauce
 (available in most
 supermarkets)
8 ounces (½ pound) fresh
 Asian noodles or American
 thin linguine
1 tablespoon lightly toasted
 sesame seeds (see Note
 page 128)

Heat the vegetable and sesame oils in a large wok or skillet. Stir-fry the vegetables until they are tender-crisp, about 3 minutes. Season them with the soy sauce and oyster sauce, blending well.

Meanwhile, boil the water and cook the Asian noodles according to the package directions. Fresh noodles take only a few minutes to cook. Drain. Spoon the noodles into a large serving dish. Top with the vegetables. Sprinkle with the sesame seeds.

Kilocalories 183 Kc • Protein 3 Gm • Fat 6 Gm • Percent of calories from fat 29% • Cholesterol 0 mg • Dietary Fiber 3 Gm • Sodium 574 mg • Calcium 59 mg

Zucchini and Scallions with Small Shells

4 SERVINGS

2 tablespoons olive oil
1 bunch scallions, trimmed
and chopped
1 medium zucchini (about
³/₄ pound), diced

8 ounces (¹/₂ pound) small
shells, cooked
¹/₄ teaspoon hot red pepper
flakes, or more to your taste

Heat the oil in a large skillet and sauté the scallions and zucchini until the vegetables are tender. Meanwhile, cook the shells according to package directions and drain. Toss them with the zucchini mixture and hot pepper flakes.

Kilocalories 288 Kc • Protein 8 Gm • Fat 8 Gm • Percent of calories from fat 24% • Cholesterol 0 mg • Dietary Fiber 2 Gm • Sodium 4 mg • Calcium 19 mg

Zucchini and Mushrooms with Penne

4 SERVINGS

3 tablespoons olive oil

2 medium zucchini (about 1¼ pounds), cut into 1-inch chunks

8 to 10 ounces button mushrooms, cleaned and halved

1 tablespoon chopped fresh flat-leaf parsley

2 teaspoons chopped fresh tarragon, or ½ teaspoon dried

Salt and freshly ground black pepper

8 ounces (½ pound) penne or ziti

¼ cup hot chicken stock or canned broth

¼ cup freshly grated Romano cheese

Heat the oil in a large skillet and stir-fry the zucchini and mushrooms until they are lightly browned and the zucchini is tender-crisp, about 3 minutes. Add the parsley and tarragon, and salt and pepper the vegetables to your taste.

Meanwhile, cook the penne according to package directions and drain. Combine the vegetables, pasta, stock, and cheese in a large serving dish, and toss to blend.

Kilocalories 356 Kc • Protein 12 Gm • Fat 13 Gm • Percent of calories from fat 32% • Cholesterol 5 mg • Dietary Fiber 4 Gm • Sodium 98 mg • Calcium 91 mg

Zucchini, Bok Choy, and Scallions with Farfallini

4 SERVINGS

1 tablespoon olive oil
2 tablespoons butter
4 stalks bok choy, without leaves, cut into 2-inch sticks
1 bunch scallions, white part only, chopped
1 large zucchini (about 1 pound), coarsely shredded

Salt and freshly ground black pepper
8 ounces ($\frac{1}{2}$ pound) farfallini (small egg bows)
3 tablespoons freshly grated Parmesan cheese

In a large skillet, heat the oil with 1 tablespoon of the butter and sauté the bok choy and scallions until they just begin to soften, about 3 minutes. Add the zucchini and stir-fry until it's tender. The total cooking time will be 5 to 7 minutes. Add salt and pepper to your taste.

Meanwhile, cook the farfallini according to package directions and drain. Toss the pasta with the remaining 1 tablespoon butter and the cheese. Spoon in the vegetables and toss them with the pasta.

Kilocalories 287 Kc • Protein 10 Gm • Fat 12 Gm • Percent of calories from fat 37% • Cholesterol 61 mg • Dietary Fiber 2 Gm • Sodium 156 mg • Calcium 109 mg

Zucchini, Prosciutto, and Rigatoni

A little prosciutto goes a long way in flavoring this delectable dish.

3 tablespoons olive oil
2 medium zucchini (about
  1½ pounds), diced
Salt and freshly ground pepper
8 ounces (½ pound) rigatoni

1 cup part-skim ricotta cheese,
  at room temperature
½ cup grated Parmesan cheese
6 thin slices prosciutto, cut in
  julienne strips

In a large skillet, heat the oil and sauté the zucchini, stirring often, until tender, 10 to 15 minutes. Add salt and pepper to your taste.

Meanwhile, cook the rigatoni according to package directions and drain. Spoon it into a large serving dish and toss it with the ricotta and Parmesan cheese. Toss again with the zucchini and prosciutto.

Kilocalories 476 Kc • Protein 24 Gm • Fat 20 Gm • Percent of calories from fat 37% • Cholesterol 35 mg • Dietary Fiber 3 Gm • Sodium 460 mg • Calcium 342 mg

Zucchini "Lasagne"

For a lighter lasagne, I use egg bows instead of the heavier noodles.

2 to 3 tablespoons olive oil
2 medium zucchini (about
    1¼ pounds), cut into ½-inch
    diagonal slices
2 cups part-skim ricotta
1 egg, beaten
1 tablespoon minced fresh
    flat-leaf parsley
Several dashes of white pepper

¾ pound (12 ounces) farfalle
    (egg bows)
2 cups tomato sauce (see A
    Fragrant Marinara Sauce or
    Tomato-Meat Sauce on pages
    318 and 322)
4 tablespoons grated Parmesan
    cheese

Coat a large skillet with olive oil and fry the zucchini slices until they are golden on both sides, adding more oil as needed. Unlike eggplant, zucchini does not sponge up a lot of oil.

Blend together the ricotta, egg, parsley, and white pepper.

Cook the egg bows according to package directions and drain.

Use a large baking dish (15 × 9 inches or equivalent, about 3 inches deep) from which you can serve. Spread ½ cup of the sauce on the bottom. Layer ⅓ of the egg bows, 1 cup of the ricotta mixture, and 1 tablespoon of the Parmesan.

Layer all the zucchini over all. Cover with half the remaining egg bows, ½ cup of the sauce, and 1 tablespoon of the Parmesan.

Complete the casserole with the remaining egg bows, 1 cup of ricotta, and 1 cup of the sauce. Sprinkle with the last 2 tablespoons of the Parmesan.

Preheat the oven to 350 degrees F. Cover the casserole with foil and bake for 30 minutes (45 minutes if the casserole has been refrigerated). Uncover and bake an additional 15 minutes.

Kilocalories 464 Kc • Protein 22 Gm • Fat 19 Gm • Percent of calories from fat 37% • Cholesterol 117 mg • Dietary Fiber 4 Gm • Sodium 455 mg • Calcium 325 mg

Zucchini-Mushroom "Lasagne"

4 SERVINGS

Sauté 10 ounces sliced mushrooms in 1 tablespoon olive oil until they are lightly browned. Season them with salt and pepper to your taste and a dash of oregano. Follow the preceding recipe, and make a layer of all the mushrooms underneath the last $^1/_3$ of the egg bows.

Kilocalories 496 Kc • Protein 23 Gm • Fat 21 Gm • Percent of calories from fat 39% • Cholesterol 117 mg • Dietary Fiber 4 Gm • Sodium 457 mg • Calcium 328 mg

Zucchini, Chilies, and Sun-Dried Tomatoes with Shells

4 SERVINGS

3 tablespoons olive oil
1 medium zucchini ($^1/_2$ to $^3/_4$ pound), cut into 1-inch chunks
2 large mild chilies (Anaheim, or California), seeded and cut into 1-inch chunks
$^1/_2$ cup slivered sun-dried tomatoes
1 garlic clove, minced

1 tablespoon minced fresh cilantro, or 1 teaspoon dried
$^1/_2$ teaspoon dried oregano
Salt and freshly ground black pepper
8 ounces ($^1/_2$ pound) medium shells
1 cup shredded Monterey Jack cheese

Heat the oil in a large skillet. Sauté the zucchini and chilies over medium-high heat, stirring often, until the zucchini begins to brown and is tender. Add the tomatoes and garlic. Lower the heat and continue to sauté for 3 minutes. Add the cilantro, oregano, and salt and pepper to your taste.

Meanwhile, cook the shells according to package directions. Drain, keeping them slightly moist, and spoon them into a large serving dish. Toss with the zucchini and chilies. Sprinkle with the cheese and serve.

Kilocalories 434 Kc • Protein 15 Gm • Fat 20 Gm • Percent of calories from fat 42% • Cholesterol 30 mg • Dietary Fiber 3 Gm • Sodium 449 mg • Calcium 222 mg

Summer Squash and Red Bell Pepper with Spinach Penne

---

4 SERVINGS

This easy dish, with its pretty color combination, is perfect as part of a relaxed summer supper.

1 medium summer squash
2 tablespoons olive oil
1 garlic clove, minced
1 red bell pepper, seeded and cut into 1-inch chunks
2 large ripe fresh tomatoes, peeled, seeded, and diced

1 tablespoon minced fresh cilantro, or 1 teaspoon dried
$1/4$ teaspoon salt
Freshly ground black pepper
8 ounces ($1/2$ pound) spinach penne

Cut the squash in half lengthwise, then into half rounds, about $1/2$ inch thick. Heat the oil in a large skillet and sauté the squash with the garlic and bell pepper until the vegetables begin to soften and are fragrant. Add the tomatoes, cilantro, salt, and pepper to your taste. Continue to cook until everything is quite tender, about 8 minutes.

Meanwhile, cook the penne according to package directions and drain. In a serving dish, toss the vegetables with the penne.

Kilocalories 305 Kc • Protein 10 Gm • Fat 10 Gm • Percent of calories from fat 28% • Cholesterol 54 mg • Dietary Fiber 5 Gm • Sodium 193 mg • Calcium 53 mg

Summer Squash, Green Peppers, and Mushrooms with Asian Noodles

4 SERVINGS

½ cup chicken stock or canned broth

2 tablespoons naturally brewed soy sauce, plus more to pass

1 teaspoon oyster sauce (available in most supermarkets)

1 tablespoon cornstarch

2 tablespoons olive oil

1 medium summer squash, cut into half-rounds

8 ounces mushrooms, cleaned and sliced thick (about 3 slices per mushroom)

2 green bell peppers, seeded and cut into triangles

1 onion, thinly sliced

8 ounces (½ pound) Asian thin flat noodles or American linguine

½ cup unsalted cashew pieces (optional)

Mix the stock, soy sauce, oyster sauce, and cornstarch in a small bowl.

In a large wok or skillet, heat the oil and stir-fry the squash, mushrooms, peppers, and onion until they are barely tender-crisp. Stir in the sauce mixture over medium heat until it thickens and coats the vegetables. Simmer over very low heat for 2 to 3 minutes.

Meanwhile, cook the noodles according to package directions and drain. Spoon them into a large serving dish and top with the vegetable mixture. Sprinkle with cashews, if using. Pass more soy sauce at the table.

Kilocalories 307 Kc • Protein 9 Gm • Fat 7 Gm • Percent of calories from fat 21% • Cholesterol 0 mg • Dietary Fiber 3 Gm • Sodium 854 mg • Calcium 52 mg

Summer Squash, Tomatoes, and Paprika with Shells

4 SERVINGS

There's a Hungarian flavor to this dish that would go well with a topping of light sour cream or nonfat yogurt.

3 tablespoons olive oil
1 to 2 garlic cloves, minced
2 large summer squash (about
  2 pounds), diced
1 cup diced fresh tomato
  (1 very large tomato)

Salt and freshly ground pepper
2 teaspoons paprika
2 tablespoons chopped fresh
  flat-leaf parsley
8 ounces ($1/2$ pound) medium
  shells

Heat the oil in a large skillet and sauté the garlic and diced squash until slightly softened, about 5 minutes. Add the tomato and salt and pepper to your taste. Stir in the paprika. Continue to sauté, stirring often, until the summer squash is tender-crisp. Remove from the heat and sprinkle with the parsley.

Meanwhile, cook the shells according to the package directions and drain. Combine the squash mixture and shells in a serving dish.

Kilocalories 348 Kc • Protein 10 Gm • Fat 12 Gm • Percent of calories from fat 29% • Cholesterol 0 mg • Dietary Fiber 5 Gm • Sodium 12 mg • Calcium 42 mg

Summer Squash-Macaroni Salad

4 SERVINGS

Follow the preceding recipe. Stir in 2 tablespoons white wine vinegar and chill the mixture. Serve cold or at room temperature.

Kilocalories 348 Kc • Protein 10 Gm • Fat 12 Gm • Percent of calories from fat 29% • Cholesterol 0 mg • Dietary Fiber 5 Gm • Sodium 12 mg • Calcium 42 mg

Summer Squash, Green Beans, and Roquefort with Spinach Fettuccine

4 SERVINGS

³/₄ cup vegetable or chicken stock, or canned broth
1 medium summer squash (about ¹/₂ pound), diced
¹/₂ pound green beans, trimmed, cut diagonally into 1-inch pieces
1 garlic clove, chopped

1 tablespoon chopped fresh tarragon, or 1 teaspoon dried
¹/₂ teaspoon salt
¹/₄ teaspoon white pepper
8 to 9 ounces (about ¹/₂ pound) fresh spinach fettuccine
3 ounces crumbled Roquefort cheese (or any blue cheese)

In a medium saucepan, combine the stock, summer squash, green beans, and garlic, and simmer the vegetables, covered, until they are tender, 5 to 7 minutes. Season them with the tarragon, salt, and pepper.

Meanwhile, cook the fettuccine according to package directions and drain. Spoon it into a large serving dish and toss it with the Roquefort and vegetables.

Kilocalories 272 Kc • Protein 13 Gm • Fat 8 Gm • Percent of calories from fat 25% • Cholesterol 57 mg • Dietary Fiber 3 Gm • Sodium 772 mg • Calcium 175 mg

Summer Squash and Cheddar Casserole with Rotelle

---

4 SERVINGS

A kid-pleasing kind of casserole to serve with a tossed green salad.

$^3/_4$ to 1 pound summer squash
$^1/_2$ cup water
1 tablespoon butter
About 1$^1/_4$ cups milk (whole or low-fat)
2 tablespoons superfine flour, such as Wondra
$^1/_4$ teaspoon salt
Several dashes of white pepper

4 ounces coarsely grated sharp Cheddar cheese
6 ounces (about $^1/_3$ pound) rotelle
$^1/_4$ cup unflavored bread crumbs
1 tablespoon grated Parmesan cheese

Cut the squash into rounds at the thin end and half rounds at the thick end. Combine with the water and butter in a saucepan. Bring to a boil, reduce the heat, cover, and simmer until tender, 5 minutes. Remove the squash with a slotted spoon.

Pour the cooking liquid into a 2-cup measure and add enough milk to make 1$^1/_2$ cups. Blend in the flour, salt, and pepper. Pour this mixture into the pan and bring it to a boil, stirring constantly. Simmer over very low heat, stirring often, for 5 minutes. Remove from the heat and stir in the Cheddar cheese.

Preheat the oven to 350 degrees F. Cook the rotelle according to package directions, undercooking it slightly; drain and mix with half of the sauce.

Layer the pasta in the bottom of a buttered 9 × 9-inch baking dish. Spread the squash over the pasta. Pour the remaining sauce over all. Top with the bread crumbs and the Parmesan. Bake the casserole on the middle shelf for 30 minutes, or until it is bubbling throughout and golden on top.

Kilocalories 402 Kc • Protein 18 Gm • Fat 17 Gm • Percent of calories from fat 36% • Cholesterol 49 mg • Dietary Fiber 2 Gm • Sodium 478 mg • Calcium 350 mg

Zucchini and Summer Squash with Pine Nuts, Feta Cheese, and Linguine

4 SERVINGS

2 tablespoons olive oil
1¹⁄₂ pounds zucchini and
  summer squash, cut into half
  rounds
1 garlic clove, minced
¹⁄₄ cup pine nuts
Salt and freshly ground
  black pepper

1 tablespoon minced fresh
  flat-leaf parsley
8 ounces (¹⁄₂ pound) linguine
¹⁄₂ cup chicken stock or canned
  broth, or pasta cooking water
1 cup diced feta cheese

Heat the oil in a large skillet and stir-fry the squash until they begin to brown and become tender-crisp. Add the garlic, pine nuts, and salt and pepper to your taste. Continue to stir-fry for 3 minutes. Sprinkle with the parsley, and keep warm.

Cook the linguine according to package directions and drain, reserving ¹⁄₂ cup of the cooking water if you do not have chicken stock on hand. Spoon the linguine into a large serving dish. Add the stock or cooking water. Toss with the squash mixture and the cheese.

Kilocalories 518 Kc • Protein 21 Gm • Fat 27 Gm • Percent of calories from fat 45% • Cholesterol 57 mg • Dietary Fiber 4 Gm • Sodium 773 mg • Calcium 355 mg

Zucchini and Summer Squash with Ziti

---

4 SERVINGS

1 medium zucchini (¹/₂ to ³/₄ pound)
1 medium summer squash (¹/₂ to ³/₄ pound)
2 tablespoons olive oil
1 green bell pepper, seeded and cut into chunks

2 garlic cloves, minced
Salt and pepper
3 tablespoons light sour cream
2 tablespoons grated Parmesan cheese
8 ounces (¹/₂ pound) ziti

Cut both squash into quarters lengthwise, then crosswise into ¹/₂-inch slices.

Heat the oil in a large skillet and stir-fry the squash and green pepper until tender-crisp, 8 to 10 minutes. Add the garlic during the last 2 minutes. Season the vegetables with salt and pepper to your taste. Remove from the heat and stir in the sour cream and Parmesan.

Meanwhile, cook the ziti according to package directions and drain. In a large serving dish, toss the ziti with the squash.

Kilocalories 319 Kc • Protein 11 Gm • Fat 10 Gm • Percent of calories from fat 27% • Cholesterol 6 mg • Dietary Fiber 3 Gm • Sodium 62 mg • Calcium 81 mg

Broiled Zucchini and Mostaccioli Salad

◼

6 SERVINGS

1 garlic clove, peeled
$1/4$ cup extra-virgin olive oil
2 medium zucchini (about
  $1^1/_2$ pounds)
2 tablespoons red wine vinegar
$1/2$ teaspoon salt
$1/8$ to $1/4$ teaspoon pepper
2 large vine-ripened tomatoes
  (1 pound), chopped

$1/4$ cup chopped red onion or
  scallions
$1/4$ cup chopped fresh flat-leaf
  parsley
6 ounces (about $1/3$ pound)
  mostaccioli

Press the garlic through a garlic press and mix it with the oil. Let the mixture stand for a half hour or so to develop its flavor.

Heat the broiler. Cut the zucchini diagonally into $1/2$-inch slices. Brush the slices lightly on both sides with the garlic oil and broil until lightly colored and tender-crisp, about 4 minutes per side. Let the slices cool to room temperature.

Mix the remaining garlic oil, vinegar, salt, and pepper in a salad dish. Stir in the tomatoes, onion, and parsley.

Cook the mostaccioli according to package directions and drain. Rinse under cold water. Add the mostaccioli and zucchini to the tomatoes and toss gently. Serve at room temperature.

Kilocalories 220 Kc • Protein 6 Gm • Fat 10 Gm • Percent of calories from fat 39% • Cholesterol 0 mg • Dietary Fiber 3 Gm • Sodium 208 mg • Calcium 32 mg

Marvelous Medleys

From the robust and hearty to the elegant and beautiful, combinations of vegetables can be tossed with pasta shapes in wonderfully varied ways. These marvelous medleys provide a blending of vitamins, minerals, and plant chemicals for some extra nutritional synergy. Many of them contain a "cocktail" of antioxidants as potent as a supplement.

Truly among the most healthful dishes you can enjoy, some of these mixtures have the star quality of an entrée and can be the centerpiece of the meal. Although most of them are quick and easy to make, get ready for some rave reviews when you serve them!

Minestrone in Minutes

◼

6 SERVINGS

A homemade broth made from the last of a roast chicken is ideal. When the ideal is not available, substitute two low-sodium 13-ounce cans of chicken broth plus sufficient water to make 6 cups, plus 1 chicken bouillon cube.

6 cups chicken broth
2 large carrots, sliced
2 celery stalks, sliced
1 fresh tomato, diced
1 garlic clove, chopped (optional)
$\frac{1}{2}$ teaspoon Italian herbs (from a jar), or a combination of dried basil, oregano, and thyme

Several dashes of black pepper
$\frac{1}{2}$ pound well-washed escarole leaves, coarsely chopped
1 cup ditali or small elbows
1 cup canned shell beans or kidney beans, drained and rinsed
Salt if needed
Freshly grated Romano cheese

Bring the broth to a boil and add the carrots, celery, tomato, garlic, herbs, and pepper. Reduce the heat and simmer the soup, covered, for 5 minutes.

Add the escarole and continue simmering for 15 minutes.

Meanwhile, prepare the ditali separately according to package directions. Cook it al dente, since it will cook a bit more in the soup. Drain. When the escarole is cooked, add the ditali and beans; simmer about 3 minutes longer. Whether or not you'll need salt depends on the broth you used; taste the soup and add $\frac{1}{2}$ teaspoon if needed. Pass the grated cheese at the table.

Kilocalories 159 Kc • Protein 10 Gm • Fat 2 Gm • Percent of calories from fat 11% • Cholesterol 0 mg • Dietary Fiber 5 Gm • Sodium 592 mg • Calcium 56 mg

Cabbage and Kidney Bean Soup with Gemellini

6 SERVINGS

Rye bread is a good accompaniment to this hearty soup.

2 tablespoons olive oil
1 large onion, chopped
1 garlic clove, minced
3 cups coarsely shredded
 cabbage
7 cups vegetable or chicken
 stock, or canned broth
1 teaspoon chopped fresh dill,
 or $^{1}/_{4}$ teaspoon dried

1 teaspoon chopped fresh
 thyme, or $^{1}/_{4}$ teaspoon dried
$^{1}/_{4}$ teaspoon salt
$^{1}/_{8}$ to $^{1}/_{4}$ teaspoon pepper
1 20-ounce can red kidney
 beans, drained and rinsed
4 ounces ($^{1}/_{4}$ pound) gemellini
 (very small twists)

Heat the oil in a large pot or Dutch oven and sauté the onion and garlic until they are soft and fragrant. Add the cabbage and sauté 5 minutes longer.

Add the stock, dill, thyme, salt, and pepper. Bring to a simmer, cover, and cook for 15 minutes. Stir in the beans and continue cooking for 5 minutes.

Meanwhile, cook the gemellini according to package directions and drain. Stir into the soup.

Kilocalories 230 Kc • Protein 11 Gm • Fat 6 Gm • Percent of calories from fat 24% • Cholesterol 0 mg • Dietary Fiber 7 Gm • Sodium 1462 mg • Calcium 55 mg

Asian Vegetable-Noodle Soup with Poached Eggs

2 cups chicken stock or
canned broth
1 cup water
2 tablespoons naturally brewed
soy sauce
2 cups chopped greens:
spinach, bok choy, and/or
Chinese cabbage

4 scallions, cut into 1-inch
pieces
4 ounces (1/4 pound) Asian
somen (thin noodles) or
American angel hair pasta
2 eggs
2 radishes, sliced, for
garnishing

Combine the stock, water, soy sauce, and vegetables in a large skillet with a cover. Bring the mixture to a boil, reduce the heat, and simmer, covered, for 5 minutes.

Meanwhile, cook the pasta separately. If there are no package directions in English, boil the noodles in a large pot of salted water, taste-testing for tenderness. They should be ready in 3 to 4 minutes (keep in mind that they will cook a little more in the soup). Remove the noodles with a slotted spoon and add them to the soup.

Break an egg into a cup and ease it into the simmering soup. Repeat with the other egg. After 1 minute, turn off the heat, cover, and let stand about 5 minutes, until the egg whites are opaque and the yolks are cooked to your taste.

Garnish each serving with some radish slices.

Kilocalories 371 Kc • Protein 19 Gm • Fat 8 Gm • Percent of calories from fat 20% • Cholesterol 216 mg • Dietary Fiber 1 Gm • Sodium 1501 mg • Calcium 113 mg

Swiss Vegetable Soup with Farfallini

6 SERVINGS

3 tablespoons olive oil
4 celery stalks, diced
1 cucumber, peeled and diced
2 carrots, diced
2 leeks, washed between rings, thinly sliced
3 to 4 cups shredded cabbage
2 large tomatoes (about 1 pound), peeled, seeded, and diced

8 cups vegetable or beef stock, or canned broth
$\frac{1}{2}$ teaspoon dried basil
$\frac{1}{2}$ teaspoon salt
$\frac{1}{4}$ teaspoon freshly ground black pepper
1 cup farfallini (small egg bows)
2 tablespoons chopped fresh flat-leaf parsley

In a large pot, heat the oil and sauté the celery, cucumber, carrots, and leeks for 3 to 5 minutes. Add the cabbage, tomatoes, stock, basil, salt, and pepper. Bring to a simmer and cook, uncovered, until the vegetables are quite tender, 20 to 25 minutes. Cook the farfallini separately according to package directions, drain, and stir into the soup with the parsley.

Kilocalories 202 Kc • Protein 4 Gm • Fat 8 Gm • Percent of calories from fat 42% • Cholesterol 6 mg • Dietary Fiber 6 Gm • Sodium 906 mg • Calcium 75 mg

Garbure
(French Vegetable Stew with Orecchiette)

Replacing the sausage traditional to this dish, I've used some robust sausage flavors: garlic, sage, fennel, and pepper.

2 tablespoons olive oil
1 large yellow onion, chopped
2 garlic cloves, minced
Several leaves of fresh
  sage, chopped, or
  $1/2$ teaspoon dried
4 cups vegetable or chicken
  stock, or canned broth
1 large carrot, sliced
2 purple-top turnips, peeled
  and sliced
1 16-ounce can tomatoes
  with juice

$1/2$ teaspoon salt
$1/4$ teaspoon black pepper
$1/4$ teaspoon fennel seeds
$1/4$ teaspoon dried thyme
$1/2$ pound fresh green beans,
  cut into 2-inch lengths
2 cups shredded cabbage
1 15- or 16-ounce can white
  kidney beans (cannellini),
  drained and rinsed
4 ounces ($1/4$ pound)
  orecchiette

Heat the oil in a large pot, and slowly sauté the onion and garlic with the sage until they are soft and fragrant but not brown, 5 minutes.

Add the stock, carrot, turnips, tomatoes, seasonings, and herbs. Bring to a simmer and cook, covered, for 15 minutes, stirring occasionally. Add the green beans and cabbage, and continue simmering for 8 minutes. Add the kidney beans and cook another 5 minutes, until everything is quite tender.

Meanwhile, cook the orecchiette according to package directions and drain. Stir the pasta into the vegetables. Serve the stew in bowls with French bread on the side.

Kilocalories 258 Kc • Protein 10 Gm • Fat 5 Gm • Percent of calories from fat 19% • Cholesterol 0 mg • Dietary Fiber 9 Gm • Sodium 640 mg • Calcium 120 mg

Very Verdi Pasta

4 SERVINGS

A combination of green beans, zucchini, spinach fettuccine, and lots of parsley makes this dish a feast of greens.

$^1/_2$ **pound fresh green beans, cut into 2-inch lengths**

2 tablespoons olive oil

1 medium zucchini ($^1/_2$ to $^3/_4$ pound), cut into 2-inch sticks

2 garlic cloves, minced

$^1/_4$ **cup chicken stock or canned broth**

Salt and freshly ground pepper

8 ounces ($^1/_2$ pound) spinach fettuccine

2 tablespoons freshly grated Parmesan cheese, plus more to pass

$^1/_4$ **cup chopped fresh flat-leaf parsley**

Parboil the green beans in a pot of salted water until barely tender, about 5 minutes. Drain.

Heat the oil in a large skillet and sauté the zucchini until it begins to brown and is tender, 5 to 7 minutes. Add the garlic during the last minute. Add the green beans and stock, and bring to a simmer. Season the vegetables with salt and pepper to your taste.

Meanwhile, cook the fettuccine according to package directions and drain. Spoon the pasta into a large serving dish, and toss with the vegetables. Sprinkle with the cheese and parsley, and toss again. Pass more grated cheese at the table.

Kilocalories 321 Kc • Protein 12 Gm • Fat 10 Gm • Percent of calories from fat 29% • Cholesterol 56 mg • Dietary Fiber 7 Gm • Sodium 120 mg • Calcium 109 mg

Tex-Mex Baked Ziti

◼

2 tablespoons olive oil
1 green bell pepper, seeded and chopped
1 medium yellow onion, chopped
2 fresh or canned jalapeño chilies, seeded and minced (wear rubber gloves)
2 garlic cloves, minced
1 16-ounce can tomatoes with juice, chopped
1 teaspoon chili powder
½ teaspoon dried oregano

½ teaspoon ground cumin
½ teaspoon salt
¼ teaspoon black pepper
1 15- or 16-ounce can kidney or pinto beans, drained and rinsed
1 10-ounce package frozen corn kernels, thawed enough to separate
8 ounces (½ pound) ziti
4 ounces shredded Monterey Jack cheese

Preheat the oven to 350 degrees F.

In a large skillet, heat the oil and sauté the pepper, onion, chilies, and garlic until they begin to soften. Add the tomatoes, herbs, and seasonings, and simmer the sauce for 15 minutes. Stir in the beans and corn.

Meanwhile, cook the ziti according to package directions, undercooking it slightly, and drain. Combine the ziti and Tex-Mex sauce in a 2-quart gratin pan or casserole. Sprinkle with the cheese. Bake on the middle shelf until the casserole is bubbling throughout and the cheese has melted, 20 to 25 minutes.

Kilocalories 582 Kc • Protein 25 Gm • Fat 18 Gm • Percent of calories from fat 26% • Cholesterol 25 mg • Dietary Fiber 12 Gm • Sodium 722 mg • Calcium 309 mg

Roasted Vegetables and Rigatoni

■

4 SERVINGS

A wooden mallet, such as an old-time potato masher, is a handy kitchen tool. In this recipe, use it to crush the olives for pitting, and also the garlic.

1 large eggplant (1 pound),
  unpeeled
4 tablespoons olive oil
1 large zucchini (³/₄ pound)
2 red bell peppers, seeded and
  cut into chunks
2 Anaheim chilies, seeded and
  cut into chunks
4 to 5 garlic cloves, unpeeled,
  crushed
12 kalamata olives, pitted, whole

1 teaspoon Italian herbs (from
  a jar), or a combination
  of dried basil, oregano,
  and thyme
Salt and freshly ground black
  pepper
³/₄ pound (12 ounces) rigatoni
¹/₃ cup warm vegetable
  or chicken stock, or
  canned broth
Grated Parmesan cheese

Cut the eggplant into eight wedges and make 1-inch deep slits in the flesh. Salt the eggplant and let it drain in a colander, cut sides down, for a half hour or more. Rinse the wedges and press them dry with paper towels. Cut the wedges in half.

Preheat the oven to 400 degrees F.

Quarter the zucchini lengthwise and cut into 3-inch chunks.

Pour 2 tablespoons of the oil into a large roasting pan. Add the eggplant, zucchini, bell peppers, chilies, garlic, and olives. Drizzle the remaining 2 tablespoons of oil over all and sprinkle with the herbs and seasonings. Bake for 30 minutes, stir well, and continue baking for 10 minutes or more, until everything is quite tender and slightly browned.

Remove the vegetables, except the garlic and olives, to a bowl; keep them warm. Peel and mash the garlic in the roasting pan.

Meanwhile, cook the rigatoni according to package directions and drain. Mix it with the garlic, olives, and oil remaining in the roasting pan, then transfer to a large serving platter. Stir in the broth. Top with the vegetables. Pass the grated cheese at the table.

Kilocalories 523 Kc • Protein 13 Gm • Fat 18 Gm • Percent of calories from fat 30% • Cholesterol 0 mg • Dietary Fiber 4 Gm • Sodium 311 mg • Calcium 52 mg

Seven-Vegetable Tagine with Couscous

---

4 SERVINGS

A tagine is a Moroccan pot for cooking stew, but the word has come to mean the stew itself.

1 cup couscous, raw
1 small eggplant (about
$\frac{1}{2}$ pound)
3 tablespoons olive oil
1 yellow onion, chopped
1 garlic clove, finely chopped
1 small zucchini (about
$\frac{1}{2}$ pound), cut into 1-inch
pieces
1 red bell pepper, seeded and
chopped
2 tomatoes, peeled, seeded,
and chopped

1 carrot, sliced thin
1 Anaheim chili, seeded and
chopped
1 cup chicken stock or
canned broth
2 tablespoons golden raisins
$\frac{1}{4}$ teaspoon curry powder
$\frac{1}{4}$ teaspoon ground cumin
$\frac{1}{4}$ teaspoon ground cinnamon
$\frac{1}{4}$ teaspoon salt
$\frac{1}{4}$ teaspoon pepper

Prepare the couscous (see page 12 for basic recipe or follow package directions); cool and separate the grains. You should have $2\frac{1}{2}$ cups cooked couscous. To serve, reheat over hot water or in a microwave-safe casserole in the microwave. Fluff well with two forks, breaking up any lumps.

Peel and slice the eggplant. Salt the slices and drain them in a colander for 30 minutes. Rinse and squeeze them dry between paper towels. Dice the slices.

Heat the oil in a large skillet and stir-fry the eggplant with the onion and garlic until slightly softened, about 3 minutes.

Add all the remaining ingredients, except the couscous, and simmer with cover ajar until the vegetables are tender and the mixture is thick, 15 to 20 minutes.

Serve the tagine over the couscous.

Kilocalories 365 Kc • Protein 11 Gm • Fat 12 Gm • Percent of calories from fat 28% • Cholesterol 0 mg • Dietary Fiber 6 Gm • Sodium 732 mg • Calcium 54 mg

Vegetarian Chili with Ditali

■

6 SERVINGS

1 tablespoon olive oil
1 large onion, chopped
1 garlic clove, minced
1 red bell pepper, seeded and chopped
1 Anaheim chili, seeded and chopped
2 celery stalks, sliced
1 28-ounce can tomatoes
1 20-ounce can kidney beans, drained and rinsed
1 medium zucchini, cut into chunks
1 carrot, sliced

2 tablespoons chopped fresh parsley
2 teaspoons chili powder
1 teaspoon dried oregano
$\frac{1}{2}$ teaspoon ground cumin
$\frac{1}{2}$ teaspoon black pepper
1 tablespoon red wine vinegar
2 cups fresh or frozen corn kernels
8 ounces ($\frac{1}{2}$ pound) ditali or small elbows
Shredded Monterey Jack cheese

Heat the oil in a 4-quart pot and sauté the onion, garlic, red pepper, chili, and celery until they are softened and fragrant.

Add all the remaining ingredients except the corn, ditali, and cheese. Bring the chili to a boil, lower the heat, and simmer, covered, for 30 minutes, stirring occasionally.

Add the corn and cook 5 minutes longer.

Cook the ditali according to package directions and drain. Spoon the chili into bowls and put a spoonful of ditali in the center of each serving. Top with the shredded cheese.

Kilocalories 335 Kc • Protein 14 Gm • Fat 4 Gm • Percent of calories from fat 11% • Cholesterol 0 mg • Dietary Fiber 11 Gm • Sodium 615 mg • Calcium 101 mg

Lasagne and Grilled Vegetable "Sandwiches"

---

1 garlic clove, very finely
minced
1/4 cup olive oil
1 medium eggplant
1 large zucchini, cut into
1/2-inch slices
8 to 10 curly-edged lasagna
noodles (cook extras in case
of breakage)

6 thick slices mozzarella
cheese
2 cups thin tomato sauce (see
A Fragrant Marinara Sauce,
page 318)
2 tablespoons grated Parmesan
cheese

Mix the garlic with the olive oil and allow it to marinate for 30 minutes or more.

Slice the eggplant, unpeeled, into 1/2-inch slices. Salt the slices and let them drain in a colander for 30 minutes or more. Rinse off the salt and press the slices dry between paper towels.

Preheat the broiler. Brush the eggplant and zucchini slices on both sides with the garlic oil. (Any leftover oil will be delicious in a vinaigrette.)

Broil the slices until they are tender but not mushy, about 5 minutes a side.

Cook the noodles according to package directions; drain.

Fold a lasagna noodle, accordion-fashion, around slices of eggplant, zucchini, and mozzarella. Do the same with the rest of the noodles. Arrange the stacks in a 9 × 9-inch baking dish. Pour the sauce over them and sprinkle with the Parmesan cheese.

Preheat the oven to 350 degrees F. Cover the baking dish loosely with foil and bake the stacks for 25 to 30 minutes.

Kilocalories 243 Kc • Protein 7 Gm • Fat 15 Gm • Percent of calories from fat 55% • Cholesterol 7 mg • Dietary Fiber 2 Gm • Sodium 345 mg • Calcium 109 mg

Jab-chae I
(Vegetable and Chicken Stir-fry with Korean Vermicelli)

4 SERVINGS

For this and all stir-fries, prepare the vegetables before beginning to cook.

1 tablespoon sesame seeds
3 tablespoons soy sauce
1 teaspoon sugar
1 teaspoon sesame oil
2 to 3 tablespoons vegetable oil
1/2 to 3/4 pound boneless
   chicken breast, thinly sliced
1 cup thinly sliced mushrooms
1 garlic clove, minced
2 cups thinly sliced fresh
   broccoli stalks and florets

1 large carrot, cut into julienne
   sticks, parboiled 1 minute
1 green bell pepper, cut into
   1/4-inch sticks
2 celery stalks, thinly sliced
1 onion, thinly sliced
6 ounces (about 1/3 pound)
   Korean vermicelli (see Note)

Lightly toast the sesame seeds in a small skillet; do not brown them; set aside. In a small pitcher or bowl, blend together the soy sauce, sugar, and sesame oil and set aside.

In a large wok or skillet, heat 1 tablespoon of the vegetable oil and stir-fry the chicken until cooked through, 3 to 4 minutes. Remove the chicken with a slotted spoon.

Add more vegetable oil if needed and stir-fry the mushrooms until lightly browned, about 3 minutes. Add the garlic during the last minute. Remove the mushrooms and garlic.

Stir-fry the remaining vegetables until tender-crisp, about 3 minutes, again adding more vegetable oil if needed. Add the soy sauce mixture and the chicken and mushrooms. Reheat briefly.

Meanwhile, prepare the Korean noodles; drain. Spoon them into the serving dish and pile the vegetables and chicken on top. Sprinkle with the sesame seeds and serve.

NOTE: Korean vermicelli is found in specialty stores. The cooking method given on the package is to pour boiling water over the noodles, soak them for 10 minutes, and drain. The method I prefer, however, is simply to boil the noodles until they are transparent and tender, 5 to 7 minutes.

Regular vermicelli or thin spaghetti can be substituted.

Kilocalories 398 Kc • Protein 21 Gm • Fat 13 Gm • Percent of calories from fat 30% • Cholesterol 48 mg • Dietary Fiber 4 Gm • Sodium 533 mg • Calcium 79 mg

Jab-chae II
(Vegetable Stir-fry with Omelet and Korean Vermicelli)

4 SERVINGS

¹/₂ pound fresh asparagus
1 bunch scallions
1 tablespoon sesame seeds
3 tablespoons soy sauce
1 teaspoon sugar
1 teaspoon sesame oil
2 eggs
Salt and pepper
About 1¹/₂ tablespoons
    vegetable oil

1 small zucchini (about
    ¹/₂ pound), cut into
    ¹/₄-inch-wide sticks
1 red bell pepper, cut into
    ¹/₄-inch-wide sticks
2 celery stalks, thinly sliced
6 ounces (about ¹/₃ pound)
    Korean vermicelli (see Note
    in preceding recipe)

Cut off and discard the tough ends of the asparagus stalks. Slice the stalks about ¹/₄-inch thick; keep the tips whole. Separate the white part of the scallions from the green tops and thinly slice.

In a small pitcher or bowl, blend together the soy sauce, sugar, and sesame oil; set aside.

Lightly toast the sesame seeds in a small skillet; do not brown them; set aside.

Beat the eggs with the chopped green scallion tops and a pinch of salt and pepper.

In a large wok or skillet, heat ½ tablespoon of the vegetable oil; tip the pan to coat it partway up the sides. Pour in the beaten egg mixture; tip the pan to make a thin omelet. Cook until set; turn the omelet (in two pieces, if necessary) to brown the second side. Remove the omelet from the pan and cut it into thin strips.

Clean out the pan and heat the remaining tablespoon of vegetable oil. Stir-fry the asparagus with the white part of the scallions until tender-crisp, about 4 minutes. Remove these vegetables with a slotted spoon.

Adding more oil if needed, stir-fry the zucchini, red bell pepper, and celery until tender-crisp, about 3 minutes. Return the asparagus and scallions to the pan. Add the soy sauce mixture.

Meanwhile, prepare the Korean noodles according to the note on page 523; drain. Spoon them into a serving dish and pile the vegetables on top. Sprinkle with the sesame seeds. Top with the omelet strips and serve.

Kilocalories 397 Kc • Protein 20 Gm • Fat 13 Gm • Percent of calories from fat 30% • Cholesterol 47 mg • Dietary Fiber 4 Gm • Sodium 854 mg • Calcium 79 mg

Mediterranean Vegetables with Fontina and Spaghetti

4 SERVINGS

1 small eggplant (about
  $1/2$ pound)
1 medium zucchini (about
  $3/4$ pound)
1 red bell pepper
$2^1/2$ tablespoons olive oil
Salt and pepper
1 garlic clove, minced
1 cup tomato sauce (see A Light
  Tomato or Summer Fresh
  Tomato Sauce, pages 317
  and 321)

Several leaves of fresh basil,
  snipped into strips
8 ounces ($1/2$ pound) spaghetti
$2/3$ cup fontina, cut into small
  dice, loosely packed

Peel and slice the eggplant. Salt the slices and drain them in a colander for 30 minutes. Rinse and squeeze out the moisture between paper towels. Dice the eggplant slices.

Quarter the zucchini lengthwise and slice the quarters into 1-inch pieces. Seed and dice the red pepper.

Heat 2 tablespoons of the oil in a large skillet and stir-fry the eggplant for 3 minutes. Add the zucchini and red pepper, and stir-fry for 7 to 8 minutes, or until the vegetables are softened. Salt and pepper the vegetables to your taste.

Add the garlic and tomato sauce, and cook, uncovered, stirring often, until the vegetables are tender, 8 to 10 minutes. Add the basil.

Meanwhile, cook the spaghetti according to package directions; drain. In a large serving dish, blend the remaining $1/2$ tablespoon of oil and the fontina into the spaghetti. Toss the pasta with the vegetables.

Kilocalories 423 Kc • Protein 14 Gm • Fat 18 Gm • Percent of calories from fat 38% • Cholesterol 21 mg • Dietary Fiber 3 Gm • Sodium 356 mg • Calcium 141 mg

Curried Vegetables with Asian Noodles

4 SERVINGS

2 large carrots, sliced diagonally into 1/2-inch pieces

1/2 pound fresh green beans, sliced diagonally into 2-inch pieces

2/3 cup chicken stock or canned broth

2 tablespoons naturally brewed soy sauce

1 teaspoon sesame oil

1/2 teaspoon sugar

1 1/2 teaspoons cornstarch

1 tablespoon vegetable oil

1 bunch scallions, cut into 2-inch lengths

2 celery stalks, sliced diagonally into 1/2-inch pieces

1 teaspoon curry powder

6 ounces (about 1/3 pound) Asian noodles or American linguine

1/2 cup chopped unsalted cashews

Parboil the carrots and green beans in boiling salted water until they are tender-crisp, about 5 minutes. Drain.

In a small pitcher or cup, mix the stock, soy sauce, sesame oil, sugar, and cornstarch until smooth.

Heat the vegetable oil in a large wok or skillet and stir-fry the scallions and celery until they are tender-crisp, 2 to 3 minutes. Add the carrots and green beans; stir-fry for 1 more minute. Stir in the curry powder until everything is evenly colored.

Pour in the soy sauce mixture all at once and stir until the thickened sauce coats the vegetables.

Cook the noodles according to package directions. Drain and spoon into a large serving dish. Top with the curry mixture. Sprinkle with the cashews and serve.

NOTE: To make this dish into a substantial meat entrée, slice 1 whole cooked chicken breast into strips and add them to the stir-fry with the carrots and green beans.

Kilocalories 348 Kc • Protein 11 Gm • Fat 13 Gm • Percent of calories from fat 32% • Cholesterol 0 mg • Dietary Fiber 4 Gm • Sodium 625 mg • Calcium 66 mg

Butternut, Broccoli, and Walnuts with Rigatoni

This is a perfect fall pasta dish, reflecting the colors and flavors of the season.

2 cups 1-inch cubes of butternut squash (about ¹/₂ pound trimmed)
2 cups broccoli florets, cut small
2 tablespoons olive oil
2 garlic cloves, minced
¹/₄ cup hot chicken stock or canned broth

Salt and pepper
¹/₂ cup toasted walnut halves or pieces
8 ounces (¹/₂ pound) rigatoni
2 tablespoons grated Parmesan cheese

Put the butternut cubes in a medium saucepan with water to cover and boil until tender, about 8 minutes. Drain.

Bring fresh water to a boil in the saucepan, add the florets, and when the water returns to a boil, cook for 3 minutes or until they are tender. Drain.

In a large skillet, heat the olive oil and sauté the garlic until it's soft and fragrant. Stir in the stock and vegetables, and salt and pepper them to your taste. Add the walnuts.

Cook the rigatoni according to package directions and drain.

In a large serving dish, toss the vegetables with the rigatoni and the cheese.

Kilocalories 433 Kc • Protein 15 Gm • Fat 18 Gm • Percent of calories from fat 35% • Cholesterol 2 mg • Dietary Fiber 5 Gm • Sodium 94 mg • Calcium 120 mg

Chicken and Vegetable Stew with Orzo

6 SERVINGS

Saffron adds a deep flavor to make this nearly fatless dish taste as rich as old-time chicken stew. Whole wheat French bread and a sliced tomato salad are perfect accompaniments.

1³/₄ to 2 pounds skinless boned chicken breasts (2 whole breasts)
1 tablespoon olive oil
1 large onion, chopped
4 large carrots, cut into 3-inch sticks
3 large celery stalks, cut into 3-inch sticks
1 quart (4 cups) water
Sprigs of fresh sage, rosemary, and thyme, or pinches of the dried herbs

1 teaspoon salt
¹/₄ teaspoon white pepper
1 cup orzo
1 cup sautéed button mushrooms
¹/₄ teaspoon saffron, well crushed between the fingers
1 cup fresh shelled or frozen peas
¹/₄ cup superfine flour, such as Wondra, dissolved in ¹/₂ cup cold water

Wash the chicken well in cold salted water; rinse and drain it. Cut the breasts into 3-ounce pieces. (If a whole breast weighs about 1 pound, that's 5 pieces per breast.)

Heat the oil in a large pot and sauté the onion until it's soft and fragrant.

Add the carrots, celery, chicken, water, herbs, and seasonings. Bring to a boil, reduce the heat, and simmer at a very low bubble until the chicken is cooked through, 25 to 30 minutes. Skim off any froth that rises to the surface.

Bring to a boil again, and add the orzo, mushrooms, and saffron. Reduce the heat and continue cooking for 8 minutes.

Add the peas and flour mixture. Bring to a boil, stirring until thickened and bubbling. Reduce the heat and simmer for 3 minutes, stirring often down to the bottom of the pot where the orzo is liable to stick.

Serve in large soup bowls.

Kilocalories 463 Kc • Protein 44 Gm • Fat 5 Gm • Percent of calories from fat 10% • Cholesterol 77 mg • Dietary Fiber 12 Gm • Sodium 516 mg • Calcium 88 mg

Broccoli and Zucchini with Small Shells

2 tablespoons olive oil
$^1/_4$ cup chopped shallots
1 small zucchini, diced
2 cups cooked chopped
  broccoli
Salt and pepper

2 tablespoons chopped fresh
  flat-leaf parsley
1 cup small shells
$^1/_2$ cup hot chicken stock or
  canned broth
Grated Parmesan cheese

Heat the oil in a large skillet or wok and stir-fry the shallots and zucchini until they are tender and slightly browned.

Add the broccoli with salt and pepper to your taste and continue to cook 2 to 3 minutes. Stir in the parsley.

Meanwhile, cook the shells according to package directions and drain. Blend the pasta with the vegetables. Stir in the hot stock.

Pass the grated cheese at the table.

Kilocalories 193 Kc • Protein 7 Gm • Fat 8 Gm • Percent of calories from fat 35% • Cholesterol 0 mg • Dietary Fiber 4 Gm • Sodium 78 mg • Calcium 53 mg

Escarole and Chickpeas with Mezzani

---

4 SERVINGS

1 bunch escarole ($^1/_2$ to $^3/_4$ pound)

2 to 3 garlic cloves, crushed

2 cups vegetable or chicken stock, or canned broth

2 tablespoons olive oil

1 red onion, peeled, sliced, and separated into rings

1 15- or 16-ounce can of chickpeas, drained and rinsed

$^1/_4$ teaspoon salt

Freshly ground black pepper to your taste

8 ounces ($^1/_2$ pound) mezzani

$^1/_4$ cup finely slivered Parmesan cheese

Wash the escarole well and chop it coarsely into 2-inch pieces. Put it into a pot with the crushed garlic and stock. Bring to a boil, reduce the heat, cover, and simmer until the escarole is tender, 10 minutes. Remove the escarole with a slotted spoon. Remove and discard the garlic. Reserve $^1/_2$ cup of the cooking liquid. (Any remaining liquid would be a fine addition to a soup.)

Heat the oil in a large skillet and sauté the onion until it is tender, 5 minutes. Add the chickpeas, escarole, reserved $^1/_2$ cup liquid, salt, and pepper; simmer 3 minutes.

Meanwhile, cook the mezzani according to package directions and drain. Spoon it into a large serving dish and toss with the escarole mixture. Sprinkle the Parmesan on top.

Kilocalories 460 Kc • Protein 16 Gm • Fat 11 Gm • Percent of calories from fat 21% • Cholesterol 4 mg • Dietary Fiber 9 Gm • Sodium 778 mg • Calcium 153 mg

Zucchini, Carrots, and Feta Cheese with Ziti

■

3 large carrots, sliced
   diagonally
2 tablespoons olive oil
1 large zucchini, quartered
   lengthwise and cut into
   1-inch chunks

1 garlic clove, minced
$^1/_8$ teaspoon salt
$^1/_8$ teaspoon pepper
6 to 7 ounces
   (about $^1/_3$ pound) ziti
$^1/_2$ cup crumbled feta cheese

Parboil the carrots in boiling salted water until tender, 5 to 7 minutes. Drain.

Heat the oil in a skillet and sauté the zucchini, stirring often, until it's tender and beginning to brown, 10 to 15 minutes. During the last few minutes, add the garlic, carrots, salt, and pepper.

Meanwhile, cook the ziti according to package directions. Drain and combine with the vegetables in a large serving dish. Stir in the cheese.

Kilocalories 341 Kc • Protein 12 Gm • Fat 14 Gm • Percent of calories from fat 37% • Cholesterol 28 mg • Dietary Fiber 4 Gm • Sodium 453 mg • Calcium 198 mg

All-Vegetable Lasagne

8 SERVINGS

2 large carrots, sliced
2 celery stalks, sliced
1 cup fresh or frozen sliced
  green beans
1 cup fresh shelled or frozen
  peas, thawed just enough to
  separate
1/2 cup water
1/4 teaspoon salt
1 cup milk (whole or low-fat)
1/4 cup superfine flour, such as
  Wondra
1/4 teaspoon Italian herbs (from
  a jar), or pinches of dried
  oregano, basil, and rosemary
White pepper
3 tablespoons grated Parmesan
  cheese

1 egg, beaten
1 15- or 16-ounce container
  part-skim ricotta cheese
1 tablespoon minced fresh
  parsley
3 cups medium-thin tomato
  sauce (see A Fragrant
  Marinara Sauce or Tomato-
  Meat Sauce recipe, page 318
  or 322—if necessary, add a
  little water or broth)
12 lasagna noodles, cooked
  according to package
  directions
8 ounces shredded part-skim
  mozzarella cheese

Put the vegetables in a saucepan with the water and salt. Bring to a boil, lower the heat, and simmer until tender, about 5 minutes.

In a 2-cup measure, mix the milk, flour, Italian herbs, and pepper to your taste. Pour all at once into the vegetables and cook, stirring constantly, until the mixture bubbles and thickens. It will be quite thick. Stir in 1 tablespoon of the Parmesan cheese. Simmer 3 minutes, stirring often, then remove from the heat. Let cool 15 minutes.

Mix the egg with the ricotta, a few dashes of white pepper, and the parsley.

In a 13 × 9 × 2-inch baking pan, spread 1 cup of the tomato sauce. Place 3 lasagna noodles crosswise over the sauce. Spread half the ricotta evenly over the noodles. Spoon another cup of the sauce over the ricotta. Sprinkle with half the mozzarella cheese.

Place 3 lasagna noodles over the mozzarella. Spread all the vegetable mixture over the noodles.

Place 3 lasagna noodles over the vegetables. Spread with the remaining ricotta.

Place 3 lasagna noodles over the ricotta. Top with the remaining cup of sauce. Sprinkle with the remaining mozzarella and 2 tablespoons of the Parmesan.

The recipe can be prepared to this point up to one day ahead. Cover with plastic wrap, then foil, and refrigerate until ready to cook.

When ready to cook, preheat the oven to 350 degrees F.

Cover the dish with foil and bake on the middle shelf for 30 minutes. Uncover and continue baking until bubbly throughout, about 20 minutes, or longer if it was refrigerated. Check that the ricotta layer is firm, not runny.

Let stand for 10 minutes before cutting into squares to serve.

NOTE: Several substitutions of vegetables are possible—broccoli, asparagus, corn, fennel, shell beans, or lima beans, for instance.

Kilocalories 359 Kc • Protein 21 Gm • Fat 15 Gm • Percent of calories from fat 38% • Cholesterol 64 mg • Dietary Fiber 4 Gm • Sodium 651 mg • Calcium 446 mg

Spinach and Chickpeas with Elbows

———————————————■———————————————

4 SERVINGS

1 10-ounce package fresh spinach

2 tablespoons olive oil

1 large yellow onion, chopped (about 1 cup)

8 to 10 leaves of fresh sage, chopped

1 15- to 16-ounce can chickpeas, drained and rinsed

¼ cup teaspoon salt

Several grindings of black pepper

8 ounces (½ pound) elbows

Wash the spinach well and steam it in just the water that clings to the leaves until wilted. Drain, reserving ½ cup of the pan liquid.

In a large skillet, heat the oil and slowly fry the onion until translucent. Stir in the sage and continue to cook for 3 minutes. Add the chickpeas and cook 5 minutes longer. Add the spinach, salt, and pepper, and heat through.

Meanwhile, cook the elbows according to package directions. Drain and spoon the pasta into a large serving dish. Stir in the reserved pan liquid and ladle the vegetable mixture on top.

Kilocalories 429 Kc • Protein 15 Gm • Fat 9 Gm • Percent of calories from fat 19% • Cholesterol 0 mg • Dietary Fiber 9 Gm • Sodium 525 mg • Calcium 130 mg

Braised Butternut and Fennel with Ziti

4 SERVINGS

2 tablespoons olive oil, or
 more if needed
1/4 cup chopped shallots
1 bulb fennel, cored and cut
 into thin wedges
2 1/2 cups butternut squash
 cubes (about 2/3 pound
 trimmed)

Salt and freshly ground black
 pepper
1 cup thin tomato purée
2 teaspoons chopped fresh
 thyme, or 1/2 teaspoon dried
8 ounces (1/2 pound) ziti
2 tablespoons grated Romano
 cheese, plus more to pass

Heat the oil in a large skillet and sauté the shallots and fennel until they begin to brown. Add the squash and, if necessary, a little more oil. Continue to sauté for 3 minutes. Salt and pepper the vegetables to your taste.

Add the tomato purée and thyme. Cover and braise over low heat for 15 minutes, or until the vegetables are very tender but still retain their shape; stir often.

Meanwhile, cook the ziti according to package directions and drain, and spoon it into a large serving dish. Gently combine with the vegetables and sauce. Sprinkle with the Romano cheese and pass more at the table.

Kilocalories 371 Kc • Protein 11 Gm • Fat 9 Gm • Percent of calories from fat 20% • Cholesterol 3 mg • Dietary Fiber 6 Gm • Sodium 74 mg • Calcium 127 mg

Armenian Vegetable Couscous with Yogurt

1 cup couscous, raw
2 tablespoons olive oil
1 large yellow onion, chopped
3 cups finely shredded cabbage
2 small purple-topped turnips,
  peeled and sliced into half
  rounds
2 carrots, thinly sliced
1 15- to 16-ounce can
  chickpeas, drained and rinsed

1 cup vegetable broth or water
1/4 teaspoon ground cinnamon
1/4 teaspoon ground cumin
1/4 teaspoon ground cardamom
1/4 teaspoon salt
Several dashes of cayenne
  pepper
Nonfat plain yogurt as an
  accompaniment

Prepare the couscous (see page 12 for basic recipe or follow package directions); fluff and separate the grains. You should have 2 1/2 cups cooked.

Heat the oil in a large skillet and sauté the onion until softened. Add all the remaining ingredients except the couscous and yogurt. Bring to a boil, reduce the heat, cover and simmer, stirring often, until the vegetables are very tender, 20 to 30 minutes.

Spread the hot couscous on a medium-size platter; spoon the vegetables on top. Serve with yogurt on the side.

Kilocalories 427 Kc • Protein 14 Gm • Fat 9 Gm • Percent of calories from fat 18% • Cholesterol 0 mg • Dietary Fiber 11 Gm • Sodium 758 mg • Calcium 84 mg

Chunky Vegetable Sauce with a French Twist on Rigatoni

4 SERVINGS

2 tablespoons olive oil, or more

8 ounces mushrooms, cleaned and cut in half, or thirds if large

1/4 cup chopped shallots

1 red bell pepper, seeded and cut into strips

1 green bell pepper, seeded and cut into strips

1 medium zucchini (about 1/2 pound), cut into 2-inch sticks

About 2 cups cabbage, cut into chunks

Salt and freshly ground pepper

1 cup tomato sauce (see Light Tomato Sauce, page 317)

1/2 cup chicken or vegetable stock or canned broth

1 teaspoon dried *herbes de Provence,* or a mixture of dried thyme, dried marjoram, dried tarragon, and dried basil

12 ounces (3/4 pound) rigatoni

Heat the oil in a large skillet and stir-fry the mushrooms until they release their juice and begin to brown. Add the shallots and bell peppers, and stir-fry for 2 minutes. Add a little more oil if needed. Add the zucchini and cabbage, and stir-fry for 2 minutes. Salt and pepper the vegetables to your taste. Add the tomato sauce, stock, and herbs. Cover and simmer for 20 minutes, or until very tender, stirring often.

Meanwhile, cook the rigatoni according to package directions and drain. Spoon it into a large serving dish and top with the vegetables. Toss gently, leaving most of the vegetables on top.

Kilocalories 453 Kc • Protein 14 Gm • Fat 11 Gm • Percent of calories from fat 22% • Cholesterol 0 mg • Dietary Fiber 5 Gm • Sodium 327 mg • Calcium 64 mg

Sweet Potato Gnocchi

■

Gnocchi are little pasta dumplings that can be prepared in the home kitchen without a lot of fuss or special equipment. In this recipe, sweet potatoes, rich in beta-carotene, pack in some extra nutrition.

1½ cups mashed cooked sweet potato (about 1½ large potatoes)
1 cup ricotta cheese
¼ cup grated Parmesan cheese, plus more to pass

1 egg yolk
About 1½ cups all-purpose flour
About 1 tablespoon oil or melted butter

Blend together the sweet potato, ricotta, Parmesan and egg yolk. (A food processor makes this step easier.) Work in enough flour to make a dough that is soft but manageable. Knead the dough into a smooth ball. Divide it into quarters. Dust your work surface with flour and roll each quarter into a 1-inch-wide roll. With a sharp knife, cut each roll into ½-inch pieces. Quickly roll each piece into a ball, as if it were a tiny meatball, and lay it on a tray covered with waxed paper.

The gnocchi can be cooked "as is" or shaped in the Italian manner, which yields a more tender dumpling. For shaping, spray a table fork with cooking spray, such as Pam. Keep some flour on your work surface to dust as needed. With the fork handle toward you, press a lump of dough against the tines with your finger, which will leave a slight indentation. Then roll the gnocchi lightly off the fork toward you. It should be slightly curved, the outside curve ribbed by the fork tines. Repeat with the rest of the dough.

Bring 6 quarts of water to a boil in a broad pot; add salt to your taste. Drop in a batch of gnocchi, about enough to cover the bottom of the pan. In a few minutes, they will rise to the surface. After they have risen, count 10 to 15 seconds, then lift them out with a slotted spoon. (I usually taste-test to get the timing exactly right.) Put the cooked gnocchi in a serving dish, drizzle on a little oil or melted butter, and keep them warm while cooking the rest.

Spoon either of the following vegetable sauces on top. Pass grated Parmesan cheese at the table.

NOTE: Uncooked gnocchi can be frozen. Freeze them in a single layer on a foil-lined tray. When they are solid, store them in a plastic bag in the freezer.

Kilocalories 354 Kc • Protein 15 Gm • Fat 11 Gm • Percent of calories from fat 29% • Cholesterol 76 mg • Dietary Fiber 2 Gm • Sodium 177 mg • Calcium 260 mg

Pea and Basil Sauce for Gnocchi

4 SERVINGS

2 tablespoons olive oil
1 shallot, chopped
1 garlic clove, minced
1½ cups fresh shelled or
    frozen peas, thawed just
    enough to separate

Several leaves of fresh basil,
    slivered, or 1 teaspoon dried
Pinch of dried mint
¼ teaspoon salt
⅛ teaspoon pepper

Heat the oil in a medium skillet and sauté the shallot and garlic until they are fragrant. Add the peas, herbs, and seasonings, cover, and cook over low heat until the peas are tender, about 5 minutes. Spoon over the sweet potato gnocchi.

Kilocalories 105 Kc • Protein 3 Gm • Fat 7 Gm • Percent of calories from fat 58% • Cholesterol 0 mg • Dietary Fiber 3 Gm • Sodium 148 mg • Calcium 16 mg

Nutmeg-scented Creamed Spinach for Gnocchi

4 SERVINGS

1 10-ounce package fresh
    spinach
2 tablespoons superfine flour,
    such as Wondra
2 tablespoons nonfat dry milk

½ teaspoon salt
⅛ teaspoon pepper
⅛ teaspoon ground nutmeg
1 cup whole milk

Wash the spinach well, discarding any tough stems, and steam it in a large pot in just the water that clings to the leaves until it's wilted. Chop it coarsely in the pot. Drain if necessary, leaving ½ cup liquid in the pot.

Whisk the flour, dry milk, and seasonings into the liquid milk. Add all at once to the pot and cook the mixture until thick and bubbling. Simmer over very low heat for 5 minutes before spooning over the sweet potato gnocchi.

Kilocalories 69 Kc • Protein 5 Gm • Fat 2 Gm • Percent of calories from fat 28% • Cholesterol 8 mg • Dietary Fiber 2 Gm • Sodium 381 mg • Calcium 153 mg

Vegetable Tetrazzini

4 SERVINGS

The vegetables can be varied, of course, if you have some leftovers—but avoid using any that are limp and overcooked already, since they will be subject to additional cooking in this casserole.

1½ cups milk (whole or low-fat)
3 tablespoons cornstarch
3 tablespoons nonfat dry milk
1 teaspoon chopped fresh thyme or tarragon
½ teaspoon salt
¼ teaspoon white pepper
1 cup chicken stock or canned broth
2 tablespoons dry sherry or dry vermouth (optional but traditional)
1 cup fresh shelled or frozen peas, thawed just enough to separate

1 cup cooked asparagus, cut into 1-inch pieces
1 cup cooked carrots, sliced
1 roasted red pepper (from a jar or homemade—see page 260), diced
½ cup mushrooms, sautéed or from a jar
8 ounces (½ pound) fettucine
½ cup fresh or dried bread crumbs
2 tablespoons grated Parmesan cheese
Dash of paprika

Preheat the oven to 350 degrees F.

In a saucepan, heat the milk but don't boil it. Whisk the cornstarch, dry milk, thyme or tarragon, and seasonings into the stock. Pour the stock all at once into the milk in the saucepan and cook over medium-high heat, stirring constantly, until the mixture bubbles and thickens. Simmer 2 minutes. Whisk in the sherry, if using. Add the peas and cook 2 minutes longer. Add the remaining vegetables.

Meanwhile, cook the fettucine according to package directions, undercooking it slightly, and drain. Combine the pasta, vegetables, and sauce in a 2-quart gratin pan or casserole. Top with the crumbs and cheese. Sprinkle with paprika. Bake on the middle shelf until bubbling throughout and browned on top, 20 to 25 minutes if the ingredients are still warm. Let rest 5 minutes; cut into squares to serve.

Kilocalories 394 Kc • Protein 17 Gm • Fat 6 Gm • Percent of calories from fat 13% • Cholesterol 14 mg • Dietary Fiber 6 Gm • Sodium 560 mg • Calcium 208 mg

Broccoli and Cauliflower with Linguine

—■—

4 SERVINGS

1 cup part-skim ricotta cheese
¼ cup freshly grated Romano
  cheese
4 cups small florets of
  cauliflower and broccoli
  (if they're large, cut them
  in half)
2 tablespoons olive oil

8 ounces mushrooms, cleaned
  and sliced
1 garlic clove, minced
Salt and freshly ground black
  pepper
Several dashes of hot red
  pepper flakes
8 ounces (½ pound) linguine

Blend the ricotta and Romano cheeses. Set aside.

Cook the florets in boiling salted water until tender-crisp, 3 minutes. Drain, reserving ½ cup of the cooking water.

Heat the oil in a large skillet and sauté the mushrooms over medium-high heat, stirring often, until they begin to brown. Add the garlic and cook 1 minute longer. Add the florets and season the vegetables with salt, black pepper, and hot pepper flakes to your taste. Add the reserved water.

Meanwhile, cook the linguine according to package directions and drain. Toss the pasta with the vegetables, right in the skillet if it's a 12-inch size or larger.

Divide the pasta among 4 plates and top each serving with a spoonful of the ricotta-Romano mixture.

Kilocalories 425 Kc • Protein 21 Gm • Fat 15 Gm • Percent of calories from fat 30% • Cholesterol 24 mg • Dietary Fiber 6 Gm • Sodium 173 mg • Calcium 281 mg

Green Beans and Bell Peppers with Mostaccioli

---

6 SERVINGS

Colorful and easy. It's okay to use any color peppers, but this combination is especially attractive.

1 pound fresh green beans, cut into 2-inch lengths
2 tablespoons olive oil
1 red bell pepper, seeded and cut into strips
1 yellow bell pepper, seeded and cut into strips
1 to 2 garlic cloves, minced
1/2 cup chicken or vegetable stock, or canned broth

2 tablespoons minced fresh flat-leaf parsley
1 tablespoon minced fresh basil, or 1 teaspoon dried
1/4 teaspoon salt
1/8 teaspoon pepper
12 ounces (3/4 pound) mostaccioli or mezzani
4 ounces smoked turkey or prosciutto, slivered (optional)

Cook the green beans in boiling salted water until tender-crisp, 5 to 7 minutes.

Heat the oil in a large skillet and stir-fry the peppers until they are beginning to brown. Add the garlic during the last minute of frying; remove from the heat. Add the green beans, stock, parsley, basil, salt, and pepper.

Cook the mostaccioli according to package directions and drain. Spoon the pasta into a large serving dish. Reheat the vegetables and toss with the pasta. Top with the slivered turkey or prosciutto, if using.

Kilocalories 294 Kc • Protein 10 Gm • Fat 6 Gm • Percent of calories from fat 18% • Cholesterol 0 mg • Dietary Fiber 5 Gm • Sodium 150 mg • Calcium 77 mg

Pasta Primavera

◼

4 SERVINGS

*P*rimavera *means springtime, so this combination celebrates the vegetables of April and May.*

2 tablespoons olive oil
1 bunch scallions, white part only, thinly sliced
1 pound new peas, shelled (1 cup)
2 baby zucchini (½ pound), sliced
½ pound fresh asparagus, cut into 1-inch pieces
1 cup seeded, chopped plum tomatoes
½ cup vegetable or chicken stock, or canned broth

2 teaspoons chopped fresh basil
1 teaspoon chopped fresh thyme
½ teaspoon salt
⅛ teaspoon pepper
8 ounces (½ pound) spaghettini
½ cup coarsely grated Asiago cheese

Heat the olive oil in a large skillet and sauté the scallions until they begin to soften. Add the vegetables, stock, herbs, and seasonings and simmer, uncovered, until everything is tender, 10 minutes.

Meanwhile, cook the spaghettini according to package directions and drain. Spoon it into a large serving dish and toss with the vegetables. Sprinkle the cheese on top.

Kilocalories 453 Kc • Protein 20 Gm • Fat 13 Gm • Percent of calories from fat 25% • Cholesterol 16 mg • Dietary Fiber 10 Gm • Sodium 538 mg • Calcium 149 mg

Harvest Casserole of Vegetables and Whole Wheat Macaroni

4 SERVINGS

A combination of vegetables you'll find in the market at harvest time— early fall.

1 pound fresh shell beans, shelled (1½ cups)
1 cup chicken or vegetable stock, or canned broth
½ teaspoon salt
Several grinds of black pepper
2 teaspoons chopped fresh marjoram, or ½ teaspoon dried oregano
2 tablespoons olive oil
1 medium zucchini (about ½ pound), sliced into half-rounds

1 green bell pepper, seeded and chunked
1 yellow onion, sliced
2 large ripe tomatoes, peeled, seeded, and chopped
8 ounces (½ pound) whole wheat elbows
¾ cup shredded part-skim mozzarella cheese

In a saucepan, combine the shell beans, stock, seasonings, and marjoram. Bring to a boil and simmer gently, covered, until the beans are tender, 15 to 20 minutes.

Preheat the oven to 350 degrees F.

Heat the oil in a large skillet and sauté the zucchini, pepper, and onion until they begin to brown. Add the tomatoes, beans, and their pan juices, and continue simmering for 5 minutes.

Meanwhile, cook the elbows according to package directions, under-cooking them slightly, and drain. Spoon them into a 2-quart gratin dish or casserole and blend in the vegetable mixture. Top with the cheese and bake on the middle shelf until bubbling throughout, 20 to 25 minutes.

Kilocalories 517 Kc • Protein 27 Gm • Fat 12 Gm • Percent of calories from fat 20% • Cholesterol 12 mg • Dietary Fiber 2 Gm • Sodium 510 mg • Calcium 244 mg

Szechuan Vegetables with Noodles

1/2 cup chicken stock or canned broth

2 tablespoons peanut butter

1 tablespoon naturally brewed soy sauce

2 teaspoons fresh lemon juice

1 teaspoon sesame oil

1/4 teaspoon hot pepper sauce, such as Tabasco, or more to your taste

1 tablespoon vegetable oil

1 large carrot, cut into julienne

2 celery stalks, cut into julienne

3 to 4 radishes, or 1 purple-topped turnip, cut into thin julienne

1 medium zucchini (1/2 pound), cut into julienne

4 scallions, sliced thin diagonally

1 slice fresh ginger, peeled and minced

6 to 7 ounces (about 1/3 pound) Asian thin flat noodles or American vermicelli

Blend together the stock, peanut butter, soy sauce, lemon juice, sesame oil, and hot pepper sauce.

Heat the oil in a large wok or skillet and stir-fry the vegetables and ginger until tender-crisp, about 3 minutes. The vegetables should still be crunchy.

Meanwhile, cook the noodles or vermicelli according to package directions and drain. Toss the pasta with the stock mixture. Blend in the vegetables.

Kilocalories 267 Kc • Protein 9 Gm • Fat 9 Gm • Percent of calories from fat 29% • Cholesterol 0 mg • Dietary Fiber 2 Gm • Sodium 380 mg • Calcium 34 mg

MARVELOUS MEDLEYS

Broccoli and Carrots with Whole Wheat Spaghetti

4 SERVINGS

2 cups broccoli florets (cut large florets in half)

2 carrots, cut into julienne

2 tablespoons olive oil

1 yellow bell pepper, seeded and cut into thin strips

2 garlic cloves, minced

$^1/_2$ cup chicken or vegetable stock, or canned broth

$^1/_4$ teaspoon salt

Several grinds of black pepper

About 8 leaves fresh basil, slivered

8 ounces ($^1/_2$ pound) whole wheat spaghetti

$^1/_2$ cup diced *ricotta salata* (a hard ricotta) or feta cheese

Bring a large pot of water to a boil, add salt, and cook the broccoli and carrots until tender-crisp, 3 minutes. Remove the vegetables with a slotted spoon and save the water for cooking the spaghetti.

Heat the oil in a large skillet and stir-fry the bell pepper until it begins to brown. Add the garlic during the last minute of frying. Add the broccoli, carrots, stock, salt, pepper, and basil, and keep warm.

Meanwhile, cook the spaghetti according to package directions and drain. Spoon the pasta into a large serving dish and toss it with the cheese. Add the vegetables and toss again.

Kilocalories 354 Kc • Protein 16 Gm • Fat 15 Gm • Percent of calories from fat 34% • Cholesterol 28 mg • Dietary Fiber 10 Gm • Sodium 587 mg • Calcium 204 mg

Succotash Chili with Elbows

4 SERVINGS

2 tablespoons olive oil
1 Anaheim chili, seeded
  and diced
1 small yellow onion, chopped
3 large plum tomatoes, seeded
  and diced
1½ cups fresh or frozen
  lima beans
1½ cups fresh or frozen corn
  kernels

2 cups chicken stock or
  canned broth
1½ teaspoons chili powder
¼ teaspoon ground cumin
¼ teaspoon salt
¼ teaspoon pepper
1 tablespoon cornstarch
1 cup small elbows

In a large pot, heat the oil and sauté the chili and onion until softened, 5 minutes. Add the tomatoes, beans, and corn with 1½ cups of the broth and all the seasonings. Bring to a boil, reduce the heat, and simmer, covered, until the vegetables are tender, 5 to 10 minutes. Blend the cornstarch with the remaining ½ cup of cold broth, and add it to the simmering vegetables. Stir constantly until bubbling and thickened. Simmer 5 minutes longer, stirring often.

Meanwhile, cook the elbows according to package directions and drain. Combine the elbows with the vegetables in a serving dish.

Kilocalories 479 Kc • Protein 23 Gm • Fat 9 Gm • Percent of calories from fat 16% • Cholesterol 0 mg • Dietary Fiber 17 Gm • Sodium 479 mg • Calcium 75 mg

Noodle Frittata with Zucchini and Bell Pepper

4 SERVINGS

2 tablespoons olive oil
1 small yellow onion, chopped
1 small zucchini (about
   $1/2$ pound), diced
1 red bell pepper, seeded and
   diced
2 cups cooked egg noodles
   (2 cups uncooked, about
   $3^{1}/_{2}$ ounces)

5 eggs
2 tablespoons water
$1/4$ teaspoon salt
Several dashes of white pepper
2 tablespoons grated Parmesan
   cheese
2 to 3 sprigs of fresh parsley,
   chopped

Heat the oil in a large nonstick skillet or well-seasoned cast-iron frying pan and sauté the vegetables until they are tender, 5 to 7 minutes. Blend in the cooked noodles.

Beat the eggs with the water, salt, and pepper. Pour the eggs evenly over the vegetables and noodles and cook over very low heat. Frequently loosen the bottom of the frittata with a spatula and tip the pan to allow the liquid to run underneath. When the egg is set, loosen the frittata again and slip it onto a plate. Invert the frittata and brown the second side. Sprinkle with the cheese and parsley.

Kilocalories 296 Kc • Protein 14 Gm • Fat 15 Gm • Percent of calories from fat 46% • Cholesterol 293 mg • Dietary Fiber 2 Gm • Sodium 281 mg • Calcium 94 mg

Asparagus, Carrots, and Almonds with Penne

4 SERVINGS

Almonds are rich in niacin (vitamin B$_3$), a heart protector and nerve builder.

1/2 **pound fresh asparagus, washed and trimmed**
1 **tablespoon butter**
1 **tablespoon vegetable oil**
4 **ounces mushrooms, cleaned and sliced**
1 **large shallot, chopped**
1/4 **cup slivered almonds**

2 **large carrots, cut into 2-inch sticks**
1/4 **teaspoon salt**
Several grinds of black pepper
2 **tablespoons minced fresh cilantro, or 1 teaspoon dried**
8 **ounces (1/2 pound) penne**

Pour 1/2 cup water into a 12-inch skillet, lay the asparagus in the pan, cover, and bring to a boil. Reduce the heat and simmer, covered, until tender-crisp, about 3 minutes. Cut the asparagus into 2-inch pieces.

Remove the asparagus and pan juices to a dish and dry the pan. Add the butter and oil, and sauté the mushrooms and shallot until they begin to brown. Add the almonds during the last minute. Return the asparagus and pan juices to the skillet.

Separately, in a saucepan of boiling salted water, cook the carrots until they are tender, 5 minutes. Drain. Add them to the asparagus. Sprinkle with the seasonings and cilantro.

Meanwhile, cook the penne according to package directions and drain. Spoon it into a large serving dish and toss with the vegetables and almonds.

Kilocalories 353 Kc • Protein 11 Gm • Fat 12 Gm • Percent of calories from fat 30% • Cholesterol 8 mg • Dietary Fiber 5 Gm • Sodium 202 mg • Calcium 59 mg

Taste-of-Spring Salad with Rotelle

4 SERVINGS

¹/₃ cup Herb Vinaigrette (see
page 10 for basic recipe)
4 scallions, chopped
1 large ripe tomato, cut into
wedges
4 ounces (¹/₄ pound) rotelle
¹/₂ pound fresh asparagus,
cooked tender-crisp, cut into
2-inch pieces

4 cups washed greens
(including fresh dandelions),
torn into bite-size pieces
1 cup whole-grain salad
croutons

In a large salad bowl, mix the vinaigrette, scallions, and tomato. Allow them to marinate at room temperature while cooking the rotelle according to package directions. Drain the pasta and rinse it until it's cold to the touch. Stir it into the vinaigrette mixture.

Put the asparagus and greens on top without tossing. Chill until ready to serve, then toss lightly. Taste to see if you want more dressing. Top with the croutons.

Kilocalories 298 Kc • Protein 9 Gm • Fat 14 Gm • Percent of calories from fat 40% • Cholesterol 0 mg • Dietary Fiber 6 Gm • Sodium 250 mg • Calcium 190 mg

Salad Niçoise with Penne

6 SERVINGS

1 red onion, peeled, sliced, and separated into rings
½ pound fresh green beans, cut into 2-inch pieces
1 10-ounce package frozen artichoke hearts, cooked according to package directions
1 pint cherry tomatoes, halved

1 yellow bell pepper, seeded and cut into triangles
1 cup pitted black olives
4 anchovy fillets, rinsed in vinegar and chopped
⅓ cup Herb Vinaigrette (see page 10 for basic recipe)
8 ounces (½ pound) penne

If the onion is too hot for your taste, soak it in ice water for a half hour or so. Drain.

Cook the green beans in boiling salted water until barely tender, about 5 minutes. Drain and rinse in cold water.

Cut the cooked artichoke hearts in half. Combine all the ingredients, except the penne, in a salad dish and toss to blend.

Cook the penne according to package directions and drain. Rinse in cold water. Stir into the vegetable mixture. Taste the salad and add more dressing if desired.

Kilocalories 333 Kc • Protein 9 Gm • Fat 14 Gm • Percent of calories from fat 37% • Cholesterol 2 mg • Dietary Fiber 6 Gm • Sodium 434 mg • Calcium 63 mg

Salad Niçoise with Tuna and Cheese

6 ENTRÉE SERVINGS

For a hearty main dish salad, follow the preceding recipe, substituting a 6- to 7-ounce can of water-packed white tuna, chunked, for the anchovies. Stir in 4 ounces *ricotta salata* (a firm ricotta, something like feta) or mozzarella cheese, cubed.

Kilocalories 388 Kc • Protein 17 Gm • Fat 16 Gm • Percent of calories from fat 37% • Cholesterol 18 mg • Dietary Fiber 6 Gm • Sodium 466 mg • Calcium 107 mg

Broccoli and Cauliflower Pasta Salad with Honey-Mustard Dressing

2 cups cauliflower florets
2 cups broccoli florets
6 to 7 ounces (about 1/3 pound)
  medium shells

1/3 cup or more Honey-Mustard
  Vinaigrette (see page 11 for
  basic recipe)

In a large pot of boiling salted water, cook the cauliflower for 3 minutes, until tender-crisp. Lift the florets out with a slotted spoon and rinse in cold water to stop the cooking action. Drain well. Cook the broccoli the same way for 3 minutes. Rinse in cold water and drain.

Cook the shells according to package directions and drain. Rinse in cold water.

In a salad bowl, combine the vegetables, the cooked shell pasta, and about half the dressing. Toss to blend. Serve at room temperature or chill, as desired. Just before serving, taste to see if you want more dressing.

Kilocalories 317 Kc • Protein 8 Gm • Fat 15 Gm • Percent of calories from fat 41% • Cholesterol 0 mg • Dietary Fiber 4 Gm • Sodium 105 mg • Calcium 34 mg

Spaghetti Salad with Watercress, Tomatoes, and Sugar Snap Peas

6 SERVINGS

2 cups fresh or frozen sugar snap peas
½ cup Herb Vinaigrette (see page 10 for basic recipe)
1 garlic clove, pressed through a garlic press
2 large ripe tomatoes, diced

8 ounces (½ pound) spaghetti
1 cup diced mozzarella, or ½ cup fontina cheese
1 bunch watercress, washed, spun dry, stemmed, and chopped

Cook fresh sugar snaps in boiling, salted water until tender-crisp, 2 minutes, or prepare frozen sugar snaps according to package directions, but undercook them slightly. Drain and rinse in cold water.

In a large salad bowl, combine the vinaigrette, garlic, and tomatoes. Allow them to marinate at room temperature while cooking the spaghetti according to package directions. Drain and rinse the spaghetti in cold water. Toss the spaghetti and cheese with the tomato mixture. Put the watercress and sugar snaps on top.

Serve at room temperature or chilled. Just before serving, lightly toss the greens into the spaghetti. Taste the salad and add more vinaigrette if needed.

Kilocalories 343 Kc • Protein 12 Gm • Fat 17 Gm • Percent of calories from fat 43% • Cholesterol 10 mg • Dietary Fiber 3 Gm • Sodium 261 mg • Calcium 196 mg

Vegetable Salad with Russian Dressing and Shells

4 SERVINGS

1 cup small shells
1 cup cooked, sliced carrots
1 cup green beans, cooked, cut into 1-inch pieces
1 cup fresh shelled or frozen peas, thawed just enough to separate

1 cup diced celery
4 scallions, sliced
8 cherry tomatoes, halved
$1/2$ cup Light Russian Dressing (see page 12 for basic recipe)

Cook the shells according to package directions and drain. Rinse them in cold water. Combine the shells and vegetables in a medium-size salad bowl. Blend in the dressing.

Kilocalories 253 Kc • Protein 8 Gm • Fat 8 Gm • Percent of calories from fat 26% • Cholesterol 3 mg • Dietary Fiber 6 Gm • Sodium 385 mg • Calcium 88 mg

Index

INDEX

TANTALIZING RECIPES

☐ **YAMUNA'S TABLE** *Healthful Vegetarian Cuisine Inspired by the Flavors of India* **by Yamuna Devi.** Drawing on the vibrant flavors of India, the author has given us a full-scale cookbook that reflects a commitment to high-flavor, lower-fat, easy-but-elegant dishes. "Devi's deft use of healthwise flavorings adds a delicious spark to an appealing range of entrées."—*Bon Appetit* (272386—$13.95)

☐ **DOWN-HOME WHOLESOME** *300 Low-Fat Recipes from a New Soul Kitchen* **by Daniella Carter.** This innovative new cookbook trims the extra fat, sugar, and salt from classic soul dishes—without sacrificing a bit of taste. Using high-flavor, low-fat ingredients like smoked turkey, sweet potatoes, leafy greens, and buttermilk, infused with vibrant flavorings like sizzling pepper bases, lemon peel, fresh herbs, and spices from around the world, the author highlights the simple pleasures of new-style down-home cooking.

(939091—$24.95)

☐ **A KWANZAA CELEBRATION** *Festive Recipes and Homemade Gifts from an African-American Kitchen* **by Angela Shelf Medearis.** The author leads us through the season, focusing on rituals and history, traditions and lore, and dishes that connect today's African-Americans to the culinary traditions of Africa, the Caribbean, South America, and the American South. Sit down with your loved ones to a Kwanzaa Karamu feast with jazzy spices and flavorings that make your cooking delicious and unmistakably African-American.

(940707—$17.95)

Prices slightly higher in Canada.
